Nutshell Series

of

WEST PUBLISHING COMPANY

P.O. Box 64526

St. Paul, Minnesota 55164–0526

Accounting—Law and, 1984, 377 pages, by E. McGruder Faris, Late Professor of Law, Stetson University.

Administrative Law and Process, 2nd Ed., 1981, 445 pages, by Ernest Gellhorn, Dean and Professor of Law, Case Western Reserve University and Barry B. Boyer, Professor of Law, SUNY, Buffalo.

Admiralty, 1983, 390 pages, by Frank L. Maraist, Professor of Law, Louisiana State University.

Agency-Partnership, 1977, 364 pages, by Roscoe T. Steffen, Late Professor of Law, University of Chicago.

American Indian Law, 1981, 288 pages, by William C. Canby, Jr., Adjunct Professor of Law, Arizona State University.

Antitrust Law and Economics, 2nd Ed., 1981, 425 pages, by Ernest Gellhorn, Dean and Professor of Law, Case Western Reserve University.

Appellate Advocacy, 1984, 325 pages, by Alan D. Hornstein, Professor of Law, University of Maryland.

Art Law, 1984, 335 pages, by Leonard D. DuBoff, Professor of Law, Lewis and Clark College, Northwestern School of Law.

Banking and Financial Institutions, 1984, 409 pages, by William A. Lovett, Professor of Law, Tulane University.

Church-State Relations—Law of, 1981, 305 pages, by Leonard F. Manning, Late Professor of Law, Fordham University.

Civil Procedure, 1979, 271 pages, by Mary Kay Kane, Professor of Law, University of California, Hastings College of the Law.

Civil Rights, 1978, 279 pages, by Norman Vieira, Professor of Law, Southern Illinois University.

Commercial Paper, 3rd Ed., 1982, 404 pages, by Charles M. Weber, Professor of Business Law, University of Arizona and Richard E. Speidel, Professor of Law, Northwestern University.

Community Property, 1982, 423 pages, by Robert L. Mennell, Former Professor of Law, Hamline University.

Comparative Legal Traditions, 1982, 402 pages, by Mary Ann Glendon, Professor of Law, Boston College, Michael Wallace Gordon, Professor of Law, University of Florida and Christopher Osakwe, Professor of Law, Tulane University.

Conflicts, 1982, 469 pages, by David D. Siegel, Professor of Law, St. John's University School of Law.

Constitutional Analysis, 1979, 388 pages, by Jerre S. Williams, Professor of Law Emeritus, University of Texas.

Constitutional Power—Federal and State, 1974, 411 pages, by David E. Engdahl, Professor of Law, University of Puget Sound.

Consumer Law, 2nd Ed., 1981, 418 pages, by David G. Epstein, Dean and Professor of Law, Emory University and Steve H. Nickles, Professor of Law, University of Minnesota.

Contract Remedies, 1981, 323 pages, by Jane M. Friedman, Professor of Law, Wayne State University.

Contracts, 2nd Ed., 1983, 425 pages, by Gordon D. Schaber, Dean and Professor of Law, McGeorge School of Law and Claude D. Rohwer, Professor of Law, McGeorge School of Law.

Corporations—Law of, 1980, 379 pages, by Robert W. Hamilton, Professor of Law, University of Texas.

Corrections and Prisoners' Rights—Law of, 2nd Ed., 1983, 384 pages, by Sheldon Krantz, Dean and Professor of Law, University of San Diego.

Criminal Law, 1975, 302 pages, by Arnold H. Loewy, Professor of Law, University of North Carolina.

Criminal Procedure—Constitutional Limitations, 3rd Ed., 1980, 438 pages, by Jerold H. Israel, Professor of Law, University of Michigan and Wayne R. LaFave, Professor of Law, University of Illinois.

Debtor-Creditor Law, 3rd Ed., 1985, 324 pages, by David G. Epstein, Dean and Professor of Law, Emory University.

Employment Discrimination—Federal Law of, 2nd Ed., 1981, 402 pages, by Mack A. Player, Professor of Law, University of Georgia.

Energy Law, 1981, 338 pages, by Joseph P. Tomain, Professor of Law, University of Cincinnatti.

Environmental Law, 1983, 343 pages by Roger W. Findley, Professor of Law, University of Illinois and Daniel A. Farber, Professor of Law, University of Minnesota.

Estate and Gift Taxation, Federal, 3rd Ed., 1983, 509 pages, by John K. McNulty, Professor of Law, University of California, Berkeley.

Estate Planning—Introduction to, 3rd Ed., 1983, 370 pages, by Robert J. Lynn, Professor of Law, Ohio State University.

Evidence, Federal Rules of, 1981, 429 pages, by Michael H. Graham, Professor of Law, University of Miami.

Evidence, State and Federal Rules, 2nd Ed., 1981, 514 pages, by Paul F. Rothstein, Professor of Law, Georgetown University.

Family Law, 1977, 400 pages, by Harry D. Krause, Professor of Law, University of Illinois.

Federal Jurisdiction, 2nd Ed., 1981, 258 pages, by David P. Currie, Professor of Law, University of Chicago.

Future Interests, 1981, 361 pages, by Lawrence W. Waggoner, Professor of Law, University of Michigan.

Government Contracts, 1979, 423 pages, by W. Noel Keyes, Professor of Law, Pepperdine University.

Historical Introduction to Anglo-American Law, 2nd Ed., 1973, 280 pages, by Frederick G. Kempin, Jr., Professor of Business Law, Wharton School of Finance and Commerce, University of Pennsylvania.

Immigration Law and Procedure, 1984, 345 pages, by David Weissbrodt, Professor of Law, University of Minnesota.

Injunctions, 1974, 264 pages, by John F. Dobbyn, Professor of Law, Villanova University.

Insurance Law, 1981, 281 pages, by John F. Dobbyn, Professor of Law, Villanova University.

Intellectual Property—Patents, Trademarks and Copyright, 1983, 428 pages, by Arthur R. Miller, Professor of Law, Harvard University, and Michael H. Davis, Professor of Law, Cleveland State University, Cleveland-Marshall College of Law.

International Business Transactions, 2nd Ed., 1984, 476 pages, by Donald T. Wilson, Professor of Law, Loyola University, Los Angeles.

International Law, 1985, about 250 pages, by Thomas Buergenthal, Professor of Law, Emory University and Harold G. Maier, Professor of Law, Vanderbilt University.

Introduction to the Study and Practice of Law, 1983, 418 pages, by Kenney F. Hegland, Professor of Law, University of Arizona.

Judicial Process, 1980, 292 pages, by William L. Reynolds, Professor of Law, University of Maryland.

Jurisdiction, 4th Ed., 1980, 232 pages, by Albert A. Ehrenzweig, Late Professor of Law, University of California, Berkeley, David W. Louisell, Late Professor of Law, University of California, Berkeley and Geoffrey C. Hazard, Jr., Professor of Law, Yale Law School.

Juvenile Courts, 3rd Ed., 1984, 291 pages, by Sanford J. Fox, Professor of Law, Boston College.

Labor Arbitration Law and Practice, 1979, 358 pages, by Dennis R. Nolan, Professor of Law, University of South Carolina.

Labor Law, 1986, about 405 pages, by Douglas L. Leslie, Professor of Law, University of Virginia.

Land Use, 1985, 356 pages, by Robert R. Wright, Professor of Law, University of Arkansas, Little Rock and Susan Webber Wright, Professor of Law, University of Arkansas, Little Rock.

Landlord and Tenant Law, 1979, 319 pages, by David S. Hill, Professor of Law, University of Colorado.

Law Study and Law Examinations—Introduction to, 1971, 389 pages, by Stanley V. Kinyon, Late Professor of Law, University of Minnesota.

Legal Interviewing and Counseling, 1976, 353 pages, by Thomas L. Shaffer, Professor of Law, Washington and Lee University.

Legal Research, 4th Ed., 1984, 452 pages, by Morris L. Cohen, Professor of Law and Law Librarian, Yale University.

Legal Writing, 1982, 294 pages, by Lynn B. Squires and Marjorie Dick Rombauer, Professor of Law, University of Washington.

Legislative Law and Process, 1975, 279 pages, by Jack Davies, Professor of Law, William Mitchell College of Law.

Local Government Law, 2nd Ed., 1983, 404 pages, by David J. McCarthy, Jr., Professor of Law, Georgetown University.

Mass Communications Law, 2nd Ed., 1983, 473 pages, by Harvey L. Zuckman, Professor of Law, Catholic University and Martin J. Gaynes, Lecturer in Law, Temple University.

Medical Malpractice—The Law of, 1977, 340 pages, by Joseph H. King, Professor of Law, University of Tennessee.

Military Law, 1980, 378 pages, by Charles A. Shanor, Professor of Law, Emory University and Timothy P. Terrell, Professor of Law, Emory University.

Oil and Gas, 1983, 443 pages, by John S. Lowe, Professor of Law, University of Tulsa.

Personal Property, 1983, 322 pages, by Barlow Burke, Jr., Professor of Law, American University.

Post-Conviction Remedies, 1978, 360 pages, by Robert Popper, Professor of Law, University of Missouri, Kansas City.

Presidential Power, 1977, 328 pages, by Arthur Selwyn Miller, Professor of Law Emeritus, George Washington University.

Procedure Before Trial, 1972, 258 pages, by Delmar Karlen, Professor of Law Emeritus, New York University.

Products Liability, 2nd Ed., 1981, 341 pages, by Dix W. Noel, Late Professor of Law, University of Tennessee and Jerry J. Phillips, Professor of Law, University of Tennessee.

Professional Responsibility, 1980, 399 pages, by Robert H. Aronson, Professor of Law, University of Washington, and Donald T. Weckstein, Professor of Law, University of San Diego.

Real Estate Finance, 2nd Ed., 1985, 262 pages, by Jon W. Bruce, Professor of Law, Vanderbilt University.

Real Property, 2nd Ed., 1981, 448 pages, by Roger H. Bernhardt, Professor of Law, Golden Gate University.

Regulated Industries, 1982, 394 pages, by Ernest Gellhorn, Dean and Professor of Law, Case Western Reserve University, and Richard J. Pierce, Dean and Professor of Law, University of Pittsburgh.

Remedies, 2nd Ed., 1985, 320 pages, by John F. O'Connell, Professor of Law, Western State University College of Law, Fullerton.

Res Judicata, 1976, 310 pages, by Robert C. Casad, Professor of Law, University of Kansas.

Sales, 2nd Ed., 1981, 370 pages, by John M. Stockton, Professor of Business Law, Wharton School of Finance and Commerce, University of Pennsylvania.

Schools, Students and Teachers—Law of, 1984, 409 pages, by Kern Alexander, Professor of Education, University of Florida and M. David Alexander, Professor, Virginia Tech University.

Sea—Law of, 1984, 264 pages, by Louis B. Sohn, Professor of Law, University of Georgia, and Kristen Gustafson.

Secured Transactions, 2nd Ed., 1981, 391 pages, by Henry J. Bailey, Professor of Law Emeritus, Willamette University.

NUTSHELL SERIES

Securities Regulation, 2nd Ed., 1982, 322 pages, by David L. Ratner, Dean and Professor of Law, University of San Francisco.

Sex Discrimination, 1982, 399 pages, by Claire Sherman Thomas, Lecturer, University of Washington, Women's Studies Department.

Taxation and Finance, State and Local, 1985, about 255 pages, by M. David Gelfand, Professor of Law, Tulane University and Peter W. Salsich, Professor of Law, St. Louis University.

Taxation of Individuals, Federal Income, 3rd Ed., 1983, 487 pages, by John K. McNulty, Professor of Law, University of California, Berkeley.

Taxation of Corporations and Stockholders, Federal Income, 2nd Ed., 1981, 362 pages, by Jonathan Sobeloff, Late Professor of Law, Georgetown University and Peter P. Weidenbruch, Jr., Professor of Law, Georgetown University.

Torts—Injuries to Persons and Property, 1977, 434 pages, by Edward J. Kionka, Professor of Law, Southern Illinois University.

Torts—Injuries to Family, Social and Trade Relations, 1979, 358 pages, by Wex S. Malone, Professor of Law Emeritus, Louisiana State University.

Trial Advocacy, 1979, 402 pages, by Paul B. Bergman, Adjunct Professor of Law, University of California, Los Angeles.

Trial and Practice Skills, 1978, 346 pages, by Kenney F. Hegland, Professor of Law, University of Arizona.

Trial, The First—Where Do I Sit? What Do I Say?, 1982, 396 pages, by Steven H. Goldberg, Professor of Law, University of Minnesota.

Unfair Trade Practices, 1982, 444 pages, by Charles R. McManis, Professor of Law, Washington University.

Uniform Commercial Code, 2nd Ed., 1984, 516 pages, by Bradford Stone, Professor of Law, Detroit College of Law.

Uniform Probate Code, 1978, 425 pages, by Lawrence H. Averill, Jr., Dean and Professor of Law, University of Arkansas, Little Rock.

Hornbook Series

and

Basic Legal Texts

of

WEST PUBLISHING COMPANY

P.O. Box 64526

St. Paul, Minnesota 55164–0526

Administrative Law, Davis' Text on, 3rd Ed., 1972, 617 pages, by Kenneth Culp Davis, Professor of Law, University of San Diego.

Agency and Partnership, Reuschlein & Gregory's Hornbook on the Law of, 1979 with 1981 Pocket Part, 625 pages, by Harold Gill Reuschlein, Professor of Law Emeritus, Villanova University and William A. Gregory, Professor of Law, Georgia State University.

American Lawyers, Legal Ethics and the Legal Profession, Wolfram's Hornbook on, 1986, about 1050 pages, by Charles W. Wolfram, Professor of Law, Cornell University.

Antitrust, Sullivan's Hornbook on the Law of, 1977, 886 pages, by Lawrence A. Sullivan, Professor of Law, University of California, Berkeley.

Civil Procedure, Friedenthal, Kane and Miller's Hornbook on, Student Ed., 1985, 870 pages, by Jack H. Friedental, Professor of Law, Stanford University, Mary K. Kane, Professor of Law, University of California, Hastings College of the Law and Arthur R. Miller, Professor of Law, Harvard University.

Common Law Pleading, Koffler and Reppy's Hornbook on, 1969, 663 pages, by Joseph H. Koffler, Professor of Law, New York Law School and Alison Reppy, Late Dean and Professor of Law, New York Law School.

Conflict of Laws, Scoles and Hay's Hornbook on, 1982, 1085 pages, by Eugene F. Scoles, Professor of Law, University of Illinois and Peter Hay, Dean and Professor of Law, University of Illinois.

Constitutional Law, Nowak, Rotunda and Young's Hornbook on, 2nd Ed., 1983, 1172 pages, by John E. Nowak, Professor of Law, University of Illinois, Ronald D. Rotunda, Professor of Law, University of Illinois, and J. Nelson Young, Late Professor of Law, University of North Carolina.

Contracts, Calamari and Perillo's Hornbook on, 2nd Ed., 1977, 878 pages, by John D. Calamari, Professor of Law, Fordham University and Joseph M. Perillo, Professor of Law, Fordham University.

Contracts, Corbin's One Volume Student Ed., 1952, 1224 pages, by Arthur L. Corbin, Late Professor of Law, Yale University.

Corporations, Henn and Alexander's Hornbook on, 3rd Ed., 1983, 1371 pages, by Harry G. Henn, Professor of Law, Cornell University and John R. Alexander.

Criminal Law, LaFave and Scott's Hornbook on, 1972, 763 pages, by Wayne R. LaFave, Professor of Law, University of Illinois, and Austin Scott, Jr., Late Professor of Law, University of Colorado.

Criminal Procedure, LaFave and Israel's Hornbook on, 1985, 1142 pages, by Wayne R. LaFave, Professor of Law, University of Illinois and Jerold H. Israel, Professor of Law University of Michigan.

Damages, McCormick's Hornbook on, 1935, 811 pages, by Charles T. McCormick, Late Dean and Professor of Law, University of Texas.

Domestic Relations, Clark's Hornbook on, 1968, 754 pages, by Homer H. Clark, Jr., Professor of Law, University of Colorado.

Economics and Federal Antitrust Law, Hovenkamp's Hornbook on, 1985, 414 pages, by Herbert Hovenkamp, Professor of Law, University of California, Hastings College of the Law.

HORNBOOKS & BASIC TEXTS

Environmental Law, Rodgers' Hornbook on, 1977 with 1984 Pocket Part, 956 pages, by William H. Rodgers, Jr., Professor of Law, University of Washington.

Evidence, Lilly's Introduction to, 1978, 486 pages, by Graham C. Lilly, Professor of Law, University of Virginia.

Evidence, McCormick's Hornbook on, 3rd Ed., 1984, 1155 pages, General Editor, Edward W. Cleary, Professor of Law Emeritus, Arizona State University.

Federal Courts, Wright's Hornbook on, 4th Ed., 1983, 870 pages, by Charles Alan Wright, Professor of Law, University of Texas.

Federal Income Taxation of Individuals, Posin's Hornbook on, 1983 with 1985 Pocket Part, 491 pages, by Daniel Q. Posin, Jr., Professor of Law, Southern Methodist University.

Future Interest, Simes' Hornbook on, 2nd Ed., 1966, 355 pages, by Lewis M. Simes, Late Professor of Law, University of Michigan.

Insurance, Keeton's Basic Text on, 1971, 712 pages, by Robert E. Keeton, Professor of Law Emeritus, Harvard University.

Labor Law, Gorman's Basic Text on, 1976, 914 pages, by Robert A. Gorman, Professor of Law, University of Pennsylvania.

Law Problems, Ballentine's, 5th Ed., 1975, 767 pages, General Editor, William E. Burby, Late Professor of Law, University of Southern California.

Legal Writing Style, Weihofen's, 2nd Ed., 1980, 332 pages, by Henry Weihofen, Professor of Law Emeritus, University of New Mexico.

Local Government Law, Reynolds' Hornbook on, 1982, 860 pages, by Osborne M. Reynolds, Professor of Law, University of Oklahoma.

New York Practice, Siegel's Hornbook on, 1978, with 1985 Pocket Part, 1011 pages, by David D. Siegel, Professor of Law, St. John's University.

Oil and Gas, Hemingway's Hornbook on, 2nd Ed., Student Ed., 1983, 543 pages, by Richard W. Hemingway, Professor of Law, University of Oklahoma.

Poor, Law of the, LaFrance, Schroeder, Bennett and Boyd's Hornbook on, 1973, 558 pages, by Arthur B. LaFrance, Dean and Professor of Law, Lewis and Clark College, Northwestern School of Law, Milton R. Schroeder, Professor of Law, Arizona State University, Robert W. Bennett, Dean and Professor of Law, Northwestern University and William E. Boyd, Professor of Law, University of Arizona.

Property, Boyer's Survey of, 3rd Ed., 1981, 766 pages, by Ralph E. Boyer, Professor of Law, University of Miami.

Property, Law of, Cunningham, Whitman and Stoebuck's Hornbook on, Student Ed., 1984, 916 pages, by Roger A. Cunningham, Professor of Law, University of Michigan, Dale A. Whitman, Dean and Professor of Law, University of Missouri–Columbia and William B. Stoebuck, Professor of Law, University of Washington.

Real Estate Finance Law, Nelson and Whitman's Hornbook on, 1985, about 950 pages, by Grant S. Nelson, Professor of Law, University of Missouri, Columbia and Dale A. Whitman, Dean and Professor of Law, University of Missouri, Columbia.

Real Property, Moynihan's Introduction to, 1962, 254 pages, by Cornelius J. Moynihan, Professor of Law, Suffolk University.

Remedies, Dobb's Hornbook on, 1973, 1067 pages, by Dan B. Dobbs, Professor of Law, University of Arizona.

Secured Transactions under the U.C.C., Henson's Hornbook on, 2nd Ed., 1979, with 1979 Pocket Part, 504 pages, by Ray D. Henson, Professor of Law, University of California, Hastings College of the Law.

Securities Regulation, Hazen's Hornbook on the Law of, 1985, 739 pages, by Thomas Lee Hazen, Professor of Law, University of North Carolina.

Torts, Prosser and Keeton's Hornbook on, 5th Ed., 1984, 1286 pages, by William L. Prosser, Late Dean and Professor of Law, University of California, Berkeley, Page Keeton, Professor of Law Emeritus, University of Texas, Dan B. Dobbs,

Professor of Law, University of Arizona, Robert E. Keeton, Professor of Law Emeritus, Harvard University and David G. Owen, Professor of Law, University of South Carolina.

Trial Advocacy, Jeans' Handbook on, Soft cover, 1975, by James W. Jeans, Professor of Law, University of Missouri, Kansas City.

Trusts, Bogert's Hornbook on, 5th Ed., 1973, 726 pages, by George G. Bogert, Late Professor of Law, University of Chicago and George T. Bogert.

Uniform Commercial Code, White and Summers' Hornbook on, 2nd Ed., 1980, 1250 pages, by James J. White, Professor of Law, University of Michigan and Robert S. Summers, Professor of Law, Cornell University.

Urban Planning and Land Development Control, Hagman's Hornbook on, 1971, 706 pages, by Donald G. Hagman, Late Professor of Law, University of California, Los Angeles.

Wills, Atkinson's Hornbook on, 2nd Ed., 1953, 975 pages, by Thomas E. Atkinson, Late Professor of Law, New York University.

Advisory Board

TORTS
IN A NUTSHELL

INJURIES TO PERSONS AND PROPERTY

By

EDWARD J. KIONKA
Professor of Law
Southern Illinois University School of Law

ST. PAUL, MINN.
WEST PUBLISHING CO.
1977

Kionka Torts

5th Reprint—1985

PREFACE

This book, like all others in the Nutshell series, is intended primarily for law students seeking a concise exposition of the basic principles of American law. Its main value will probably be to first-year students taking the course in torts, who are struggling to get a glimpse of the elusive "big picture" to which my former dean and colleague Dean John Cribbet of Illinois so often refers. (Every law student and lawyer should know his famous "big picture" story. See J. Cribbet, Principles of the Law of Property ix–x (2d ed. 1975).) It may also be useful to lawyers and others who wish to refresh their recollection of this subject or some part of it.

This Nutshell, again like all others, must be used with caution and with a clear understanding of its limitations. Overall, I believe that it presents an accurate "big picture" of the subjects discussed. But many of the rules are subject to minor exceptions and qualifications which space does not permit to be mentioned. Some rules and subrules, not essential to an understanding of the basic principles, have been omitted altogether. Some hard problems are only alluded to. In addition, the tort law of every jurisdiction is a little bit different from that of every other, and each contains its own idiosyncrasies, judicial and sometimes statutory. This text must not be taken as the law of any particular jurisdiction, but rather as a composite view.

The law student would be ill-advised not to base his or her study of tort law primarily on other sources. There is no substitute for a careful analysis of casebook materials for a more thorough treatment and for a necessary perspective of tort law in action. And it would be wise to flesh out one's knowledge of the various areas by study of a more complete text, such as Dean Prosser's classic Hornbook, and also of the Restatement (Second) of Torts. Reference to other sources available in the law library is sometimes necessary in areas where enlightenment seems slow to come. Nevertheless, it is my firm belief that law students (as all of us are) must have a clear view of the forest before they can truly understand and assimilate the various trees. I hope that this book will help to provide that overview, a solid structural framework of concepts to which the elaborations and refinements of ever more specific rules can be attached. May it serve as an entree into the proverbial seamless web.

No single Nutshell could do justice to all of tort law. This one's focus is the basic principles of liability defenses, and damages for physical harm. The volatile area of products liability, discussed briefly here, is the subject of a separate Nutshell (D. Noel & J. Phillips, Products Liability in a Nutshell (1974)). The law governing the liability of those who provide medical services is now undergoing rapid growth and change, and there are important statutory developments in this area.

See J. King, Law of Medical Malpractice in a Nutshell (1977). And harms to relational interests—survival and wrongful death, defamation, certain kinds of invasions of privacy, misuse of legal procedure, business torts, and interference with family relations—are covered in a Nutshell which is now being written by Professor Wex Malone.

On the other hand, I have covered some subjects not normally included in basic torts texts and courses (see, e. g., Chapter 1 and §§ 8-14, 8–15, 8–21, and 8–22) because I believe that they are important to an accurate overview.

I am deeply grateful to all those—students, lawyers, and legal scholars—who have helped me learn about tort law and its processes, and to my colleagues, friends and family who supported me in this project. Many thanks are also due to the law schools of Southern Illinois, St. Louis, and Washington Universities and to those who provided administrative and secretarial services, especially Jan and Nancy, often above and beyond the normal call of duty. And special thanks to Prof. James F. Meara, S.J., who graciously volunteered to help edit the manuscript and who taught me the difference between "inferable" and "inferrible."

Portions of the Restatement of the Law, Second, Torts (copyright 1965, 1971, 1972, 1976, 1977 by the American Law Institute) are reprinted herein with the permission of the American Law Institute.

EDWARD J. KIONKA

Carbondale, Illinois
May, 1977

EXPLANATORY NOTES

The following notes may be helpful in using this book.

Cases. For obvious reasons, cases have been cited sparingly. In general, the cases cited are either (1) leading authorities on a particular point, (2) landmark cases, or (3) illustrative cases, particularly recent ones in developing areas.

Only the name, court of decision, and date are cited in the text. The full citation may be found in the Table of Cases. If only the name of the state is given, it is the highest court of that state.

Restatement of Torts. The Restatement of Torts has been particularly well regarded by the courts, and it is highly authoritative in many jurisdictions. Frequent references to it are given, but I have not cited every relevant section. Ordinarily it is cited where the provision or its comments provide further illumination of the point under discussion. In *all* instances, citations are to the Restatement (Second) (unless otherwise noted), even though only the first half (§§ 1–503) is now in print in final form. The remainder has been tentatively approved, and Volume 3 will be published in 1977 and the final volume in 1978. Therefore the Restatement (Second) will be available in its entirety during most of the time this Nutshell is in use. As to sections later than § 503 quoted herein, the reader should check the final version in the Restatement (Second) when it is published, as there may be minor changes in wording from the tentative drafts heretofore approved.

For simplicity and to save space, the Restatement (Second) of Torts is cited throughout as "R. § _____."

Texts. Texts and articles are cited only occasionally. It is generally agreed that the most authoritative and useful text is the Hornbook by the late Dean William L. Prosser, now in its fourth edition (W. Prosser, The Law of Torts (4th ed. 1971)). For convenience, it is cited as "Prosser." There is also a useful three-volume treatise, F. Harper & F. James, The Law of Torts (1956, with 1968 supplement to volume 2). Texts on individual subtopics are also available (e. g., V. Schwartz, Comparative Negligence (1974)).

References to Parties. For convenience and consistency, the terms "plaintiff" and "defendant" are used throughout to include not only persons who technically have that status (i. e., those who have been sued or who have brought suit) but also persons who *potentially* occupy one status or the other—one who has been harmed, or one who is arguably a tortfeasor. Also, plaintiffs and defendants are personalized by use of the pronouns which refer to natural persons (e. g., "he"), which should be read to include, where appropriate, legal entities such as corporations. And "he" and "man" are used throughout in a generic sense to include both men and women.

Where appropriate, "plaintiff" may refer to one who was *fatally* injured, and therefore would not, technically, ever be a party to a lawsuit. The more correct term would be "plaintiff's decedent," but it would be too awkward to use both terms. Similarly, the terms "injury" or "harm" include fatal injuries unless the context otherwise requires.

*

OUTLINE

OUTLINE

OUTLINE

OUTLINE

PART IV. IMMUNITIES

*

TABLE OF CASES

References are to Pages

TABLE OF CASES

C

D

E

F

TABLE OF CASES

G

H

I

K

TABLE OF CASES

R

S

Y

†

TORTS

IN A NUTSHELL:

Injuries To Persons And Property

PART I

INTRODUCTION

CHAPTER 1

PROLOGUE: ORIGINS, OBJECTIVES AND OVERVIEWS OF TORT LIABILITY

§ 1—1. The Definitional Dilemma

"Tort" is an elusive concept. The word is not used in common speech. Although it describes one of the major pigeon-holes of the law, the concept has defied a number of attempts to formulate a useful definition. The dilemma is that any definition which is sufficiently comprehensive to encompass all torts is so general as to be almost meaningless.

Closely related to the definitional dilemma is the classic question, is there a general principle of tort liability? Or are there only the laws of the individual "torts," a miscellaneous and more or less unconnected collection of nominate civil actions grouped together merely for convenience of reference? Legal scholars have debated this issue for more than a century, without resolving it satisfactorily.

If there is any such general principle, it has yet to be adopted by Anglo-American courts and legislatures. The common law developed as a system of individual named torts—trespass, deceit, slander, and later assault and battery, conversion, and so on—each with its own more or less unique rules. In fact, until 1859 there was no legal treatise bearing the name "torts." As yet, except for the tort called "negligence," there has been little synthesis of the nominate torts into larger categories.

The one common element of all torts is that someone has sustained a loss or harm as the result of some act or failure to act by another. Beyond this, accurate generalization becomes impossible. Virtually all of the infinitely diverse forms of human activity—driving a vehicle, engaging in business, speaking, writing, owning and using real or personal property, making love—may be a source of harm and therefore of tort liability. This diversity of conduct resists broad generalizations, and so does the tort liability on which it is based.

Tort law is perhaps the last bastion of the common law. Even in this age of legislation, with its proliferation of codes and uniform acts, tort law remains uncodified and in large part unaffected by statute. This may tell us something about its fundamental nature. In any event, in view of the fact that it evolved a posteriori, inductively, from particular cases, and not a priori, it is not surprising that a number of diverse and independent torts emerged. And perhaps this very diversity results, overall, in a closer approximation of justice than could be achieved by the application of more general rules.

Sometimes it is suggested that a common element of tort liability is *fault,* that tortious conduct is that which falls below accepted community standards of behavior. Some sort of fault is common to many torts, although it might more accurately be described as conduct which creates an unreasonable or unacceptable risk of harm. But even in this sense, fault cannot be said to be a universal principle of liability. Various kinds of blameworthy conduct resulting in damage do not give rise to tort liability. Conversely, the law sometimes imposes tort liability simply because a particular activity can and should bear the cost of damage associated with it, regardless of the fact that the conduct of the "tortfeasor" was morally blameless.

The common law system of nominate torts does not seem to have impeded the creation of new causes of action. For example, the action for invasion of privacy, now well established, had its genesis in a law review article published in 1890. Nor has this system stifled change. Within the confines of the nominate torts, the law has persistently evolved toward expanded liability by modifying existing rules. In less than a century, the law of product-caused injuries has moved from rules highly favoring the manufacturer (caveat emptor) to a form of strict liability.

One may well ask whether there is need for a general principle of tort liability. The boundaries of the spheres of the nominate torts intersect, often overlap. If one's damage is not actionable, it is almost certainly not for lack of a name or a general principle, but rather because the existing law deliberately refuses to shift the loss.

One might also ask whether our law would be appreciably different even if such a general principle were announced. The codes of the European and other civil law countries usually contain a provision such as § 1382 of the French Civil Code:

> Every act whatsoever of an individual which causes injury to another obliges the one by whose fault [*faute*] it has occurred to make reparation for it.

Yet the tort law of these countries is remarkably similar to ours. The California Civil Code (§§

1708–1720) includes some general tort liability provisions, but the structure and rules of California tort law are indistinguishable in form from those of other states.

If a definition of "tort" is necessary, it will have to be something in the nature of this:

> A civil wrong, wherein one person's conduct causes a compensable injury to the person, property, or recognized interest of another, in violation of a duty imposed by law.

Obviously, this does not tell us very much. To say that the breach of a law-imposed duty creates tort liability begs the question. Moreover, not *all* violations of legal duties are torts. This does not even distinguish tort from breach of contract, since in the final analysis the binding effect of contractual duties is limited to that imposed by law. Some have defined "tort" by excluding "mere" breaches of contract, but this glosses over the fact that the breach of a contractual duty under certain circumstances can be the basis for tort liability.

Even the simple term "cause" has no external reference. Many times courts have denied liability because of the absence of legal cause, even though the conduct in question was rather clearly a substantial cause in fact of the harm.

Tort law is a complex machine for shifting human losses. Like other complicated machinery, for most practical purposes it is best understood as the sum of its individual component parts. Efforts to change these parts to make them more similar may only impair their individual performance.

§ 1—2. Functions, Goals and Justifications of Tort Law

Tort law has three main functions or goals: (1) compensating persons sustaining a loss or harm as a result of another's conduct; (2) placing the cost of that compensation on those who, in justice, ought to bear it, but only on such persons; and (2) preventing future losses and harms.

Compensation. The victim of a tort has sustained certain harm(s) or loss(es) which we shall call "costs". Tort law is predicated on the idea that all these costs—tangible and intangible—can be measured in money. The basic (and usually exclusive) tort remedy is to require the tortfeasor to pay the victim the sum of these costs as "compensatory damages".

Note that in most tort cases—the automobile "accident" is a typical example—the loss to the victim is also a net loss to the economic system. The loss-producing event ordinarily does not result in a corresponding economic gain to the tortfeasor which could be returned to the victim. The main jurisprudential issue in tort law is, under what circumstances can we justify compelling another to compensate the victim for these costs?

[6]

If compensation—relieving the victim of the sudden and substantial burden of these costs— were our only goal, there are more efficient ways than tort litigation. The law permits (and presumably could require) first party insurance— life, health and accident, disability, fire, theft, etc. Or government could impose a tax-financed compensation system, similar to social security. A portion of the tangible costs of physical harm to persons and property are already reimbursed by insurance, employment benefits, and governmental benefits. The trend is for these to increase. By expanding the coverage and limits, such compensation could be made to serve as a substitute for tort damages in the vast majority of cases now processed through the tort system. Why use the more cumbersome, inefficient and expensive method?

The answer is found in our notions of justice, which include the idea of fairness and to some extent other considerations.

Justice.

Fairness. Fundamentally, justice is the result of the application of current community standards of fairness. If a loss-producing event is a matter of pure chance, then the fairest way to relieve the victim of the burden of its costs is insurance or governmental compensation. In this way the risk and its costs are shared by all. If the risk differs for different groups but is more or less random within each group, premium classifications can equitably adjust these differences.

But where (1) we can identify a particular person as responsible for the creation of the risk (the "tortfeasor"), (2) the risk is not inconsequential nor of a type which the community customarily accepts, and (3) the tortfeasor is at least theoretically capable of reducing or eliminating the risk or its consequences, the balance of fairness shifts. At some point on the continuum of these factors, it becomes more just to impose the loss on the tortfeasor than to permit it to remain on the victim or to be shared by the community. Ideally, at precisely this point tort liability attaches.

Cause In Fact. Causation is, for obvious reasons, the sine qua non. Tort liability is only just if the actor's conduct was a substantial factor in bringing about the victim's loss or harm.

Fault. Fault is usually a necessary element of the liability equation. It is not enough that one has caused harm to another; ethically, we find it difficult to justify liability unless the actor's conduct was somehow culpable. One is not required —in most cases—to insure others against the risks inherent in socially accepted conduct. But the requisite "fault" need not be narrowly defined, nor need the actor be subjectively aware that his conduct carries an unacceptable risk of harm. Clearly, if one intentionally harms another, or knows (or is presumed to know) that his conduct creates a substantial certainty of harm, liability naturally follows. Motive (actual or inferred) can thus be an element of fault. However, "fault" also includes conduct where no harm was intended or even foreseen, where an ordinary person *should have foreseen* that such conduct created an *unreasonable* risk to others. According to Learned Hand's classic formula, conduct is wrongful if the burden of alternative conduct which would have prevented the harm is less than the foreseeable probability and gravity of the harm. In measuring this burden we may consider the necessity and utility of the harm-producing conduct as compared to its alternatives. Thus, fault may lie in merely creating an unnecessary or unreasonable risk, however unknowingly. In this sense, one can find a fault element even in some forms of so-called strict liability.

Fault Substitutes. Sometimes other factors may partly or entirely substitute for the fault requirement. These include:

(1) Economic efficiency. Principles of economics suggest that, in general, the costs of an activity should be internalized. Where an activity causes harm, the cost of that harm ought to be reflected in the overall cost-price structure of that activity. Workmen's compensation statutes and products liability rules to some extent reflect this idea. It is also suggested that the law may consider the relative capacity of the parties

to absorb or spread the costs. Thus, as between (a) one who carries on an insurable activity or an activity with respect to which income is received and (b) an injured person with limited resources, the former is deemed better able to absorb and distribute the costs of harm resulting from the activity, thereby reducing what Calabresi calls the "secondary costs" of the injury.

A corollary principle is that it is more efficient to require an *activity* to be insured against the non-intentional harms it causes than to require an *individual* to insure generally against such harms and others.

(2) Vicarious liability. Tort liability is sometimes imposed on one in the absence of any fault on his part for a tort committed by another who is acting on his behalf or with his express or implied permission—most commonly employees, and sometimes independent contractors and others. In addition to the economic efficiency reasons, and the justification that such liability promotes care in the selection, training and supervision of one's agents (which is doubtful), the principal basis for vicarious liability is the simple idea that one, in justice, ought to be liable for the torts of those who act in his stead—in effect, their acts are his when committed in that capacity.

(3) Economic benefit. Earlier it was noted that in most tort cases, the harm results in a net economic loss. But this is not always so. In many situations, the creation of the risk is of

benefit to the creator. Speeding saves time, which we are fond of saying is the equivalent of money. Cornercutting of all kinds often reduces the costs of the activity. This benefit to the actor is not often articulated as a justification for liability, but there is some evidence that courts and legislators will more readily impose liability where this element is present.

There are other cases where defendant's wrongful conduct causes a direct pecuniary loss to plaintiff and a corresponding direct pecuniary gain to defendant—for example, misrepresentation in a sales transaction or conversion of a chattel. In such cases compensation may also be termed reimbursement or restitution, and here, too, it is more readily awarded.

Fault Without Liability. There are cases where the actor's conduct is a cause in fact of another's harm, and all of the usual fault requirements are met, but for reasons of social policy no tort liability exists. The concepts *duty, proximate cause, privilege,* and *immunity* are the means by which the courts (and legislatures) balance the burden of liability against other social values.

Contributory Fault. The victim's tort recovery may be reduced or denied when he has consented to encounter the risk or when his own fault contributed to his injury. Where there has been a true consent or a knowing and voluntary assumption of the risk, denial of all recovery may be just. However, until very recently most jurisdictions denied recovery entirely in cases where defendant's conduct was negligent or even "reckless" (a twilight zone between negligent and intentional) if the victim's conduct of the same kind contributed, however slightly, to the unfortunate result. Under prevailing notions of justice, this is unsound. The victim's fault is by definition only a portion of the total loss-producing fault; it does not negate or supersede the fault of others. The more logical approach is to compare the fault of all parties to the loss-producing event and reduce the damages of each in proportion to his own contributory fault. This is now accomplished by statute or court decision in a majority of the states, and frequently by juries ad hoc in the remainder.

Prevention of Future Costs. The third major function or goal of tort law is to prevent future torts by regulating human behavior. In this respect, the law serves an educational function, and operates prospectively. Theoretically, a tortfeasor held liable for damages will himself be more careful in the future, and the general threat of tort liability is an incentive to all to regulate their conduct in accordance with the established standards. To this extent tort law supplements and extends the criminal law; indeed, tort sanctions can often be more potent. Punitive damages, allowable in most tort actions involving intentional or reckless misconduct, are intended to reinforce this function.

Although this function is frequently asserted to be a justification for tort liability, no one really knows whether it works. Does tort liability—actual or prospective—in fact affect human behavior, and if so, to what extent? Perhaps future empirical research will provide some answers, but for now we can only speculate.

Other Justifications. These are not the only functions, goals or justifications of rules of tort law, but merely the principal ones. There are others. For example, in some cases the provision of a remedy in tort will serve to vindicate plaintiff, quite apart from any compensation he may receive. And it is widely assumed that it deters individual retaliation and resort to violent or otherwise improper self-help remedies for a perceived wrong.

The Real World. All of the foregoing justifications for the existing rules of tort liability are to some extent based on an idealization of the operation of the tort system. The underlying assumptions need to be tested to determine whether they have any basis in fact. We need to know more about external influences—for example, the widespread availability and use of insurance. And we need better information about the results of the system in actual operation in the real world. Litigation is an expensive, time-consuming and uncertain means of compensation which can be justified only if it adequately achieves other goals. Many proponents of "no-fault" compensation systems assert that tort law has failed this test. Some also suggest that in certain kinds of cases —notably auto crashes—our basic assumptions about fault and its determinability are erroneous. The fundamental question which must continually be asked is, does the tort system achieve its stated goals—compensation, justice, deterrence—sufficiently well to justify its costs?

§ 1—3.　The Evolution of Tort Concepts and Remedies

Evolution of Tort Remedies. English law in its earliest stages did not differentiate between tort and crime; indeed, such terms were unknown. Where one person was harmed by another, the remedy was a private war or "feud" in retaliation, the object being to cause an equivalent harm to the wrongdoer. As the law began to intervene in these private disputes, it first merely provided incentives for the parties to settle by an agreed compensation. Soon it began to require resort to a primitive form of trial (by ordeal or oaths) in lieu of the feud. If plaintiff won, defendant had to pay some fixed sum to the plaintiff (called "bot") and to the king ("wite"), computed on the basis of plaintiff's value ("wer") and the nature of the injury, or on the value of the property. If the defendant could not pay (which was probably the usual case), he was punished.

The Anglo-Saxon courts were local and applied local laws. After the Norman Conquest (1066), the royal courts were created and gradually took limited jurisdiction over a specified list of wrongs —primarily felonies where there was a breach of the "king's peace," and disputes involving land. Minor wrongs (what we now call misdemeanors) continued to be handled in the local courts as before. (It is well to remember that even as late as the thirteenth century, there was little "common law"—that is, law which was uniform throughout the country—except with respect to land. Both local laws and the royal law were customary law, and in most matters local customs varied.)

At first, all prosecutions for "wrongs" in the king's courts were brought by the individual harmed (or his representative). Plaintiff accused defendant of a wrong in open court and offered the appropriate form of trial—combat, ordeal or oaths, depending on the type of wrong and other factors. This procedure was known as the "appeal of felony." If plaintiff won, defendant was punished, but no compensation was awarded to plaintiff in this action, except that in an appeal of larceny, the goods (if available) were returned to the plaintiff. In 1166, the presentment (grand) jury was instituted, and a century later lesser crimes could be prosecuted by public officials upon an information, but the appeal of felony remained optional for many years.

Much of the king's business was accomplished by royal writ, and this included the administration of justice. At first, most writs merely commanded the local courts to do justice between certain parties so that the king would hear no more complaints about the matter. Soon such writs became the grant of jurisdiction to a royal court to adjudicate a case. Gradually, a formal system of named writs evolved, and it became necessary for the plaintiff to purchase an appropriate writ from the king's chancellor in order to commence his action. As the result of various political and judicial pressures, the writs became crystallized into certain forms and contents, corresponding to the available actions, and if plaintiff could not fit his case into one of the prescribed writs, he had no action in the royal courts. By the fifteenth century it had become possible, and common, to commence an action by bill (complaint) instead of royal writ; but plaintiff's declaration still had to state a cause of action in the recognized form, corresponding to the writs that could have been selected.

The most important personal civil action was trespass, called by Maitland "that fertile mother of actions." Its origins are obscure, but shortly after 1250 it seems to have been in common use and to have been one of the writs of course. For some time, its limits were not clearly defined, and it was used in a variety of cases where one person had harmed another. Its great significance lay in the fact that plaintiff recovered his actual damages, if any, rather than damages according to a fixed scheme of compensation. For many years it also retained a quasi-criminal character in that a vanquished defendant was usually imprisoned or fined. In a short time it became immensely popular and largely supplanted the "appeal" in felony cases except, curiously, for homicide. No civil action was permitted in the king's court for wrongful death until the passage of Lord Campbell's Act in 1846. In addition, it provided a remedy in the royal courts for a number of lesser harms which theretofore could be redressed only in the less effective local courts.

Three common forms of the writ soon developed: (1) trespass *vi et armis* (with force and arms) for assault, battery, and false imprisonment; (2) trespass *de bonis asportatis* (taking of goods) for trespass to chattels; and (3) trespass *quare clausum fregit* (breach of the "close") for trespass to land. In time the criminal penalties were dropped, but plaintiff could still recover in trespass even though he could not prove actual damage.

Concurrent with the growth of trespass there developed a practice of issuing and honoring writs for wrongs which did not fit within the confines of the designated trespass actions. Such writs eventually became classified as an action of trespass on the case or, more correctly, "action on the case." Unlike the trespass writs which had been developed into inflexible forms, the "case" writs set forth the facts of plaintiff's particular case in considerable detail. By the sixteenth century, case had become a distinct and generic form of action.

As time went on, certain of the recurring case actions crystallized and were separated into named actions having rules and writs of their own. Trespass, together with case and its progeny, account for virtually all the actions to which we now refer collectively as the law of torts.

Assumpsit, which eventually became the primary remedy for breach of contract, began life as a special form of case. In the fourteenth century (some believe even earlier), case provided a remedy where one undertook to provide a service and expressly agreed to exercise care and skill but instead damaged the plaintiff or his property. (Where a "common calling" was involved, the undertaking was implied by law.) The breach of this promise or *assumpsit* was a wrong. Gradually assumpsit became a means for enforcing other contracts not under seal. It then became an independent contract action, while case remained an alternative remedy in tort for breach of certain kinds of contractual undertakings, primarily involving misfeasance (as opposed to a total failure to perform).

Case also came to provide a remedy for deceit. There was an original writ called deceit, but it concerned abuse of legal procedure, construed as a fraud on the courts. But as the idea of assumpsit developed in case, a related case action for deceit developed for breach of an express warranty. During the nineteenth century implied sales warranties developed, and the law of warranty became classified as a part of the law of sales, but some of its tort origins remain visible. In the meantime, the tort action for deceit continued to develop under the aegis of case.

Trover began to emerge as an action separate from case during the sixteenth century. It developed as a remedy for conversion and certain kinds of damage to chattels in situations where replevin, detinue, or trespass *de bonis asportatis* did not apply or where these remedies were inadequate. Eventually it became concurrent with all of them.

Case was the general form of action under which most other torts evolved. Nuisance, defamation, interference with economic relations, and malicious prosecution were case actions. So were certain kinds of strict liability, such as that of certain classes of bailees or for the spread of fire. And so was the most important of the tort causes of action, negligence, when it finally emerged as an independent basis of liability.

Evolution of Theories of Liability. In the final stages of their evolution, there were three basic differences between trespass and case so far as tort remedies were concerned.

(1) Trespass was applicable when the injury was *direct* and *immediate;* case was the remedy for *indirect* or *consequential* harm. The best known articulation of this principle is the oft-cited Scott v. Shepherd (K.B.1772), but the principle clearly pre-dates that case.

(2) Case actions required proof of *actual damages,* whereas trespass actions did not.

(3) Proof of defendant's *fault* was required in case, but not in trespass.

Trespass. The English court system in its early stages consisted of not one but many courts— royal, feudal, and communal—each with a jealously guarded jurisdiction of its own. The jurisdiction of the royal courts, from which came our common law, was at first quite limited, and had to be justified on some theory pertaining to the king's business. The royal courts first entertained the action of trespass on the theory that it involved a breach of the king's peace, which was for a time a necessary allegation. These courts' jurisdiction was thus limited to the more serious and inflammatory civil wrongs, and to actions to try title to property, for which trespass was often used. Eventually it became established that the essence of trespass was that defendant had committed some *affirmative* act which caused a *direct* and *immediate* injury to the plaintiff. Assault and battery "with force and arms," a forcible entry onto plaintiff's land, or the forcible taking of his chattels were the types of cases for which the action was most clearly designed. But it was not so limited. The requirement that plaintiff prove a *forceful* trespass was eventually dropped, although for a time it was still formally alleged.

Thereafter, plaintiff could recover for any direct and immediate trespass to his person or property, however slight the contact or harm, and if he could not prove actual damages nominal damages were awarded. Moreover, liability was strict, or nearly so. Plaintiff did not have to prove defendant's fault. Ordinarily the only defense available was a plea of not guilty—"I did not do it"—although other defenses were recognized, such as self defense and the use of force to repel a trespass or to effect a lawful arrest. In addition, there is occasional dictum that "inevitable accident" would excuse a trespass (e.g. Weaver v. Ward (K.B.1616)) but apparently this defense was never successfully invoked prior to the nineteenth century so long as the act of the defendant was voluntary. And it must be remembered that these were defenses; a prima facie case did not require that they be negated.

Case. The action on the case was the remedy for indirect injury. The classic illustration of the distinction between trespass and case is that of the log thrown onto a highway. One struck by the log as it fell could maintain trespass against the thrower; but one hurt by stumbling over it as it lay in the road was required to sue in case. In addition, case required allegation and proof of a breach of a duty, ordinarily by proof of defendant's fault—that is, that his conduct was illegal, intentionally wrongful, or unreasonably dangerous. And being wholly a civil action, actual damages were essential.

Negligence. The action on the case in most instances required proof of fault to establish a breach of duty to plaintiff, in a sense as a substitute for the missing element of a direct trespass. This fault could be the performance of a lawful act in a dangerous manner. Thus negligence (often under a different name) was, until recently, merely one basis of liability in a number of different civil actions for which case was the appropriate writ.

There is no clear path by which we can trace the development of the negligence concept from the emergence of case in the thirteenth century to the latter part of the eighteenth century when negligence came to be recognized as a special form of the action. From the beginning the common law had no difficulty in imposing liability for a wrongful act even though the harm it caused was indirect or delayed in time. Not so, however, if the wrong was instead a *failure* to act. Liability for nonfeasance was first imposed on those who undertook to perform some service and breached an express promise to exercise care or skill. This was extended to those engaged in "common callings"—common carriers, innkeepers, public warehousemen and other public servants (and for a time surgeons, smiths, carpenters, tailors and barbers). As to them, in the absence of an express promise a promise to exercise care and skill was implied. Gradually the idea was extended to the neglect of other duties, and with it came the tendency to allege that defendant had acted "negligently and recklessly" or similar words. During the eighteenth century liability for nonfeasance was considerably expanded, and the term "negligence" changed from a mere descriptive term to the standard characterization of the wrongful conduct, whether action or inaction.

By 1800, "case for negligence" was a common expression, and soon thereafter writers began to classify a large number of previously unclassified tort actions under that heading. As the vitality of the forms of action declined, intentional harms, direct and indirect, came to be grouped as a separate field of liability, and a general concept of negligence took hold. Thus, negligence came to be regarded as itself an independent tort. It is important to remember, however, that the term continues to be used in both senses. It is the name of a tort cause of action, and it also describes the actor's conduct in this and other torts.

United States. In this country, all of the states (except Louisiana) received the common law of England including its forms of action. But during the formative period of American law, significant changes occurred. One was the abolition, to a greater or lesser extent, of the forms of action which were replaced either by a single civil action at law or by a limited number of actions such as trespass (for all torts) and assumpsit (for contracts). Another was the restriction of tort liability.

Fault became a necessary element of plaintiff's case in a trespass action, both in this country and in England. The leading American case was

Brown v. Kendall (Mass.1850). Defendant raised a stick to separate two fighting dogs, and in doing so accidentally struck the eye of plaintiff who was standing behind him. Plaintiff sued in trespass for assault and battery. Under the English common law plaintiff should have won, since the injury was directly caused by defendant's voluntary act. Although the court held that trespass was the proper form of action, it found for defendant, holding that liability in trespass required either intentional or negligent misconduct. The *Brown* case was widely cited and followed. Eventually most states applied the same rule in cases of trespass to land and chattels.

Liability was limited in other ways as well. Charities and units of government were given total immunity for the torts of their employees. Employers generally were protected from liability to their injured employees by the strict application of the doctrines of contributory negligence, assumption of the risk of known hazards in the work situation, and the fellow-servant rule. American courts in the nineteenth century largely rejected the English doctrine of strict liability for harm caused by abnormally dangerous activities (§ 3—3). A consumer injured by all but the most dangerous products had a cause of action, if any, only against his immediate vendor. The fault ethic was so strong that the New York Court of Appeals in 1911 held the state's first workmen's compensation statute unconstitutional because it imposed liability without fault.

The past fifty years have seen a dramatic reversal of this attitude. Workmen's compensation statutes have been passed and sustained in every state. Charitable and governmental immunities have crumbled. Strict liability for abnormally dangerous activities is now the general rule. Manufacturers as well as retailers are strictly liable for defective products in most states. Comparative negligence in lieu of contributory negligence has become the majority rule. New causes of action, such as for invasion of privacy and negligent infliction of psychic trauma, have been created. Procedural reform, such as the abolition of the forms of action in almost all states and improved discovery procedures, has removed many of the barriers to the successful prosecution of meritorious claims. Vestiges of its ancestry are still discernible, but the tort law of today, like society itself, is far different from that which our forefathers knew.

§ 1—4. The Roles of Judges and Juries

In the United States, the vast majority of tort (and especially accident) cases are settled prior to filing suit or prior to trial, but they are settled largely on the basis of counsel's judgments as to what a jury verdict in the case is likely to be. In those tort cases which reach the litigation stage, trial by jury is usually demanded. The remainder of this book will briefly outline the rules of tort law, but it is well to remember that for the most part, these rules do not decide actual cases.

The preeminent power in resolving tort cases lies with the "trier of fact" which is customarily a jury.

It is commonly said that questions of *law* are for the court and questions of *fact* are for the jury. This is not entirely true, and can be a little misleading, since judges possess the ultimate power to decide which is which. But through well-established rules and customs, and by use of the general verdict, juries are given wide latitude to decide these controversies without court interference.

Jury questions are of three kinds. R. § 328C. First, the jury must determine what in fact occurred—was the light red or green when defendant drove through it, did defendant utter certain words, did plaintiff look before he stepped, and the like. Then, in most cases, the jury is required to make one or more decisions as to the *legal consequences* of these facts—was plaintiff or defendant negligent, were the words defamatory, was plaintiff a trespasser, licensee, or invitee, etc. —usually on the basis of some general legal definition given by the court. Finally, the jury must determine whether plaintiff was damaged by defendant's tortious act and the dollar value of plaintiff's compensable damages.

Questions of law for the court are also of three kinds. R. § 328B. First, certain issues are invariably issues of law, such as (1) whether defendant owed plaintiff any recognized legal duty, or, conversely, whether plaintiff has a legally protected right; (2) the elements of proof necessary to establish liability (or nonliability) and the measure of damages; and (3) whether, on the facts, some particular rule of law imposes or excuses liability as matter of law—for example, the rule that violation of a certain safety statute is negligence per se, or that false statements of intent are not actionable misrepresentations. The latter are sometimes stated in terms of duty or "proximate" (i.e., legal) cause, but they are more particularized standards of conduct than the broad general rules usually associated with the term "duty," such as the duty to exercise reasonable care in operating a motor vehicle. It will be seen that by embodying particular standards of conduct in rules of law, courts take from the jury the power to determine the legal consequences of certain facts, and thereby transform questions of fact into questions of law and enable the court to decide the case instead of the jury.

Second, all issues which are ordinarily questions of fact for the jury become questions of law for the court if the judge decides that the evidence on that issue so overwhelmingly favors one conclusion that reasonable men could not reach the opposite conclusion.

Third, judges alone apply rules of procedure which may have an important effect upon the outcome of the case, especially rules concerning the admission and exclusion of evidence, burden of proof, presumptions, and the applicability of res ipsa loquitur.

However, in spite of the ultimate powers of decision retained by the courts, the fact is that courts do permit juries to render the ultimate judgment in a substantial proportion of tort cases, particularly where the controlling issues involve disputes as to what occurred or mixed questions of law and fact such as breach of duty, status, damages, causation, and the like.

Thus, it is important to understand that tort law is not merely a system of rules of actionable or nonactionable conduct, but also of rules which determine when the law will *not* decide cases and instead will leave the decision whether to impose liability to the more or less unfettered discretion of the jury. In fact, one scholar has suggested that "nearly all legal theory in negligence cases is designed to serve the ends of allocating the power of judgment respectively to judge and jury." (L. Green, Judge & Jury 261). In many—perhaps even most—tort cases, rules of law take one only so far, and the lawyer or judge cannot determine the ultimate liability question. In such cases, it is necessary and entirely appropriate to say that beyond a certain point, the remaining issues are jury questions, and therefore whether or not the particular defendant is liable to the particular plaintiff is merely an educated guess.

See generally R. §§ 285, 328B, 328C; Harper & James c. 15; Prosser, §§ 37–40, 45.

CHAPTER 2

CAUSE IN FACT

§ 2—1. Cause in Fact

Obviously, the most basic element of any tort
cause of action is some causal connection between the act or omission of the tortfeasor and
plaintiff's injury. Yet the application of this
simple concept has proved one of the most
troublesome tasks in all of tort law. No other
topic has occasioned so much controversy and
confusion among both courts and legal scholars.

One source of confusion has been the common
tendency of judges to discuss all causation problems under the misleading term "proximate
cause." It is preferable to divide causation problems into two distinct categories: (1) cause in
fact and (2) legal cause. Both must be established before liability may be imposed. Legal
cause is primarily a device for limiting the scope
of liability to those consequences of defendant's
conduct which bear some reasonable relationship
to the risk he created. Problems of legal cause
arise most often in cases of nonintentional physical harm, and therefore will be discussed in § 4—
4, infra.

In its simplest form, cause in fact is established
by evidence which tends to show that defendant's
act or omission was a necessary antecedent to
plaintiff's injury. Many courts express this in

the form of a rule commonly known as the "but for" or "sine qua non" rule: defendant's conduct is not a cause of the event, if the event would have occurred without it.

Proof. A large number of cause in fact problems are merely problems of proof. Plaintiff's decedent is found at the bottom of defendant's stairway, obviously killed by a fall. The stairway is littered with debris and poorly lit. Was the negligent maintenance of the stairway the cause of decedent's death? The usual rules of circumstantial evidence apply, and if the jury can draw a reasonable inference of causation, its determination is final. Compare Wolf v. Kaufmann (N. Y.App.1929) (cause not proved) with Wright v. Stech (Ill.App.1972) (jury question). And where a resolution of the cause issue requires special knowledge beyond that possessed by the average juror, plaintiff must produce satisfactory expert testimony. E.g., Stubbs v. City of Rochester (N. Y.1919) (cause of typhoid fever).

Multiple Causes. In real life, of course, every occurrence has many causative antecedents. Recognizing this, the test for tort liability is whether the cause for which defendant was responsible was a *material element* and a *substantial factor* in bringing about the event. It need not be the sole cause, nor (contrary to the implication of the term "proximate") the last or nearest cause, and thus there may be two or more causes which were material and substantial.

Such multiple causation cases often present special problems.

A defendant is not relieved of liability merely because others are also responsible for the same harm. Where the negligence of two drivers concurs to produce a collision which injures a bystander, both may be held jointly and severally liable, even though there was no concert of action and despite the fact that the negligence of neither driver alone would have resulted in injury.

Going one step further, there may be two culpable acts or omissions which concur to cause plaintiff's harm, either one of which alone would have been sufficient to produce the same result. For example, two fires, each negligently set, combine to destroy plaintiff's property; either one alone would have done the same thing. In such cases, the "sine qua non" rule is inapplicable, and both defendants may be held jointly and severally liable for the whole loss.

Suppose, however, there are two sufficient causes and one is blameless—in the last example, one of the fires was set by lightning. The better rule holds the negligent defendant liable, since the fortuitous intervention of a natural event ought not to exonerate him when he would have been liable without it, and he would have been jointly and severally liable if the other cause were the culpable act or omission of another.

If there are two or more causative agents and each is responsible only for a divisible part of plaintiff's harm, the law will hold each culpable defendant liable only for his respective portion of the damages, unless the defendants were acting in concert or engaged in a joint enterprise. For example, if several riparian owners pollute a stream, each is liable only for that portion of the damage caused by his contribution.

The exception to this principle is where A's act injures plaintiff and also foreseeably exposes him to an increased risk of further injury by B. Driver A runs down plaintiff and renders him helpless in the roadway where he is struck again by B, who was also negligent; A is liable for plaintiff's entire damage, but B only for that portion he caused. Another relatively common example is where A negligently injures plaintiff and B, a doctor, aggravates the injury by negligent treatment. A is again liable for all of plaintiff's damages, including those caused by B's malpractice, for which B is also jointly and severally liable.

Subject to this exception, plaintiff's damages must be apportioned where they are even theoretically divisible. In other words, in any case where a given defendant was *in fact* responsible for less than all of plaintiff's damages, plaintiff may have judgment against that defendant for no more than his share, and the burden is on the plaintiff to prove his contribution or fail to recover against him at all. As a practical matter, in many cases adequate proof is impossible, with the result that plaintiff may have been seriously damaged by several defendants and be unable to recover anything from any of them.   However, courts have often come to plaintiff's rescue with the aid of various devices, such as finding concerted action, or an indivisible injury for which all are jointly liable, by relaxing standards of proof, or, sensibly, by shifting the burden of apportionment to the defendants.

A special variation of this case is where there is clearly established double fault and alternative liability.   Suppose two defendants negligently and simultaneously fire shotguns in the direction of plaintiff, and he is struck by the shot from only one, but cannot prove which.   Rather than find a dubious concert of action (as a few courts have done), the California Supreme Court in such a case shifted the burden of proof on the issue of causation to the defendants, and imposed liability on both unless and until one or the other could prove his innocence.   Summers v. Tice (Cal. 1948).

See, on cause in fact, R. §§ 430–434.

PART II

PHYSICAL HARM

CHAPTER 3

STRICT LIABILITY

§ 3—1. Basis of Strict Liability

Modern tort law classifies the cases involving physical harm to persons and property according to the degree of fault inherent in the tortious conduct: intentional, negligent (including reckless or "wilful and wanton" misconduct), and a third category called "strict liability," "absolute liability," or "liability without fault."

As previously noted (§ 1—3) it is generally thought that strict liability was the prevailing rule of the early common law. Certainly it was where the proper form of action was trespass. Gradually the negligence concept emerged, carrying with it the requirement that defendant's conduct be blameworthy in the sense of creating an unreasonable risk of harm. The intentional torts became a separate category. Ultimately, the fault ethic became predominate. But there remained certain cases where the historically-rooted strict liability was preserved.

Writers have disagreed as to whether there is any liability without an element of fault. The issue is largely definitional. Legal fault is not the same as moral blame; it is merely a deviation from some standard of conduct required by society for the protection of its members. If the departure is innocent, or if defendant cannot help it, he may be *morally* blameless but he is nonetheless *legally* at fault.

The activities which give rise to strict liability —e.g., blasting, storing dangerous substances, keeping dangerous animals—are not so unreasonable as to be prohibited altogether; indeed, they may be socially useful or necessary. But they are sufficiently dangerous or create sufficiently *unusual* risks that the law requires them to be carried on at the actor's peril. Thus, it has been suggested that the fault is *conditional,* arising only if and when harm results, or that there is an element of fault in carrying on the activity at all but that the activity is privileged so long as it does not cause harm. Such analyses are, of course, somewhat tautological; they equate fault and legal liability. It may be just as valid to ignore "fault" and to say that certain activities, for reasons of social policy, may be conducted only if the person conducting them is willing to insure others against the harm which results from the risks they create.

There are a number of instances in the law of liability without fault, besides those (discussed in this chapter) which traditionally are collected under the heading "strict" or "absolute" liability.

Certain statutes (e.g. workmen's compensation) create it. It is found in an employer's liability for the torts of his employees, in common law liability for defamation, and in liability for selling defective products. The common thread which runs through all forms of strict liability is that, irrespective of the care with which it is conducted, a particular activity ought to carry with it the costs of the risks it creates. If it helps one to stretch the concept "fault" to include the creation of these risks, perhaps no harm is done, but it would seem preferable to view strict liability as special instances of mandatory insurance against particular designated risks imposed as a matter of policy irrespective of fault.

§ 3—2. Animals and Fire

Harm caused by animals and fire are early examples of common law strict liability.

Animals. To primitive law, a man and his chattels were an entity, and liability without fault was imposed on the owners of animals and other personal property which caused harm. Strict liability for damage caused by animals has survived (with modifications) the general shift to the fault requirement, probably because of the special risks they create. Since animals have no conscience with which to restrain themselves, and possess great capacity to do mischief if not restrained, those who keep them have a duty to restrain them or pay.

Trespassing Animals. In most jurisdictions, the general rule is that keepers of all animals, including domesticated ones, are strictly liable for damage resulting from the trespass of their animals on the property of another.

There are three principal exceptions:

(1) Owners of dogs and cats are not liable, absent negligence, for their trespasses, except where strict liability is imposed by statute or ordinance.

(2) Highways are properly used for moving livestock, and hence there is no liability without negligence for damage caused by the trespass on property adjoining a road by animals straying from the road on which they are being lawfully driven.

(3) In some parts of the western United States, certain farm animals (especially cattle) by custom or statute are permitted to graze at large on the range, and their owners are not strictly liable for their trespasses. In some states there are "fencing out" statutes which require landowners who wish to exclude such animals to construct a certain type of fence; having done so, the animals' owner is strictly liable for subsequent trespasses. In other states, "fencing in" statutes relieve the animal's owner of strict liability if he has constructed a certain fence to keep his animals on his own property.

The basis of liability for animal trespass is possession and control. Hence, if the owner surrenders possession to another, the bailee becomes liable. Except perhaps as to wild or known danger-ous animals, the bailment relieves the owner's lia-bility.

Liability Apart From Trespass. For purposes of liability for harm other than trespass, the law distinguishes between animals domestic and wild. In the case of animals which are customarily do-mesticated and kept in that region (e.g., in the U.S., dogs, cats, cattle, sheep, horses, etc.) the keeper is strictly liable for the harm they cause only if he had actual knowledge (or had knowl-edge of facts which ought to have given him no-tice) that the animal had the particular trait or propensity which caused the harm. The trait must be a potentially harmful one, such as vicious-ness or destructive tendencies (as opposed to, e. g., excessive playfulness), and the harm must cor-respond to the knowledge; notice that a dog will attack other dogs is not, of itself, notice that he will attack humans. Thus, it is often said that "every dog is entitled to one bite," but this is not necessarily true since the keeper may be on no-tice by reason of other known facts. In some jurisdictions, statutes impose absolute liability for certain types of damage (e.g. dog bites) without requiring scienter.

Keepers of species which are normally consid-ered "wild" in that region (e.g., in the U.S., bears, lions, elephants, monkeys, etc.) are strictly liable for the harm they cause if they escape, whether or not the animal in question is known to be dangerous. And because such animals are known to revert to their natural tendencies, they are considered to be wild no matter how well trained or domesticated. However, where the injury occurs on the owner's premises while the animal is confined or restrained, the cases tend to deny strict liability, commonly on a theory of assumed risk.

Fire. The early common law probably imposed something close to strict liability for damage caused by the spread of a fire for which defendant was responsible. In the case of domestic fires, the rule was changed in England by statute (1774) to require at least negligence. But if the fire had its origin in an activity which was itself abnormally dangerous (§ 3—3), strict liability remained the rule. No such strict liability has been adopted in the United States, except by statute in certain cases (railroad fires, prairie fires, fire started in dry season).

§ 3—3. Abnormally Dangerous Activities

Strict liability for harm resulting from abnormally dangerous conditions and activities is a relatively recent development in tort law, but its roots are found in earlier forms of liability without fault. The doctrine originated in the leading English case styled Rylands v. Fletcher (Exch. Ch.1866, aff'd, H.L.1868). Defendants, mill owners in the coal mining area of Lancashire, constructed a reservoir on their land. The water broke through the filled-in shaft of an abandoned coal mine and flooded along connecting passageways into plaintiff's active mine nearby. The trier of fact found that defendants were ignorant of the abandoned mine shaft and free of negligence. The lower court held for defendants.

On appeal, the Exchequer Chamber decided to impose strict liability, but the case did not fit into the existing tort pigeon-holes. There was no trespass since the flooding was not direct or immediate (the premises of plaintiff and defendants did not adjoin) nor any nuisance (as the term was then understood) since there was nothing offensive to the senses and the damage was not continuous or recurring. Using analogies to strict liability for trespassing cattle, dangerous animals, and "absolute" nuisance, Justice Blackburn concluded:

> We think that the true rule of law is, that the person who for his own purposes brings on his lands and collects and keeps there anything likely to do mischief if it escapes, must keep it in at his peril, and, if he does not do so, is prima facie answerable for all the damage which is the natural consequence of its escape.

Defendants appealed to the House of Lords, which affirmed, but the rule of the case was more narrowly stated by Lord Cairns:

> The Defendants . . . might lawfully have used that close for any purpose for which it might in the ordinary course of the enjoyment

of land be used; and if, in what I may term the
natural user of that land, there had been any
accumulation of water, either on the surface or
underground, and if, by the operation of the
laws of nature, that accumulation of water had
passed off into the close occupied by the Plaintiff, the Plaintiff could not have complained
.   .   ..

On the other hand, if the Defendants, not
stopping at the natural use of their close, had
desired to use it for any purpose which I may
term a non-natural use, for the purpose of introducing into the close that which in its natural condition was not in or upon it, for the purpose of introducing water either above or below ground in quantities and in a manner not
the result of any work or operation on or under
the land,—and if in consequence of their doing
so, or in consequence of any imperfection in
the mode of their doing so, the water came to
escape and to pass off into the close of the
Plaintiff, then it appears to me that that which
the Defendants were doing they were doing at
their own peril .   .   ..

Thus, the emphasis was placed upon the activity's non-natural or abnormal character, and subsequent English cases have turned on this distinction.   There is strict liability for harm resulting
from the miscarriage of an activity which,
though lawful, is unusual, extraordinary, excep-
tional or inappropriate, in light of the place and

manner in which the activity is conducted. Thus, water collected in household pipes or a stock watering tank or a cistern is a natural use; but water collected in large tanks in dangerous proximity to plaintiff's land is not. Gas or electricity in household pipes or wires is a normal use, but not so gas stored in large quantity or high-voltage electricity under the street. Although the automobile is manifestly dangerous, the risks of harm it creates, absent negligence, are common and accepted; but those created by a ten-ton traction engine or a steam roller are not. The storage in quantity of explosives or flammable liquids, blasting, accumulation of sewage, emission of creosote fumes, and pile driving all have been held to be sufficiently unusual and excessive under the circumstances to justify strict liability.

The same activity may be appropriate or normal in one location but not in another. This suggests that the primary basis of liability is the creation of an extraordinary risk, either in kind or degree. A water reservoir is an inappropriate use of land in a coal mining area (Rylands v. Fletcher), but not in West Texas (Turner v. Big Lake Oil Co., Tex.1936). The storage of explosives in quantity, or blasting, create unusual and unacceptable risks in the midst of a large city, but not in remote rural areas. An oil well in the oil fields of Pennsylvania is a natural use of the land and there is no strict liability for resulting harm; but the opposite is true of an oil well drilled in a thickly settled residential area of Los

Angeles. If the activity is appropriate to the
area, there is strict liability only if it is conducted in an unusual or abnormal way (e.g. crop
dusting).

Until 1947, the English cases had applied the
doctrine broadly. While the rule was originally
framed in terms of an "escape" of that which
caused the harm, subsequent cases imposed no
such requirement. And the rule was extended to
cover personal injuries as well as property damage. But in Read v. J. Lyons & Co., Ltd. (1947),
the House of Lords refused to impose strict liability in favor of a government inspector injured in
an explosion at defendant's munitions plant on
the ground that there had been no escape of a
dangerous substance from defendant's land. In
addition two of the judges thought that the rule
did not apply to personal injuries. It is not yet
clear whether this case is aberrational or represents a change in the law's direction in England.

At first, the doctrine was widely rejected by
American courts. (Interestingly, a number of
cases spurning the "rule" rejected it in the broad
form stated by Justice Blackburn, ignoring or
overlooking the fact that the final formulation by
Lord Cairns was somewhat narrower.) Much of
the earlier hostility to the rule was probably due
to the strength of the fault ethic and to a desire
to protect emerging industries. More recently, of
course, the policy pendulum has swung to the
view that hazardous enterprises, however useful,

must pay their own way. At present, a majority of U.S. jurisdictions accept the rule, in name or in fact, and it remains rejected by name in only seven states. However, in comparison to the English decisions, American cases have been slightly less liberal in applying the rule. For example, no U.S. case has yet applied the doctrine to electricity in any form or place (although they uniformly require a high degree of care commensurate with the danger). But see Ferguson v. Northern States Power Co. (Minn.1976) (rule cited with approval).

Even where *Rylands v. Fletcher* is expressly rejected or narrowly applied, the same result may be reached by other means. The principal theory is "absolute nuisance," under which negligence or intent to do harm need not be proven. Prosser states (§ 78):

There is in fact probably no case applying Rylands v. Fletcher which is not duplicated in all essential respects by some American decision which proceeds on the theory of nuisance; and it is quite evident that under that name the principle is in reality universally accepted.

Trespass is another. In cases involving damage caused by blasting (an activity often cited to typify a *Rylands v. Fletcher* situation) some courts (e.g. New York) imposed strict common law trespass liability for harm caused by debris thrown off defendant's premises, in lieu of adopting *Rylands*. The catch was that under this theory, there was no strict liability for damage caused solely by vibration or concussion, since there was no trespass. Most of the jurisdictions which once made this distinction have now repudiated it and impose strict liability for all blasting-caused damage, direct and indirect, with or without accepting *Rylands*.

Aviation has been a source of controversy. So far as passengers and cargo are concerned, the usual rules of negligence law have always been applied. But as to ground damage caused by falling aircraft or objects or forced landings, various rules have been applied or suggested. Some early cases imposed strict liability on a trespass theory. The Uniform Aeronautics Act, promulgated in 1922, provided for strict liability, and it was adopted (sometimes with modifications) in several states. So did the Restatement (First) of Torts § 520, Comment *b* (1939). However, as the industry has passed from its infancy and become a common and safe means of transportation, there has been something of a retreat toward negligence.

The Uniform Act was withdrawn in 1943. Several state statutes have been modified or repealed. Some strict liability decisions have been overruled (e.g., see Wood v. United Air Lines, Inc., N.Y.1962).

Even though it now is generally agreed that aviation no longer creates abnormal or unusual risks, it has also been recognized that there remain good reasons to justify strict liability for ground damage. The probability of harm is small, but the potential gravity is great and there is simply no way for those on the ground to avoid the risk. Thus, the Restatement (Second) Torts § 520A provides strict liability for ground damage caused by "the ascent, descent or flight of any aircraft, or by the dropping or falling of any object therefrom." It must be remembered, however, that statutes in almost half the states supersede the common law to a greater or lesser extent.

The advance of technology will likely provide new illustrations of this rule. Two cases have imposed strict liability for damage caused by rocket testing. And it seems certain that the same result will be reached if the case ever arises involving nuclear energy.

In this area, the Restatement of Torts has been of questionable value, and has not accurately mirrored the case law. The first Restatement limited strict liability to "ultrahazardous" activities which the actor "should recognize as likely" to cause harm "by the unpreventable miscarriage of the activity" (§ 519). An activity was said to be ultrahazardous if it "(a) necessarily involves a risk of serious harm .   .   . which cannot be eliminated by the exercise of the utmost care, and (b) is not a matter of common usage." (§ 520) Generally speaking, the case law did not require that the harm be unpreventable, that the risk necessarily be a "serious" one, nor that the plaintiff prove the foreseeable *probability* of the harm. In addition, the formulation was misleading, as noted by the reporter to the Restatement (Second), since there is probably *no* activity which is not perfectly safe if the *utmost* care is used in conducting it (including the choice of location). The Restatement (Second) §§ 519, 520, approved in 1964, simply provides strict liability for activities which are "abnormally dangerous," to be determined by considering six factors:

(a) whether the activity involves a high degree of risk of some harm to the person, land or chattels of others;

(b) whether the gravity of the harm which may result from it is likely to be great;

(c) whether the risk cannot be eliminated by the exercise of reasonable care;

(d) whether the activity is not a matter of common usage;

(e) whether the activity is inappropriate to the place where it is carried on; and

(f) the value of the activity to the community.

This formulation is far superior, and gives much needed flexibility; but it should be noted that not all courts will consider all factors, and some factors are of greater significance than others.

§ 3—4.　Scope of Strict Liability

All forms of strict liability have similar limits and defenses.

Scienter. Unless otherwise provided by statute, defendant must *knowingly* engage in (or authorize) the activity. Fairness dictates that if liability is strict, at least the risk must be consciously assumed.

Proximate Cause. For similar reasons, courts tend to invoke a narrower rule of proximate cause than in negligence cases (see § 4—4, infra). Thus, liability is confined to those consequences, the risk of which made the activity abnormally dangerous in the first place (R. § 519 (2)), and to those persons foreseeably within the zone of danger, the courts applying a slightly more restrictive view of what is foreseeable.

In negligence cases, defendant is ordinarily not excused by the fact that the harm was brought about by an unforeseeable intervening cause (such as an "act of God") so long as the result is within the scope of the risk he created. However, in strict liability cases unforeseeable intervening cause is a defense. See, e.g., Madsen v. East Jordan Irrigation Co. (Utah 1942) (blasting caused frightened mother mink to kill her kittens); Kaufman v. Boston Dye House (Mass. 1932) (flammable liquid discharged into stream ignited by sparks from passing truck). The Restatement and Restatement (Second) § 552 are contra, but so far the courts have refused to follow this section, apparently on the theory that one who is held to the liability of an insurer at least ought to be able to predict the limits of his risk with reasonable certainty.

Contributory Negligence, Assumption Of Risk. Contributory negligence is not a defense in a strict liability case. R. § 484(1). At first glance, this may seem incongruous; plaintiff's fault will excuse defendant's liability when he is also at fault but not when he is innocent. But recall that strict liability is based on the *wilful* creation of an abnormal risk by unusual conduct; inherent in the creation of such a risk is the possibility that others may fail to anticipate or guard against it.

"At the same time, the defense which consists of voluntarily and unreasonably encountering a known danger, and in negligence cases passes more or less indiscriminately under the names of contributory negligence and assumption of risk, will, in general, relieve the defendant of strict liability." Prosser, § 79; R. § 484(2). Thus, one who brings himself within the reach of, or provokes, a dangerous animal cannot recover if he knew of the danger or if it was obvious. And while strict liability ordinarily extends to invitees, licensees, and even known trespassers on defendant's premises (R. § 512) such persons cannot recover if they knew of the danger and proceeded to bring themselves within its zone.

Note, however, that the encountering of the risk must be both voluntary and *unreasonable*. Defendant, by creating a patently dangerous condition, may not unreasonably limit plaintiff's freedom of action or unreasonably restrict the use of neighboring land. And in many situations (e.g. a circus) plaintiff may reasonably assume that defendant will protect him against the obvious risks.

Legislative and Public Duty Privileges. When legislation expressly authorizes or imposes a duty to carry on an activity, strict liability is usually not imposed. R. §§ 517, 521. E.g., Pumphrey v. J. A. Jones Constr. Co. (Iowa 1959) (blasting under state contract); Guzzi v. New York Zoological Soc'y. (N.Y.1922) (custodian of public zoo); Pope v. Edward M. Rude Carrier Corp. (W.Va. 1943) (common carrier required to accept dangerous cargo). Contra: Smith v. Lockheed Propulsion Co. (Cal.App.1967) (rocket testing under government contract).

Federal Tort Claims. The Federal Tort Claims Act waives the sovereign immunity of the United States for harm caused by the "negligent or wrongful act or omission of any employee of the Government," but this language has been construed to exclude claims based on strict or absolute liability. Laird v. Nelms (U.S.1972).

CHAPTER 4

LIABILITY FOR NEGLIGENT CONDUCT

§ 4—1. Standards of Conduct: Of Risks and Reasonable Persons

The term "negligence" is used in two senses. First, it is the name of a tort cause of action, notable for its breadth. It is the closest thing there is to a general principle of tort liability. As a general rule, all persons are under a duty to conduct themselves in all of their diverse activities so as not to create unreasonable risks of harm to others. In certain cases, as will be noted later, this duty is limited or denied, but unless such a special exception exists one may be held liable for the injurious consequences of his negligent conduct.

Second, "negligence" describes that form of wrongful conduct itself which is an element of various tort causes of action (or defenses), including the action of that name. Thus, the components of the cause of action for negligence are:

(1) A *duty* owed by defendant to plaintiff (or, more accurately, the absence of any rule limiting the general duty of ordinary care) (§ 4—5);

(2) A violation of that duty by defendant's failure to conform to the required standard of conduct (i.e., *"negligence"*);

(3) A sufficient *causal connection* between the negligent conduct and the resulting harm (§§ 2—1, 4—4); and

(4) Actual *loss* or *damage*.

Plaintiff's *contributory negligence* will reduce or defeat his claim. In most jurisdictions, contributory negligence is a defense to be pleaded and proved by defendant, but in some plaintiff must allege and prove his freedom from contributory negligence as a part of his prima facie case.

In analyzing the negligence cause of action, we will first consider the nature of negligence itself. What criteria do we use to determine whether defendant's act or omission may be deemed to be negligent?

General Characteristics of Negligence. According to the accepted definition, "negligence is conduct which falls below the standard established by law for the protection of others against unreasonable risk of harm."   R. § 282.

To laymen, "negligence" imports the absence of carefulness as a state of mind.   The root word "neglect" implies forgetfulness or inattentiveness, determined subjectively and individually.   In this sense, negligence and moral fault coincide.

But this is not the accepted legal concept. As the definition indicates, legal negligence is *conduct*.   If one's conduct creates an unreasonable risk of harm, he may be held negligent even though his actual state of mind was one of anxious concern for the safety of others.   In such cases, legal fault and moral blame diverge.

This is not to suggest, however, that the actor's state of mind is irrelevant.   Whether or not his conduct in question was reasonable may depend, in part, on what he actually knew. For example, whether one who operates an automobile with defective steering is negligent may depend upon whether he knows of the defect. The distinction, so far as negligence liability is concerned, is between (1) knowledge and perception and (2) motive and intent. In judging whether conduct is negligent, the actor is charged with what he actually knew and actually perceived, as well as what he ought to have known and perceived. However, we do not permit the actor to defend his conduct by proof that his subjective intent or motive was to act nonnegligently. The ultimate issue is the reasonableness of his conduct, not the reasonableness of his belief that he was acting with appropriate care. Conversely, if defendant's *conduct* did not subject plaintiff to an *unreasonable* risk of harm defendant was not negligent, even though his state of mind was that of total obliviousness to the safety of others.

The Reasonable Person. In general, in judging whether conduct is negligent the law applies objective standards of reasonableness. It does not make special allowance for the particular weaknesses of the actor. The clumsy, rash, timid, forgetful, the chronically careless person, the fool, the ignorant, the slow reactor, the person with low intelligence—all are held to the general standard of reasonable care, whether or not they are capable of meeting it. Conduct which creates an unreasonable risk of harm is no less dangerous simply because the actor lacked the capacity to conform to an acceptable level of performance. While it may be somewhat unfair to such persons to hold them to a standard which they cannot always meet, it would be more unjust to require the innocent victims of their substandard conduct to assume such risks.

The standard is usually stated as "ordinary care" or "due care" or "reasonable care," measured against the hypothetical conduct of a hypothetical person—the "reasonable man of ordinary prudence." The question is, what would the "reasonable man" (sometimes the "ordinarily prudent person") have done under the same circumstances as those in which defendant found himself? R. § 283.

The reasonable person is, of course, a creature of the law's imagination. He is not the average or typical person, but rather an idealized image of such a person. He is a composite of the community's judgment as to how the typical community member *ought* to behave in each of the infinite variety of circumstances and activities in which there is a potential or actual risk of harm to himself or others. The test is not what the typical respectable citizen in fact does, nor what the majority of the community does, since the behavior (e.g. jaywalking) may fall below the community's standards of safety.

On the other hand, the reasonable person is not perfect or infallible. He is permitted errors of judgment, mistakes in perception; he may even be momentarily distracted. He is human. But such errors must have been reasonable or excusable under the circumstances; they must have been consistent with the exercise of ordinary care.

Attributes of the Reasonable Person.

Knowledge, Experience and Perception. Tort liability for physical harm is founded upon defendant's knowledge (actual or constructive) of the risk and of some degree of probability that it will be realized (harm to the plaintiff). In negligence (as distinguished from intentional torts), the actor does not desire the injurious consequences of his conduct; he does not know that they are substantially certain to occur, nor believe that they will. There is merely a risk of such consequences sufficiently great that the ordinarily prudent person will anticipate them and guard against them. Thus, the normal actor (plaintiff or defendant) is charged with his *actual* knowledge and perceptions, and also with certain basic knowledge common to the community and with the ability to observe and understand his environment.

Obviously, conduct must be judged in light of what the actor *actually* knows and observes, since the reasonable person always takes this into account. If he by chance discovers that a product has a latent dangerous defect, if he sees another vehicle approaching his without lights at night, he must act accordingly, even though he would not have been negligent in failing to discover or observe these things. R. § 289.

In addition, most persons are deemed to have the knowledge and experience, and the ability to perceive, understand and remember, of the hypothetical reasonable person. Thus, in the absence of overriding extenuating circumstances, one must see the clearly visible and hear the clearly audible. A driver approaching a railroad crossing where the view is unobstructed will not be heard to say that he did not see the approaching train or hear its whistle. And one cannot deny personal knowledge of those things which are commonly known in the community: basic principles of physics (materials which are combustible, the danger of electricity, principles of leverage), the limits of the body's physical capacity, the natural propensities of children and animals, the dangers of common sports, the effects of intoxicating beverages, and the like. R. § 290. Moreover, one must take notice of what he does *not* know (such as when walking in a strange dark hallway, or using an unfamiliar product or substance) and exercise caution commensurate to his ignorance.

One who undertakes an activity ordinarily is charged with the knowledge common to those who regularly engage in it. A product manufacturer must know the characteristics and dangers of his product, at least to the extent that they are generally known in the industry or reasonably knowable. A motorist must know the rules of the road. And knowledge must keep reasonably current.

Special Skills. If the actor has chosen to engage in an activity requiring special skills, education, training or experience, then the standard by which his conduct is measured is that of the reasonably skilled, competent and experienced person who is a qualified member of the group authorized to engage in that activity. R. §§ 299, 299A. Typically (though not necessarily) these are activities which are licensed—physicians and surgeons, lawyers, architects, barbers, pilots, motorists, and the like—in general, the professions and skilled trades. The public properly relies upon the special expertise of those who engage in such activities, so that persons who undertake (even gratuitously) to perform them are judged by the standards of conduct of those properly qualified to do so, whether or not the actor is in fact a recognized member of the group in question. For example, a druggist who undertakes to diagnose and prescribe medication for an illness described to him by a customer will be judged by the standards applicable to a physician.

With respect to medical doctors (and sometimes dentists), the standard of care has been limited by the so-called "locality rule." A doctor has been required only to possess and apply the knowledge and use the skill and care that is ordi-

[57]

narily used by reasonably well-qualified doctors *in the locality in which he practices* or, usually, in "similar localities". This frequently made it difficult or impossible for plaintiff to prove the applicable standard since other doctors in the same locality are reluctant to testify against their professional colleagues.   However, with the advent of improved communication and continuing medical education, the reason for the rule has abated, and today the trend is toward its abolition.

Where the profession recognizes specialists—as do medicine and dentistry—a certified specialist is held to the higher standard of the specialist subgroup.   And, like all reasonably prudent persons, the actor who possesses more than the minimum level of knowledge, skill, training or experience for that activity is required to apply it, especially where he holds himself out to the public as possessing such special competence.

In earlier times, when medical knowledge was less advanced, courts were forced to recognize divergent medical theories represented by different "schools" of medicine.   Thus, the conduct of a doctor who followed the teachings of a respectable "school" was judged by the tenets of that group.   Today, however, the accepted standards of diagnosis and treatment tend to be uniform nationally, although there are still many specific matters on which respectable medical authorities differ.   This is largely a matter for expert testimony, and there would seem to be little need to recognize "schools" as such. Of course, where the legislature has expressly sanctioned other types of healers, such as chiropractors and osteopaths, members of these groups will be judged by their own standards when acting within the areas of their competence.

As to all specialized activities, the law generally has refused to create a subgroup for novices. The learner, the beginner, the trainee—pilot, automobile driver, employee, professional—is held to the standard of conduct of persons who are reasonably skilled, learned and experienced in the activity. The law does not require the general public to assume the risk of the neophyte's lack of competence. True, these activities typically are socially useful and, of necessity, all those who would engage in them must be more or less unskillful and incompetent at first. The beginner is thus held to a standard which he sometimes cannot meet. But at least the beginner can take his lack of skill and experience into account and act accordingly, whereas the public is usually defenseless against these risks. Of course, in a given case the victim may be found to have knowingly and voluntarily assumed this risk (e.g. his instructor), but this does not affect the general standard of care to which the novice is held.

Physical Characteristics. Of necessity, the "reasonable person" standard is subjective to the extent that the actor's actual *physical* characteristics are taken into account. The test is, what is reasonable conduct for an ordinarily prudent person with the actor's physical characteristics? Or, what would the reasonably prudent person do under the circumstances, his physical handicap constituting one of those circumstances? R. § 283C. The blind, the deaf, the crippled, and all others physically impaired are no less entitled to live in the world because of their handicap, and it would be an unfair burden to require them to conform to a standard of conduct physically impossible for them to meet. At the same time, the physically handicapped person must act prudently in light of his infirmity, and he may be negligent in taking a risk which is unreasonable in view of his known physical limitations.

Mental Capacity. In judging the actor's conduct, no allowance is made for subjective deficiencies in the actor's mental capacity to conform to the standard of the reasonably prudent person. The fact that one is mentally deficient (in intelligence, judgment, memory, emotional stability, etc.), voluntarily intoxicated, or even insane does not generally excuse his failure to act as a reasonably prudent sane, sober and normal person would have acted under the same circumstances. R. §§ 283B, 895J. Although this imposes a standard of behavior which such persons often cannot possibly meet, their mental incapacity itself poses a threat to the general security and increases the risk of unreasonably dangerous conduct. As between such persons and their innocent victims, it is deemed preferable that the former (or those responsible for them) should bear this risk.

However, as to contributory negligence the reason for the rule does not apply with equal force, and some courts have applied a subjective standard and permitted the jury to excuse a plaintiff who lacked the mental capacity to appreciate the risk or avoid it (other than by intoxication). In particular, the elderly whose mental faculties are impaired by senility may qualify for subjective treatment.

Evidence of intoxication is frequently admitted on the issue of negligence, but the better view is that drunkenness is not negligence per se but does not excuse conduct otherwise negligent. Its true function in such cases is probably to aggravate the wrong. It is usually negligent (or even reckless) to undertake certain activities at all (e. g. driving) while intoxicated.

Minors. Children, like other incompetents, are liable for their torts. R. § 895I. But children as a class are expected to be more or less incapable of meeting adult standards of behavior, and of necessity are judged by a lesser standard. Thus, where plaintiff or defendant is a minor, the test is, what is reasonable conduct for a child of the actor's *age, intelligence* and *experience*. R. § 283A. Aside from society's general tolerance for the unintended misdeeds of its youth, there are several justifications for applying a subjective standard. For the most part, children do not engage in the high-risk activities of adults. Due to their smaller size and subjection to adult supervision and control, their negligence overall does not create the same magnitude of risk as that of adults. Also, children as a group are readily identifiable on sight, and thus others can frequently adjust their conduct to make allowance for them and their "childish" behavior.

A number of courts have gone so far as to establish arbitrary age ranges within which children are "presumed"—rebuttably or conclusively—to be incapable of negligence. In many states, children below a certain age (usually seven) are legally ("conclusively presumed") incapable of negligence. In the next higher range (usually seven to fourteen) they are rebuttably presumed incapable; above that, no presumption operates, which means that they are capable of negligence as a matter of law. Sometimes these presumptions apply only to the minor's contributory negligence. These multiples of seven were borrowed from rules of criminal responsibility, which in turn were derived from the Bible, and there is little justification for their use. It would seem preferable to leave the question of capacity to the jury in each case.

Tort law applies the statutory age of majority (which is now eighteen in most jurisdictions) for purposes of these rules and all those this age or above will be held to adult standards of conduct.

There is one major exception to the standard for minors. If the child is engaging in what is deemed to be an "adult" activity—such as operating an automobile or flying an airplane—he will be held to an adult standard of care. It is doubtful that the courts really intend to use the appellation "adult" in any literal sense, since minors are freely permitted to engage in them and regularly do so. Rather, this is merely an application of the rule, previously discussed, that *whoever* engages in an activity which requires special skill, experience, training, or education will be judged objectively by standards of reasonable competence for that activity, for the protection of the public, regardless of age.

Emergencies. The law recognizes that even the reasonably prudent person is susceptible to errors of judgment in emergency situations. Thus, in such cases the test is, was the actor's conduct in the emergency a reasonable response under the circumstances, even though in retrospect another course of action might have avoided the injury. R. § 296.

It must be remembered, however, that failure to anticipate an emergency may itself constitute negligence. The owner of a theater must consider the possibility of fire; the proprietor of a swimming pool or beach cannot ignore the likelihood of emergencies that threaten drowning; a certain level of "defensive" auto driving is required.

Moreover, the actor may have been negligent in creating the emergency in the first place, in which case he may be held liable for that negligence, even though his conduct in the emergency was acceptable.

Conduct of Others. The reasonable person will regulate his conduct in light of his expectations of the conduct of others. This is merely an application of the principle requiring him to know his environment.

This duty includes anticipating not only the reasonably prudent conduct of others, but in some cases their negligence or even unlawful conduct, at least where such conduct is reasonably foreseeable. It is sometimes said that an actor may assume that others will act lawfully and carefully. This may be true in specific situations, but it is equally clear that if he has reason to anticipate the contrary he must act accordingly. Thus, it may be negligence to leave one's car unlocked with the keys in the ignition due to the foreseeable risk of theft, or to fail to slow down in the vicinity of a school yard where children may negligently dart into the street. R. §§ 302A, 302B.

When Is A Risk "Unreasonable"? In general, and in the absence of some more specific rule of conduct, negligence is the doing of an act (or omitting to do an act which some duty requires), without wrongful intent, under circumstances where our hypothetical reasonably prudent person would foresee that he is thereby exposing another (or himself) to an *unreasonable* risk of harm. R. § 284. (Of course, the harm must be to a legally protected interest. This is a matter of duty, which will be discussed in § 4—5, infra, and throughout this book.)

When is the risk unreasonable? The classic formulation is that of Judge Learned Hand— when the foreseeable *probability* and *gravity* of the harm outweighs the *burden* to the actor of alternative conduct which would have prevented the harm. Conway v. O'Brien (2d Cir. 1940); United States v. Carroll Towing Co. (2d Cir. 1947). Compare Terry, Negligence, 29 Harv.L. Rev. 40 (1915); R. §§ 291–292.

The *probability* or likelihood that harm will result together with the *gravity* or seriousness of the potential harm, in combination, determine the magnitude of the risk (sometimes called the "hazard" or "danger"). R. § 293. Thus, it may be negligence to dash across a little-traveled highway without looking for traffic, even though the statistical probability that you and a fast-moving car will reach the same point at the same time is very low; the potential harm is very great. Conversely, the failure to repair a hole in a rarely-used sidewalk might not be negligence, whereas it would be if the sidewalk is heavily traveled. The gravity of the harm includes both the extent of the damage and the relative societal value of the protected interest; for example, one such value is that people are more valuable than property. R. § 293(a).

Note particularly that the actor's conduct is judged by the *foreseeable* risk, viewed at the time and place of the conduct.

The *burden* of reducing or eliminating the risk by alternative conduct is placed on the other side of the scale. A number of considerations may be relevant: (1) the importance or social value of the activity or goal of which the actor's conduct is a part (for example, rescuers are often held not negligent in situations where similar conduct would clearly have been negligent for any other purpose); (2) the utility of the conduct as a means of conducting the activity or reaching the goal; (3) the feasibility of alternative, safer conduct; (4) the relative cost (in money, time or effort) of safer conduct; (5) the relative utility of safer conduct as a means of achieving the same end; (6) the relative safety of alternative conduct; and perhaps others as well. For example, suppose the question is whether it was negligence to give a transfusion of whole blood which (unknown to the hospital) contained hepatitis virus. So far as the *burden* aspect is concerned it would be relevant to consider: (a) the purpose of the transfusion; (b) its anticipated medical value; (c) whether other blood was available; (d) whether a substitute (e.g. plasma) would have worked as well; (e) whether it was possible to detect the virus, and at what cost; (f) whether better screening of donors would have significantly reduced the risk; and the like. Thus, all of these factors are proper subjects of proof.

Reducing the risk does not always require that the conduct or condition creating it be modified. In certain cases, this can be accomplished by an adequate warning of the danger. And where a warning would be appropriate and effective, the burden of providing one is ordinarily very slight, and in such cases negligence may thus be found if there is any significant risk of harm at all.

Judge and Jury. Whether conduct was negligent is preeminently a question of fact, which means it is ordinarily for the jury (see § 1—4). Fundamentally, the attributes of the reasonable man are matters of common sense and community values, and so are the factors which determine whether a risk was unreasonable. Thus, it is common practice to give the jury merely a short general definition of negligence and the reasonable man test, leaving it to the jury to apply its common experience to the evidence. R. § 285. It is left ignorant of the elaboration of these concepts which fill the pages of lawbooks.

However, in certain cases, the decision is one for the court. The judge may decide, based on his own experience and his legal knowledge of the underlying principles, that there is no question for the jury because the conduct in question so clearly was or was not negligent that no reasonable person could reach any other conclusion. The elaboration of the attributes of the reasonable person and of the balancing test for determining reasonableness of the risk derive mainly from appellate decisions in cases where the trial court decided the question, or one of the parties contends that it should have.

There are situations, however, in which the jury receives further guidance.　The jury will be told if some special variation of the reasonable man test applies, such as in the case of physicians, minors, etc.　Further, courts will sometimes go so far as to declare that certain kinds of conduct in certain situations are (or are not) negligence as a matter of law, or presumptively negligent, or evidence of negligence, and the jury will be so instructed.　Sources of these specific standards of conduct will be discussed in the section which follows.

§ 4—2.　Sources of Standards of Conduct

Rules of Law.　As we have seen, the standard of conduct required of plaintiff or defendant in the circumstances of the particular case is ordinarily fixed by the trier of fact (the jury), and is derived from its own knowledge and experience. Thus, each jury is usually free to make its own independent ad hoc determination of what the reasonable person would or would not have done, subject only to the court's power to decide the case when it feels strongly one way or the other (by directing a verdict).

However, in reviewing trial court rulings appellate courts are frequently required to state whether or not, as a matter of law, certain conduct was negligent or nonnegligent in particular circumstances. Under principles of stare decisis, these decisions become precedents in future cases. As similar fact situations recur, there is an inevitable tendency to generalize, with the result that some types of conduct become fixed as standards by rules of law.

Within proper limits, this is necessary and desirable. Jury trials of clear cases are a waste of time and resources, and occasionally (due to prejudice or sympathy) the jury will reach an improper result. A certain amount of judicial control lends stability, certainty and meaning to the negligence concept.

Occasionally, however, courts and scholars have gone too far and attempted to establish rules of conduct of universal application to which no exceptions are permitted. Invariably, the rule eventually breaks down in the face of the obvious necessity of basing the standard on the particular circumstances of the case, the apparent risk, and the actor's opportunity to deal with it. No fixed rule can be justly applied in every case, nor ignore the changing conditions and expectations of society.

The classic example is the so-called Pennsylvania rule concerning the standard of care of motorists approaching railroad crossings. In Baltimore & Ohio Ry. v. Goodman (U.S.1927), Mr Justice Holmes (a leading advocate of setting standards by rules of law) attempted to "lay down a standard once for all" requiring a driver to stop, look and listen and, if necessary, to leave his vehicle and walk out onto the tracks to ascertain whether a train is coming. It soon became apparent that such a rule was too harsh and unjust in many cases, and made it virtually impossible to recover for a crossing accident. Moreover, the standard was clearly unworkable, since compliance would often unreasonably delay vehicular traffic, might itself be dangerous, and in some situations would not even accomplish the desired result. Finally, in Pokora v. Wabash Ry. (U.S. 1934), *Goodman* was overruled. "Illustrations such as these," said Mr. Justice Cardozo, "bear witness to the need for caution in framing standards of behavior that amount to rules of law . . .. Extraordinary situations may not wisely or fairly be subjected to tests or regulations that are fitting for the commonplace or normal."

Similar rules—such as that it is *always* negligent to drive at such a speed that it is impossible to stop within the range of vision, that a motorist must *always* sound his horn when a pedestrian is in or about to enter his path, and the like—have met a similar fate.

This is not to say, of course, that courts may not take the case from the jury where there would be general agreement that on the particular facts the conduct in question clearly was negligent (or was not). But given the infinite variety of fact situations in which injuries occur, virtually all rules of conduct must be sufficiently flexible to admit of exceptions and excuses.

Legislation. Legislation—federal and state statutes, municipal ordinances, even administrative regulations—will often prescribe standards of conduct for the protection of others from harm. For purposes of tort law, such legislation may be classified in two categories: (1) statutes which expressly or by necessary implication themselves create a civil cause of action for damages; and (2) those which do not, ordinarily providing criminal penalties for their violation.

If the statute itself provides for a civil remedy, it creates in essence a statutory tort cause of action, and the only questions are whether the statute is valid and whether the facts of the case are within its terms. Examples include the Federal Employers Liability Act, the Jones Act, and state employee safety and dram shop acts. In a proper case, a civil remedy may be found to have been given by necessary implication, even though not expressly provided. See, e.g., Mowe, Federal Statutes and Implied Private Actions, 55 Ore.L. Rev. 3 (1976); R. § 874A.

In the second category, where no civil remedy is expressly or impliedly provided, courts will nevertheless permit the statute to be introduced into evidence to establish the standard of conduct. Some courts have constructed the doubtful fiction that this is what the legislature intended. Others have suggested that the reasonable man obeys the criminal law; while this is no doubt often true, this rationale does not account for all the cases. Perhaps the most satisfactory justification is that the statute embodies a legislative judgment that certain conduct either is required or is unreasonable (depending on the type of statute) which the courts will apply in civil cases where logic dictates that the issue is directly analogous. Negligence is the breach of a duty imposed by law, and in most cases it matters not whether the law is of judicial or legislative origin.

When is the statute a relevant standard? The fundamental limitation is legislative purpose. The court must first find that the statute was intended, at least in part, to protect a class of persons which includes the plaintiff (or defendant, as the case may be) against the particular hazard and kind of harm which resulted. R. §§ 286, 288. If the legislature's standard is to be adopted, then the court must also adopt the limits of the purpose for which the statute was intended, for those are presumably the limits of its validity. Thus, a statute prohibiting certain activities on Sunday is intended to protect the public peace and morals, and therefore is irrelevant on the issue whether the activity was conducted negligently. Violation of a speed limit enacted solely to conserve gasoline is irrelevant in determining whether the excessive speed was unreasonably dangerous. An act requiring certain safety features in factories may be held to be for the protection of employees, not casual visitors or trespassers. A statute, intended to prevent the spread of disease, requiring separate pens for animals transported by ship was not admissible in an action for loss of plaintiff's sheep which were washed overboard during a storm at sea, even though as chance would have it the required pens would have prevented the loss.

On the other hand the class of those protected may be construed very broadly, especially where the danger is great. Thus, statutes regulating the sale of firearms, gasoline, explosives, intoxicants and poisons have been held to protect all those likely to be injured by the violation, including those injured as a result of subsequent criminal acts.

Legislative purpose is, of course, whatever the courts say it is, and their predilections vary. Thus, different courts have held that similar statutes requiring that upon leaving an auto the driver must remove the key and lock it were, and were not, intended for the protection of persons struck by a thief operating the car. In general, however, courts have taken a reasonably broad view of safety statutes. For example, a statute requiring open elevator shafts to be fenced, obviously intended primarily to prevent workmen accidentally falling into them, was held to encompass protection against a radiator placed near the opening being accidentally knocked into the opening and killing a workman below. De Haen v. Rockwood Sprinkler Co. (N.Y.1932). Moreover, statutes by their terms not applicable to the case at bar may be invoked by analogy, more or less as a statutory custom, as where a statute setting safety standards for a private power company was admitted as tending to establish a standard for one municipally owned.

Licensing statutes—such as for doctors, lawyers, auto drivers, etc.—present a special problem. Most courts have held that defendant's failure to comply with a licensing statute is not admissible, since it does not tend to prove that he was negligent on the occasion in question. This is consistent with the evidentiary rule that one's reputation for a particular character trait (e.g. as a careless driver) is not admissible to prove that he was careless at the time and place in question. This has troubled some courts and dissenters, since such a rule seems to authorize violations and exposes the public to the very risk—lack of skill and competence—against which the licensing statute was intended to protect. A better rule might be to permit the violation of a licensing statute to create a presumption of negligence, which would shift to the defendant the burden of establishing that he exercised the requisite care and skill.

Where a statute is used to establish the standard of care in a negligence case, what weight should it be given and how is it to be invoked? Preliminarily, the court must determine whether the statute is applicable. If it is, most jurisdictions hold that violation of the statute is *prima facie* negligence or negligence *per se*. R. § 288B. Thus, in the absence of evidence excusing the violation, negligence is conclusively established and the jury is so instructed. However, in a considerable minority of jurisdictions the violation is merely *evidence* of negligence, which the jury may consider together with all other evidence in the case in determining the standard of care and whether it was breached. In such cases the statute is not binding on the jury even in the absence of evidence by defendant excusing the violation.

Even in those states which follow the "negligence per se" rule, most statutes have the effect of establishing negligence but no more. Plaintiff must still establish proximate cause—for example, that the violation of a speed statute was a cause of the collision. And in most cases, contributory negligence and assumption of the risk (if otherwise available) are defenses. There are, however, statutes such as child labor laws, factory safety laws, and laws regarding the operation of school buses which are intended to protect a particular class of persons against their own inability to protect themselves, where the courts refuse to permit such defenses. And courts will sometimes apply expanded versions of the proximate cause rule, particularly where the statute creates a civil remedy for its violation.

When may a violation of the statute be excused?

A few statutes are held to impose an absolute duty of compliance, where to hold otherwise would be inconsistent with a strong legislative safety purpose. In such cases, any violation, however innocent or well-intentioned, is negligence, and to this extent the liability is strict. These include some types of statutes for the protection of workers (the Federal Safety Appliance Act, child labor laws, some factory and construction safety acts), pure food acts, building regulations, and some motor vehicle equipment and maintenance laws.

However, as to most statutes courts properly hold that in proper circumstances a violation may be excusable, in recognition of the fact that the civil standard of *reasonable* care will not invariably require obedience to the letter of the criminal law. In those jurisdictions where violation of a statute is merely *evidence* of negligence, any countervailing evidence which tends to excuse or justify the violation is, of course, admissible. Moreover, even in those states in which the violation is negligence *per se,* certain types of excuses are recognized. These include physical circumstances beyond the actor's control, innocent ignorance of facts which make the statute applicable, sudden emergencies not of the actor's making, and even situations where it would be more dangerous to comply with the statute than to violate it. See R. § 288A. Sometimes courts merely require the exercise of reasonable care to attempt to comply. And although there is authority to the contrary, the better rule would refuse to recognize obsolete, unenforced or clearly unreasonable legislation which remains on the books solely because of legislative inaction.

The converse issue is, may defendant show *compliance* with a statute as proof that he exercised reasonable care.   He may, but (except for statutory torts) such proof is ordinarily not conclusive and is merely some evidence for the trier of fact to weigh, since the statute prescribes only minimum standards of conduct which may or may not have been sufficient under the circumstances.   R. § 288C.

§ 4—3. Proof of Negligence

Burden of Proof and Presumptions.   In order to win a negligence case, plaintiff must produce sufficient evidence to tip the scales of probability in his favor with respect to each "element" of his cause of action—duty, negligence, causation and damages.   R. § 328A.   In some jurisdictions he is also required to prove his own freedom from contributory negligence.   The ordinary rules of evidence apply and these are beyond the scope of this discussion.   However, a few rules of proof which regularly arise in negligence cases are worthy of special note.

Negligence law has its own set of legal presumptions.   Most presumptions are merely formalized rules of circumstantial evidence.   Upon proof of a certain fact or facts (*A*), called the "basic" facts, the law presumes the existence of fact *B*, the "presumed fact." In other words, fact *B* is established by proof of *A*, unless and until disproved by other evidence. For example, the fact that a person properly addressed, stamped and mailed a letter (*A*) gives rise to a presumption that the letter was received by the addressee (*B*). Some presumptions merely codify common knowledge, for lack of better evidence, such as the presumption that the instinct for self-preservation has induced the plaintiff (normally a careful person) to exercise due care for his own safety. And some presumptions are mainly designed to shift the burden of producing evidence where the fact to be presumed is statistically probable and the true facts are within defendant's control (sometimes called "smoking out" presumptions). Examples of the latter include the presumption of a carrier's negligence when a passenger is injured by a cause within the carrier's control, the presumption that the discharge of a firearm was intentional or negligent which occurred while the firearm was in defendant's possession and control, and the presumption that a vehicle normally used in the owner's business was being driven by the owner's employee within the course and scope of his employment. The authorities are split as to the procedural effect of a presumption in the face of contrary evidence; see McCormick, Evidence § 345 (2d ed. 1972).

Experts and Opinion Evidence. Expert witnesses are frequently necessary or desirable in tort litigation. Their chief functions are: (1) to provide the jury with facts beyond the common knowledge of jurors, such as scientific data, computations, tests, experiments, and the like; and (2) in professional negligence cases, to establish the standard of care.

The general rule of evidence is that witnesses must testify only to *facts,* not opinions or conclusions, since the inferences to be drawn from the evidentiary facts are for the jury. The rule was particularly strong against opinions on so-called "ultimate issues," e.g., whether defendant was negligent. However, the prohibition was never absolute; and at least as to intermediate issues, such as whether plaintiff's injuries were caused by the occurrence in question, whether defendant was intoxicated, and the like, the necessity of conclusory testimony outweighs any possible prejudicial effect and hence it is admissible. Recognizing that the jury is never bound by the witness's conclusions anyway, the rule is presently in the process of further erosion, and where the underlying facts are such that the witness is better able (by reason of his expertise or experience) to evaluate them than the jury, courts are increasingly permitting the witness to assist the jury by giving his opinion, even on the ultimate issue. Thus, experts have been permitted to testify that a railroad crossing was "extrahazardous," that a product was unreasonably dangerous, and even that a doctor in a malpractice case was negligent.

Res Ipsa Loquitur and Circumstantial Evidence.
Like the rules of presumptions, res ipsa loquitur
is basically a rule of circumstantial evidence, and
the doctrine can only be understood as such. It
does not shift the burden of proof, nor change the
standard of care. It is merely a method of indirect proof of negligence.

Virtually any fact can be proved circumstantially, and it is probably the rare lawsuit in which
one or more facts are not so proved. Speed can
be inferred from skid marks; age from appearance; the point of collision from the position of
the vehicles afterward. The classic illustration is
that of the careless cross-examiner who asked
one question too many. After eliciting from the
witness testimony that he did not actually see defendant bite off plaintiff's nose, he asked, "How do
you know he did?" The witness replied, "I saw
him spit it out." In that case, the fact that defendant bit off plaintiff's nose was proved circumstantially. If other facts or conditions are
used to establish the happening of some event in
lieu of direct, eyewitness testimony of the event
itself, then such event is being proved by circumstantial evidence.

Res ipsa loquitur ("the thing speaks for itself") is merely a special application of this rule
to proof of defendant's conduct—perhaps more
accurately, it sanctions circumstantial evidence
that defendant must have performed some act (or
omitted to perform some act) under circum-

stances where such conduct may be deemed negligence. See R. § 328D.

The three basic requirements for invoking the doctrine are merely codifications of common sense principles of circumstantial evidence.

(1) *Control by Defendant.* It must be shown that plaintiff's injury or damage was caused by an instrumentality or condition which was under defendant's exclusive management or control at the relevant time(s). Some courts have applied this requirement restrictively, ruling that such control or management must have existed at the time of the injury. However, the better and logical rule requires only that the jury be able to find that the negligence, if any, occurred while the instrumentality was within defendant's control. In cases where the injury occurred after the instrumentality had left defendant's control, this requirement is usually met by evidence which tends to exclude other possible causes subsequent to defendant's possession. For example, res ipsa is often invoked in exploding bottle cases upon a showing of careful handling between the time the bottle left the possession of defendant bottler and the time of the explosion.

This requirement ordinarily precludes use of res ipsa against multiple defendants, except in cases of vicarious liability or shared responsibility for the same instrumentality or condition such that either all were similarly negligent or none were. A striking exception is Ybarra v. Spangard

(Cal.1944) where plaintiff, unconscious during an appendicitis operation, sustained a traumatic injury to his shoulder, and res ipsa loquitur was applied against all of the doctors and hospital employees connected with the operation although clearly not all of them were negligent. Given the special relationship between medical personnel and patients and the notorious reluctance of the former to testify against one another, the court decided to shift the burden of explanation under such circumstances to those with sole knowledge of the true facts. Accord: Anderson v. Somberg (N.J.1975) (burden of proof shifts to defendants).

(2) *Inference of Negligence.* The circumstances must be such that, in the ordinary course of events, the plaintiff's harm would not have occurred if defendant had used ordinary care while the instrumentality was within his management or control. In other words, it must be inferable that some negligence on the part of defendant was the cause of the damage. Note that other possible causes need not be excluded to a certainty; plaintiff need only show that defendant's negligence is the most probable explanation. There are many possible reasons for the explosion of a bottle; but upon proof that it was properly and carefully handled after leaving the bottler's possession, we are left with the inference that the bottler must have been negligent somewhere in the bottling process. Note also that the inference need not be of any *particular* negligence; it is

sufficient if the jury can find that of the several possible causes which might have occurred while the instrumentality was under defendant's control, the possibilities for negligence outweigh the nonnegligent possibilities. A bottler may have failed to detect a defect in one of its bottles, or it may have overcharged a sound bottle; if negligence in one process or the other is more probable than the sum of the remaining (nonnegligent) possibilities, this requirement is satisfied.

If the inference of negligence depends on facts beyond the common knowledge of jurors, such facts may be supplied by testimony, and in appropriate cases (e.g. professional negligence) an expert witness may testify directly to the inference itself—for example, that plaintiff's injury would not have occurred if the doctor had not been negligent.

(3) *Plaintiff's Conduct.* The event must not have been due to any cause for which plaintiff is responsible. Older formulations required the absence of any "voluntary act" by plaintiff, but it is now clear that he need not be completely inactive but merely that his conduct did not significantly contribute to the event. In practice, evidence to satisfy this requirement is virtually indistinguishable from proof of freedom from contributory negligence and this is probably all that is really required.

Courts sometimes say (almost always in dictum) that res ipsa applies only where evidence of the true facts of the occurrence is more accessible to the defendant than to the plaintiff. However, this is more properly a *policy justification* for the rule than a requirement, and very few courts have elevated it to the latter.

Whether a particular case is appropriate for the application of res ipsa loquitur is decided in the first instance by the court, but the credibility and weight of the inference is for the jury. In other words, once plaintiff introduces sufficient evidence to raise a jury issue on each requirement, the court instructs the jury on res ipsa loquitur and the decision whether it has been sufficiently proved and what inferences should be drawn is for the jury, the same as in any other circumstantial evidence case. Most courts require res ipsa to be specifically pleaded in the complaint, but will permit alternative pleading and proof and will permit the case to go to the jury on both theories, proof of specific acts of negligence and res ipsa, so long as they are consistent—that is, so long as plaintiff's proof of specific negligence does not itself negate the res ipsa inferences or requirements.

Once a res ipsa case is established prima facie, what is the procedural effect? While courts occasionally have held that it creates a presumption or otherwise permits a directed verdict for plaintiff in the absence of sufficient explanatory evidence by defendant to overcome it, most courts hold that the weight and credibility of the inference is for the jury and the jury is free to decide for defendant even in the absence of explanation by defendant, unless the inference is so strong that reasonable jurors could reach no other conclusion.

Suppose defendant introduces explanatory evidence. In most cases, unless defendant's evidence destroys the inference of negligence so completely that a directed verdict for defendant is proper, both the res ipsa inference and defendant's explanation must be weighed by the jury. In other words, the res ipsa inference ordinarily survives the introduction of contrary evidence by defendant and the jury must decide which is stronger.

There is an analogous circumstantial evidence rule applied in strict product liability cases which holds that plaintiff need not prove the exact defect in the product which caused the occurrence in question, so long as the evidence tends to show that the product malfunctioned in such a way that the existence of a defect may be inferred and also tends to exclude possible causes other than a product defect.

Custom and Habit. Evidence of the usual and customary conduct or practice of others under similar circumstances is normally admissible as tending to establish the proper standard of reasonable conduct. R. § 295A. Such evidence is frequently used in cases of alleged negligence in some business activity, where the nature and operation of the business or industry are beyond the common knowledge of jurors. For example, evidence that all other manufacturers of punch presses incorporate a certain safety switch in their machines would tend to show that its absence from defendant's press was unreasonable and therefore negligent. And conversely, evidence that defendant (or plaintiff) conformed to the usual and customary practice is some evidence that his conduct was reasonable and therefore not negligent. However, in neither case is evidence of conformity or nonconformity conclusive, since the jury is the final arbiter of whether the reasonably prudent person would have done more or less than was customary.

On the other hand, evidence of habit—that plaintiff or defendant customarily behaved in a certain way—is normally inadmissible to show that he probably behaved the same way on the occasion in question. Its slight probative value is outweighed by its prejudicial effect. However, such evidence may occasionally be admissible on a narrow issue, where relevant, such as to show notice or knowledge of a condition, custom, or some other fact in issue. And in those states which require plaintiff to prove his own freedom from contributory negligence, evidence of plaintiff's "habits of due care" (i.e., his character trait of carefulness) may be admissible where plaintiff is incapable of testifying and there were no eyewitnesses to the occurrence.

Trade Rules and Standards. Rules and standards for the conduct of an activity are frequently available. Sources include accrediting agencies, trade associations, safety organizations (e.g. the National Safety Council, Underwriters' Laboratories), federal and state agencies, and even the rules and bylaws of the defendant himself. Like evidence of custom, these are normally admissible (if sufficiently authoritative) as some evidence of the proper standard of conduct, but are not conclusive.

§ 4—4. Proximate Cause

"Proximate cause" is one of the more elusive concepts in tort law. As previously noted (§ 2—1), the term is loosely (and confusingly) used to encompass both (1) questions of cause in fact and (2) issues which might better be called "legal cause" or "responsible cause." More properly (and as used herein) it refers to the latter only —those more or less undefined policy considerations which limit a defendant's liability to persons and consequences which bear some reasonable relationship to the tortious act or omission.

Ironically, issues of proximate cause have little to do with either proximity (in time or space) or causation. They are not questions of fact; they arise only after cause in fact is established. The term "proximate cause" is descriptive only in the sense that it refers to those rules which require that there be a *legal* proximity, a proximity in the sense of justice or fairness, between the cause of the harm (the tortious conduct) and its consequences.   Suppose that defendant negligently drives his car so as to strike another auto, causing it to leave the roadway and knock down an electric utility pole.   The wires break, and electricity is shut off to a certain area.   Clearly, defendant's negligence is the cause in fact of any harm which results from the electrical failure. But rules of proximate cause will be applied to excuse defendant from liability for at least some of those consequences, simply because fundamental notions of fairness tell us that they are too far removed from the risks of negligent driving.   The principal cause in fact of the Great Chicago Fire may have been Mrs. O'Leary's negligent placement of her lantern, but obviously no court would impose tort liability upon her for the full consequences of that negligence.

Thus, at bottom, proximate cause is essentially a question of *duty*—was the defendant under a duty to protect this particular plaintiff against the particular event which injured him or the consequences of that event?   The trouble is, courts often do not see it or articulate it as such. They will sometimes say that defendant's conduct was not the proximate cause of plaintiff's harm when they really mean that defendant was not negligent at all, or that plaintiff was contributorily negligent, or assumed the risk, or misused the product.   As Prosser says, " 'Proximate cause' .   .   .   has been all things to all men.   'Having no integrated meaning of its own, its chameleon quality permits it to be substituted for any one of

the elements of a negligence case when decision
on that element becomes difficult. . . . No
other formula . . . so nearly does the work
of Aladdin's lamp.' " (Prosser, § 42.)

Leon Green has logically proposed (with little
success) that *all* limitations on liability other
than those imposed by the cause in fact requirement be administered as a part of some issue other than cause.

Even when properly characterized as a policy
question, the concept has defied attempts to articulate workable general rules or formulae to use in
deciding cases. For example:

Nearest cause. It has long been recognized
that proximity in time or space has little bearing;
causes remote in that sense may be legally proximate because they are directly and foreseeably
related to the result.

Last Human Wrongdoer. The last human
wrongdoer may or may not be liable depending
upon intervening causes and the scope of the risk
he created; and an earlier tortfeasor may not be
relieved of liability by the conduct of a later one
if the former was under a duty to protect the
plaintiff against the risk of the latter.

Cause vs. Condition. Some courts have sought
to distinguish active "causes" from passive "conditions" upon which they operate, and hold that a
defendant who merely creates the latter is not
liable. Besides the fact that such a characterization is purely arbitrary in many cases, this test

overlooks the fact that a failure to act when there is a duty to do so may be just as culpable as active wrongful conduct.

Substantial Factor Test. The substantial factor test is useful on the issue of cause in fact, but it has little value on the question of proximate cause, which is not factual or quantitative.

Clearly, all such "tests" are inadequate and even misleading. Proximate cause cannot be reduced to absolute rules. The best statement concerning the problem is that of Street:

> It is always to be determined on the facts of each case upon mixed considerations of logic, common sense, justice, policy, and precedent . . .. The best use that can be made of the authorities on proximate cause is merely to furnish illustrations of situations which judicious men upon careful consideration have adjudged to be on one side of the line or the other. [1 Street, Foundations of Legal Liability 110 (1906).]

Thus, it is better to view proximate cause as several distinct problems, more or less unrelated. Excluding cause in fact, the principal ones are (1) unforeseeable consequences, and (2) intervening causes.

(1) Unforeseen Consequences. Perhaps the most troublesome and controversial proximate cause problem is that of liability for the unforeseen and unforeseeable consequences of admittedly wrongful conduct. Conduct is said to be negligent (or reckless or intentional) because it involves a *foreseeable* and unreasonable risk (or certainty) that it will cause harm. Suppose that certain conduct is negligent, but the resulting harm is different in kind or degree from that which was or should have been foreseen. Defendant negligently operates his auto and thereby collides with a truck. He did not know (and had no reason to suspect) that the truck was carrying dynamite. The ensuing explosion injures plaintiff, two blocks away. Obviously, the contemplated risk of negligent driving, to the reasonable man, would not include any injury to plaintiff. Is defendant liable for plaintiff's harm?

There are two competing schools of thought. The prevailing view limits a defendant's liability (1) to those consequences, the foreseeability of which made defendant's conduct negligent in the first place, and (2) to persons within that foreseeable zone of danger. In other words, the test for whether a given result is proximately caused by defendant's negligence is essentially the same, so far as foreseeability limitations are concerned, as for determining whether defendant's conduct was negligent at all.

Frequently, and especially in jury instructions, this test is stated, the harm must be the "natural and [or] probable" consequence of the tortious act.

The opposing view—held by fewer courts and writers—is that a consequence is proximate to a

cause if it occurs as a *direct* result of the tortious
act (regardless of whether it was foreseeable).
The result is direct if it follows in an unbroken
natural sequence from the effect of defendant's
act upon conditions existing and forces already in
operation at the time, without the intervention of
any external forces which were not then in active
operation.   And direct consequences are *always*
proximate.

The classic case on proximate cause is Palsgraf
v. Long Island R.R. (N.Y.1928).   Two of defendant's employees helped a passenger board a train
as it pulled away from the station.   In doing so,
one of them negligently dislodged a package,
wrapped in newspaper, which the passenger was
carrying.   The package contained fireworks,
which exploded when it fell.   The explosion
caused some scales located on the platform some
distance away to tip over on Mrs. Palsgraf and
injure her.

Clearly, while defendant's employees could
have foreseen some harm (e.g. to the contents of
the package or to the passenger) as a result of
their negligence, they had no reason to foresee
any harm to the plaintiff.   Should defendant be
liable to her?

A judgment for plaintiff was reversed, 4–3.
Writing for the majority, Judge Cardozo saw the
problem as one of duty, not causation (although
as previously noted proximate cause is basically a
duty question).   Negligence toward *someone* is

not enough; there must be a breach of a duty (negligence) toward the *plaintiff,* and there is none unless harm to the plaintiff was *foreseeable.* Plaintiff must "sue in her own right for a wrong personal to her, and not as the vicarious beneficiary of a breach of duty to another." And the question is one of law. See R. § 281.

Judge Andrews, for the dissent, took a broader view. The duty to exercise care is owed to all. If defendant's conduct unreasonably creates a risk of harm to others, it is negligent. And within broad limits (set by rules of proximate cause), one is liable for the consequences of that negligence, foreseeable or not. Proximate cause establishes the point beyond which the law declines to trace a series of events, and is determined by considerations of "convenience, of public policy, of a rough sense of justice." Foreseeability may enter in, but only as one factor; it is never determinative. Thus, Andrews' idea of proximate cause closely approximates the "direct causation" test noted above. And he would permit the jury to set the limits.

The *Palsgraf* case has been extensively discussed and debated. Although essentially a problem of the "unforeseeable plaintiff," it has been cited in connection with almost every conceivable proximate cause problem because it so effectively contrasts the ideas of limitations based on scope of the risk and foreseeability of harm on the one hand, and the directness of the consequences on the other.

A series of English cases illuminate the problem in terms of foreseeability of consequences. In In re Polemis and Furness, Withy & Co. (K.B. 1921), the negligence of defendant's stevedores caused a wooden plank to fall into the hold of defendant's ship, striking a spark which ignited petrol vapor in the hold. The ensuing fire destroyed the ship. Although the arbitrators specifically found that the spark was not foreseeable, recovery was allowed because the damage was a direct consequence of the negligence. *Polemis* was overruled in 1961 by a case commonly known as Wagon Mound No. 1 (the ship involved), where the court refused to impose liability for the destruction by fire of plaintiff's dock caused by the ignition of an oil spill because the trier of fact found that it was not foreseeable that the oil would catch fire and burn. However, in a later action for damage to some ships caused by the same fire (Wagon Mound No. 2) there was evidence that defendants should have been aware of some *slight* risk of fire, and in view of the total lack of utility of defendant's conduct, it was not justified in ignoring even this slight risk and was therefore liable.

Even though liability be limited to foreseeable consequences within the risk and to foreseeable plaintiffs, there is still much room for flexibility and for the application of special rules.

(a) *Definition of "foreseeable."*   Obviously, courts have ample maneuverability even within the foreseeable consequences rule, depending upon how broadly or narrowly the foreseeable event is defined and how probable it has to be.   Thus, it is usually held that it is not necessary that the exact manner in which the harm occurs be foreseeable, but only that harm of the same general type as that sustained by plaintiff be foreseeable. R. § 435. For example, if one of the foreseeable risks of negligent driving is broadly defined as *injury* to pedestrians, then a negligent driver may be held liable where he strikes a utility pole and knocks it on a pedestrian, or perhaps even where he incapacitates a traffic control device and thereby contributes to a separate car-pedestrian collision.   On the other hand, if the risk is narrowly defined as *colliding* with pedestrians, the latter would not be included. Further, few consequences of a negligent act are *entirely* unforeseeable, especially in retrospect. As illustrated by *Wagon Mound No. 2,* a willing court can attach liability to consequences which are mathematically rather improbable.   This is sometimes facilitated by characterizing the result as "not unforeseeable" rather than marginally foreseeable.

(b) *Definition of "hazard."*   Liability may be expanded or contracted depending upon how one defines the hazard or risk which makes the conduct wrongful.   Thus, it is usually held that a tortious act which threatens only property dam-

[*95*]

age will nevertheless support liability for personal injury, even though unforeseeable. (However, liability based on violation of a statute is generally limited to consequences against which the statute was intended to protect.) And it is often held that where some harm is foreseeable, defendant will not be excused from liability because the harm is greater in degree than was foreseeably within the risk. Some writers have sought to explain the *Polemis* case on this basis, since some damage to the ship or its cargo might have been expected from knocking the plank into the hold; therefore, defendant is in no position to complain that the damage was merely greater in amount than foreseen.

(c) *Rescuers.* It is generally held that rescuers, as a class, are always foreseeable when defendant's negligence endangers anyone, including himself. Wagner v. International Ry. (N.Y.1921) (Cardozo, C. J.). This appears to be more a matter of policy than foreseeability, as even rescuers of rescuers are protected.

(d) *Physical consequences.* It is uniformly held that defendant takes the plaintiff as he finds him, and is liable for all the physical consequences of his injuries, however unusual or unforeseeable (sometimes referred to as the "thin-skulled" or "eggshell" plaintiff rule). R. §§ 435(1), 458, 461. Thus, if plaintiff has hemophilia or some other special susceptibility to harm, and dies from what would be a minor injury to almost everyone else, defendant is nevertheless liable for his death. A corollary principle is that defendant is liable for damages based on plaintiff's actual income (where this is one element of damages) even though defendant had no reason to foresee that his income was very large.

(e) *Intentional torts; strict liability.* Courts tend to expand proximate cause limits where the tort is intentional. R. § 435A. For example, defendant shoots at *A*, misses him and hits plaintiff, whom he had no reason to expect to be in the line of fire. Under the doctrine of transferred intent, plaintiff has a cause of action for battery. Conversely, where liability is strict, courts tend to restrict liability to foreseeable consequences and persons.

(2) **Intervening Cause.** Intervening cause describes the second important category of proximate cause problems. See R. §§ 440–453. In these cases, there are two (or more) causes in fact of plaintiff's harm; one is defendant's tortious conduct, and another is a subsequent act or event which *intervenes* between defendant's conduct and the injury. The intervening cause may be human conduct (tortious or not) or a natural force or event. The question is, under what circumstances does the intervening cause *supersede* defendant's tortious conduct and excuse his liability. If it does, the term "superseding cause" is applicable.

A cause is intervening, by definition, only if it comes into active operation as a cause *subsequent* in time to the tortious conduct of the defendant. If it was operating at the time of defendant's conduct, then it is a concurrent cause, and as we saw in § 2—1, will not excuse defendant's liability.

The essence of an intervening cause is that it changes the fact situation which existed when defendant acted. Therefore, if defendant is to remain liable, it must be because he ought to have *foreseen* the intervening cause and taken it into account in his conduct. Thus, the test is again one of foreseeability (seen, as always, in hindsight). Was the intervention of the later cause so significant a part of the risk involved in defendant's conduct, or so closely connected to it, that defendant's responsibility for his own conduct ought not to be terminated by it?

Obviously, defendant remains liable if the risk of the intervening cause was the very thing which made his conduct negligent. Thus, one is negligent in spilling a large quantity of gasoline because of the risk that it will be ignited, and he is not relieved of liability merely because the ignition occurs by the independent act of another. And he also remains liable if his negligence was the sufficient cause in fact of the harm, in spite of the fact that a foreseeable act or omission of another (or a natural force) intervened, altering the effects of the harm or failing to prevent it. The risk of negligently starting a fire will ordi-

narily include the risk of delays by others in noti-
fying the fire department, or of foreseeable
changes of wind direction or velocity.

Foreseeability of subsequent events—like foreseeability of consequences, previously discussed
—is often improved by hindsight. Courts will
sometimes say that an intervening cause was
foreseeable because it was not unforeseeable or
abnormal, even though it seems clear that no ordinary person would actually have had such an
event within his contemplation. A driver who
negligently strikes a pedestrian does not usually
consider in advance the fact that he may be left
unconscious in the roadway and run over by another car, or negligently treated by a physician,
but these events are not so bizarre or improbable
as to constitute superseding causes. R. §§ 457,
460.

Foreseeable events include forces of nature
(such as wind, rain, lightning, freezing temperatures, etc.) so long as not abnormal, as well as
human conduct. In appropriate cases, negligence
and even criminal conduct by others is deemed
foreseeable. Thus, one who spills gasoline must
anticipate that another will negligently ignite it.
And one who leaves an automobile on a city
street, unlocked with the keys in the ignition, creates a foreseeable risk that it will be stolen. Rescuers—even negligent ones—are to be expected.
And a defendant who negligently creates an
emergency must anticipate negligent (but not

fool-hardy or unreasonable) defensive acts by those in peril. Even suicide has been held not to be a superseding cause of the victim's death when it results from an insanity, caused by defendant's tort, which prevents the victim from realizing the nature of his act or controlling his conduct. R. § 455.

Conversely, superseding causes are those which are unforeseeable and which produce unforeseeable results. The abnormal, the unpredictable, the highly improbable—whether forces of nature or acts of people—will relieve defendant of liability, so long as the results they produce are also unforeseeable. A defendant who negligently requires plaintiff to make a detour is not liable for his death caused by an airplane falling upon him, or by an unexpected flood, or by a robber (so long as defendant had no reason to know he was subjecting plaintiff to an increased risk of such an attack). An owner who negligently facilitates the stealing of his car is generallly held not liable to a victim of the thief's negligent driving unless he should have foreseen a greater than normal risk of such harm (e.g. he leaves his auto in a neighborhood populated by derelicts and drunks).

Suppose that the *result* is foreseeably within the risk created by defendant's negligence, but is actually brought about by an unforeseeable intervening cause. For example, defendant negligently maintains its rotten telephone pole so as to create an unreasonable risk that it will fall over of its own accord and injure a pedestrian; instead, however, a negligent driver strikes the pole and knocks it upon the plaintiff. Or explosive gas is negligently permitted to accumulate in an oil barge, but it is unforeseeably ignited by lightning. In such cases, defendant is held liable, even though the intervening cause was unforeseeable, because the result was within the foreseeable risk for which defendant is responsible.

There are two exceptions, if they may be called that, to the foregoing rule. First, if the intervening cause is the intentional or criminal conduct of a third person, defendant is excused. Thus, if in the preceding examples someone intentionally ignited the gas, or intentionally pushed the pole over on the plaintiff, considerations of justice require that the third person and not the defendant be held responsible. Second is the situation where a third person discovers the danger which defendant has created, under circumstances where the third person has some duty to act. There are two groups of such cases. Defendant permits some dangerous chattel (e.g. dynamite caps) to get into the hands of a child. The parent discovers the danger, takes the chattel away from the child, but fails to prevent him from obtaining possession of it again and the child is then injured. Similarly, a third person discovers the danger which defendant has created, and *deliberately* ignores it and thereby exposes others to its risks. For example, a retailer discovers that certain bottles of defendant's product marked "kero-

sene" actually contain dangerous amounts of gasoline, but he continues to sell them without any
warning. In all of these cases, the intervening
cause is deemed sufficiently strong and independent to shift liability from defendant to the intervening third person, and defendant is exonerated.

§ 4—5. The Concept of Duty

The duty concept is not limited to negligence
law. In fact, all rules of law which define the
boundaries of one's legal liability to another may
be phrased in terms of some duty, whatever the
conduct or activity. One has a duty not to utter defamatory falsehoods; to refrain from un-
excused breaches of valid contracts; to support
one's minor children. The difference is that in
areas other than negligence law the liability rules
are sufficiently specific that there is ordinarily
no occasion to create rules which further limit the
scope of these already narrowly defined duties.
This is not to say that there are not exceptions
and limitations to such liability rules, but merely
that courts do not find it necessary to use a
"duty" analysis.

In contrast, negligence is a broad and pervasive
principle of liability. The general rule is that one
is under a duty to all persons at all times to exercise reasonable care for their physical safety
(and that of their property). At the same time,
justice considerations require that particular
classes of persons and particular activities be sub-

ject to greater or lesser standards of liability. For example, in most jurisdictions a product manufacturer is strictly liable for the physical harm caused by product defects, even though the manufacturer was not negligent. On the other hand, there is as yet no general liability for negligent conduct which causes only mental suffering, or which causes harm to a trespasser. Those rules which create exceptions to the general principle of negligence liability by narrowing its scope can best be analyzed as duty limitations.

It is sometimes stated that in order for negligence to be actionable, it must constitute a violation of some *legally recognized duty* to another. This is true, but it misplaces the emphasis. It is preferable to view duty in negligence law in terms of a broad *general duty* of reasonable care with *exceptions,* rather than as a series of specific duties which vary according to the facts of the case.

Confusion often results from the loose use of the term "duty" as a substitute for a proper analysis of some other element of the negligence equation. For example, court may hold that a bottler has a "duty" to inspect its bottles for defects; strictly speaking, its failure to do so is merely a specific illustration of negligent conduct.

The scope of one's legal duty is a *question of law* to be decided by the *court,* and never by the jury. Thus, perhaps it is only natural for courts to speak in terms of duty when they are promulgating fixed rules of conduct as rules of negligence, causation, or contributory negligence of general application. In fact, if the court really intends to establish a fixed rule of liability or nonliability with respect to certain specific conduct, it probably does no harm to characterize these rules as duties. But there is danger in using the term when no such arbitrary rule is intended, for judicial approval of the finding of a jury may thereby become transformed unwittingly into a static rule of general application in future cases. While some legal scholars (e.g., Leon Green and Justice Holmes) have favored the proliferation of such specific standards of conduct and the consequent narrowing of the role of the jury, experience has shown that many such arbitrary rules are too rigid and inflexible. See § 4—2, supra. Thus, they must be developed cautiously and deliberately, and clarity is facilitated if the term "duty" is used only with respect to general liability limitations imposed by law.

Numerous duty limiting rules are sprinkled throughout the negligence cases; some are statutory. Some are broad and general, others quite narrow and specific. Each jurisdiction has a few peculiar to itself. The principal common ones include the following.

Relationship Between Plaintiff and Defendant. The principal development of negligence as a separate tort cause of action occurred during the nineteenth century when the fault ethic was particularly strong and liability rules tended to favor defendants. This may explain the fact that early in this development both English and American courts developed the rule that no action could be founded on the breach of a legal duty owed to some person other than the plaintiff. In other words, there must be some *relationship* between defendant and his victim sufficient for the court to find that defendant's duty to exercise reasonable care ought to run in favor of that particular person. "Negligence in the air, so to speak, will not do." The catch is, of course, that there is no standard except the judge's conscience for determining when the relationship is sufficient to raise a duty. The basic question remains a philosophical one: whether plaintiff's interests are entitled to protection against defendant's conduct. It would be hard to conceive of a case where the court could not find such a relationship if it chose to do so. In cases where the connection between defendant's negligence and plaintiff's harm is tenuous, the rules of proximate cause previously discussed (see § 4—4) are adequate protection.

In fact, recall that in the *Palsgraf* case discussed in § 4—4 Judge Cardozo saw the issue as whether the negligence of defendant's employees was a breach of a duty to Mrs. Palsgraf, and concluded that it was not; Andrews on the other hand saw the issue as one of proximate cause. Proximate cause rules themselves may be seen as duty limitations; one may well ask why two separate sets of liability limiting rules are necessary.

Perhaps it is because some courts confuse legal cause and cause in fact and send questions of proximate cause to the jury. Nevertheless, both sets exist, and on similar facts some courts will analyze the issues in terms of duty while others will use proximate cause. The desired result can be reached with either concept.

Nature and Scope of the Risk. Suppose defendant's conduct threatens harm to a particular interest or of a particular kind, but results in harm to a different interest or of a different kind. For example, an act may be negligent only because it threatens property damage, but it results in some unforeseen personal injury (e.g. *Palsgraf*). Or it may be negligent to entrust a child with a pistol because of the danger of accidental discharge, but instead he drops it on plaintiff's foot—a risk as to which (let us assume) the entrustment was not unreasonable. In such cases, many courts will say that there was no duty to protect plaintiff against the harm which actually resulted, or to protect the interest which was actually invaded. As we have seen, other courts will reach the same result by applying principles of proximate cause. Again, either way the result is the same.

Of course, not all courts would deny liability in these situations. As we saw in our discussion of proximate cause, the nature and scope of the risk may be broadly defined so as to encompass the harm which occurred. Duty is no less elastic than proximate cause.

Interest Invaded. Certain types of interests for various reasons have been afforded relatively little protection against negligent invasion. Interests of a solely pecuniary nature, such as the right to have a contract performed, the expectation of financial advantage, damage caused by negligent misrepresentation, and other kinds of pecuniary harm present special problems which are discussed elsewhere.

There are interests which traditionally have been given less than full protection even though the harm is physical, although the scope of these limitations appears to be narrowing. For example, until 1946 recovery was denied for injuries to an unborn child. Some courts said that a fetus was not a "person" to whom a duty of care was owed, but the real reason was that courts were skeptical of the medical proof of cause and effect. This duty limitation has now been overturned, provided the child is born alive, and the child may recover for his personal injuries or his survivors for his subsequent death. The courts are still split, however, on whether a wrongful death action may be maintained if the child is killed while still in the womb, but the recent trend has been in favor of permitting suit. See § 8—20, infra.

American courts have also been slow to allow recovery for illnesses resulting entirely from negligently-caused psychic trauma. This subject is discussed in § 8—19, infra.

Misfeasance vs. Nonfeasance. The law of negligence, from its inception, has distinguished between liability for the consequences of affirmative acts—"misfeasance"—and liability for merely doing nothing—"nonfeasance." The early law of wrongs was concerned only with the more important forms of misconduct, and was less concerned with punishing inaction. Courts have hesitated to force people to act affirmatively to prevent physical harm to others, however strong the *moral* duty may be. Affirmative negligent acts create a new risk of harm, but nonfeasance at least does not make matters worse and perhaps merely fails to benefit another by interfering in his affairs.

The problem is that almost any inaction can be characterized as "misfeasance" if the court is so disposed, and often inaction is substantially the equivalent of active misconduct. The failure to blow a horn may be seen as active negligence in the operation of a train or auto. A failure to repair may be deemed active mismanagement on the part of one responsible for that which is broken. Thus, as in other duty issues, the fundamental question is whether there is a sufficient relationship between the one who failed to act and the one injured thereby that the court deems it just to impose liability. In an oft-quoted case, Cardozo characterized the problem as whether the defendant has gone so far in what he has actually done, and has got himself into such a relation with the plaintiff, that he has begun to affect the interests of the plaintiff adversely, as distinguished from merely failing to confer a benefit upon him. H. R. Moch Co. v. Rensselaer Water Co. (N.Y.1928).

A common example of this limitation is the absence of a duty to go to the aid of one in peril, in the absence of some pre-existing status or relationship which would require it. R. § 314. Thus, an expert swimmer with a boat and rope at hand is not required—so far as American tort law is concerned—to attempt to rescue one who is drowning, unless the swimmer happens to be a life guard hired for that purpose. A physician who by chance happens upon the scene of an accident is under no duty to render emergency medical care, unless the victim also happens to be the doctor's patient. This rule has troubled many courts and writers, at least in cases where aid could be offered or a rescue attempted with little or no risk to the actor, especially since such a duty is imposed by legal systems of other countries. Thus, American courts will tend to find that this duty exists if there is any sort of pre-existing relationship between the parties such that the victim might reasonably expect aid, such as carrier-passenger, innkeeper-guest, employer-employee, jailer-prisoner, school-pupil, parent-child, husband-wife, and even store-customer and host-guest. R. §§ 314A, 314B. The requisite relationship is found where defendant's conduct is responsible for plaintiff's peril, whether or not defendant's conduct was negligent. R. § 322.

Moreover, duties of affirmative action which would not otherwise exist may be voluntarily assumed. It is commonly held that one who gratuitously undertakes to render aid to another assumes a duty to act with reasonable care, a duty which once assumed may not be abandoned at will. R. § 324. While consistent with the principles of negligence law, this rule is said to have the negative effect of stifling charitable impulses and deterring would-be rescuers, and has resulted in the enactment of "Good Samaritan" acts in many states which relieve physicians who render emergency medical aid from all liability for negligence.

While early cases held that there was no tort liability for failure to perform a gratuitous promise, more recent cases have permitted recovery where there was reasonable detrimental reliance. And once defendant has commenced performance, it is clear that he has assumed a duty to perform with reasonable care. R. §§ 323, 324A.

The principle of voluntary duty assumption has been broadly applied, and is by no means confined to rescue situations. It has been extended to landlords who make repairs on leased premises, railroads which provide extra protection at crossings, and even to workmen's compensation liability insurers who undertake safety inspections of the insured's premises. Liability is usually justifiable on the ground that defendant has increased the danger, or misled the plaintiff into a false sense of security, or deprived plaintiff of the possibility of help from other sources. However, liability need not depend upon the existence of these factors; the better approach is simply to impose liability on the basis of the general duty of reasonable care.

Relationships of the kind referred to above (carrier-passenger, innkeeper-guest, employer-employee, etc.) may give rise to other duties of affirmative action, such as to protect the subordinate or dependent party against harm which may be foreseeably caused by third persons (other passengers, guests, employees, etc., or others outside the relationship) or to protect those outside the relationship from harm caused by those under defendant's control (e.g., the parent's duty to control his child, the duty of the owner-passenger of an auto to exercise control over the driver). See R. §§ 315–320.

Special Duty Rules. Tort law has created special duty rules for certain kinds of defendants or activities. These include owners and occupiers of land, manufacturers and suppliers of products, automobile owners and operators, and others. The trend is toward abolishing these special duty rules, insofar as they arbitrarily restrict the duty of ordinary care. These rules will be discussed in Chapter 8.

In addition, there are certain status immunities, such as sovereign immunity, charitable immunity, and intra-family immunities. Strictly speaking, these are not duty limitations but limitations on the availability of a remedy. However, as a practical matter, they have the same effect. These will be discussed in Chapter 11.

§ 4—6. Degrees of Negligence

Regrettably, negligence law has been the victim of attempts to refine the negligence concept by subdividing negligent conduct into narrower categories. There are two closely-related but distinguishable approaches—degrees of care, and degrees of negligence.

High Degrees of Care. Common carriers (operators of airplanes, ships, buses, railroads, taxicabs, and even elevators, escalators, and amusement devices) are said to owe their passengers "the highest degree of care consistent with the mode of conveyance used and the practical operation of its business." Similarly, those responsible for certain dangerous instrumentalities (e.g., explosives, high-voltage electricity) must, say the courts, exercise a "high degree of care," commensurate with the danger, to protect others from harm.

While these and other similar statements might be interpreted as creating a higher duty of care, in most cases this is not what is intended. Negligence is the failure to exercise reasonable care. The amount of care—that is, the conduct—which is *reasonable* for a given situation depends on various factors, including the relationship between the parties and the nature and extent of the risk inherent in that situation. Brain surgery requires greater care in the wielding of the knife than does carving a turkey. Transporting dynamite or paying passengers on a public conveyance requires different conduct than does hauling potatoes. But even though a high risk or a heavy responsibility may be involved, there is no logical reason to depart from the usual standard of *reasonable care under the circumstances,* and there is no such departure so long as the jury is instructed in the usual way.

However, most jurisdictions have authorized jury instructions phrased in terms of the "highest degree of care" standard in suits by passengers against common carriers, and occasionally "high degree of care" instructions are permitted in other cases. Such instructions are in theory objectionable as giving undue weight to the obligations of these defendants, since the law only requires, for example, a carrier to behave as would a reasonably prudent carrier under the same or similar circumstances. Instructions like these may well result in a heavier burden of liability by encouraging the jury to find liability for conduct which would not otherwise constitute a breach of the duty of reasonable care.

Degrees of Negligence. The idea that negligence may be classified as slight, ordinary, or gross apparently found its way into the English law of bailments from the Roman law, and thence into our law, where it has persisted. For an injury to the goods bailed, a bailment for the benefit of the bailee (such as in the case of a bailee for hire) results in liability for slight negligence. A bailment for the mutual benefit of both parties requires ordinary care. And a gratuitous bailment for the benefit of the bailor makes the bailee liable only for gross negligence.

Except for bailments, however, American courts have almost entirely rejected as unworkable the notion of degrees of negligence. For a time during the nineteenth century, Illinois and Kansas tried a form of judicially-created comparative negligence in which these concepts were used, but the system had to be abandoned when the decisions as to which was which became hopelessly confused. The idea of degrees of negligence has been almost uniformly condemned by the legal writers.

Apparently, however, the state legislatures did not get the word, and there are statutes in many jurisdictions in which the term "negligence" is preceded by some adjective, usually "gross." Some automobile guest statutes are of this type. In most cases, the statute applies only to a particular situation, activity, or type of defendant; but the general comparative negligence statutes of Nebraska ("slight" and "gross") and South Dakota ("slight") use them. Thus, the courts are forced to continue to deal with these concepts.

"Slight" negligence is the failure to exercise *great* care; it is *not* a slight departure from ordinary care (except in the comparative negligence context).

Some jurisdictions, rather than (or in addition to) making common carriers liable for failure to exercise the "highest degree of care," hold them liable for slight negligence. Is there a distinction? Technically, yes; practically, no. Technically, slight negligence is the failure to exercise *greater* care than the circumstances would ordinarily demand; whereas the "highest degree of care" is itself, by definition, the standard which the circumstances require, and therefore one who does not conform to that standard is, strictly speaking, guilty of ordinary (not slight) negligence. However, as a practical matter, while the form of the instructions to the jury may be different depending upon which approach is used, the net effect is the same in either case, since the ultimate question is whether defendant failed to exercise a high degree of care.

"Gross" negligence is an even more troublesome concept. Any definition, such as "the failure to exercise even slight care," is virtually indistinguishable from wilful and wanton misconduct (see § 4—7, infra). Some courts have therefore treated these concepts as identical, but most have struggled to preserve some distinction between them. The best that can be done is to say that gross negligence is something more than ordinary negligence but only in degree; and it is something less than recklessness, which is a different kind of conduct evincing a conscious disregard of the safety of others. The distinction is important, since contributory negligence is not a defense to wilful and wanton misconduct but is to gross negligence, and a finding of wilful and wanton misconduct will usually support an award of punitive damages whereas gross negligence will not.

§ 4—7. Wilful and Wanton Misconduct

Lying on the fault continuum between mere negligence and the intent required for liability for one of the intentional torts (see § 6—1) is a gray area known by various names, such as "wilful and wanton" or "reckless" conduct. "Wilful and wanton" is the term most commonly used by the courts and lawyers in practice; the Restatement uses the term "reckless." See R. §§ 500–503. The term "wilful" in this context can be misleading, since no intent to cause injury is required, and the cases do evidence some confusion of terminology. Bear in mind that "wilful and wanton" cannot be taken literally; it is an idiom for that conduct which can best be described as characterized by a reckless disregard of the safety of others.

Definitions of reckless or wilful and wanton conduct vary among the jurisdictions, and sometimes within the same jurisdiction depending upon the type of case. The most common general definition is unreasonable conduct committed under circumstances in which the actor knew or had reason to know (that is, had knowledge of facts from which he ought to have been aware) that (1) his conduct created an unreasonable risk of physical harm, and (2) that risk was relatively high, either in degree or in the probability that harm would occur. Compare R. § 500. It is sometimes said that it is conduct which evidences a conscious disregard or indifference to the safety of others. The actor is aware of the danger but he is indifferent to it, or he recklessly disregards the fact that his conduct has created a substantial risk of harm.

Thus, such conduct differs from negligence not only in degree, but also in kind. It differs in degree in the sense that the risk of harm is greater; and it differs in kind because of the different mental state of the actor. He is (or is presumed to be) *conscious* of the risk, and yet chooses to proceed (or to fail to act) in spite of his awareness. In contrast, mere negligence ordinarily consists of inadvertence, inattention, thoughtlessness, or incompetence; there is no awareness of an imminent and considerable danger. Recklessness also differs from intentional tortious conduct (see § 6—1), in that the latter requires an awareness that the injury is certain or substantially certain to occur so that we may infer that the actor intended to bring about that result. In contrast, the reckless actor did not intend to injure anyone, but he knew or had reason to know that the *risk* of harm was quite substantial.

Reckless conduct is a hybrid, with attributes of both negligence and the intentional torts. It will often support a claim for punitive damages (see § 9—3). Contributory negligence is not a defense to reckless conduct, although of course contributory reckless conduct is. But in those jurisdictions which have adopted comparative negligence, plaintiff's contributory negligence will reduce his recovery even against defendant's reckless conduct. See § 5—4.

As in the case of negligence, an action based upon wilful and wanton misconduct requires that plaintiff establish that defendant owed him a duty of care, and the same duty limitations apply. See §§ 4—5, and Chapter 8. Proximate cause rules, in a form slightly more favorable to the plaintiff than in negligence cases, are applicable (see § 4—4). And actual damages must be shown.

In certain situations, a finding that defendant's conduct was reckless is a prerequisite to liability. For example, the general rule (subject to various exceptions) is that a possessor of land is liable to a trespasser or licensee injured on the premises only for wilful and wanton misconduct. And there are numerous statutes which exempt certain defendants from liability for ordinary negligence, thereby requiring at least recklessness—e. g., automobile and airplane guest statutes, certain governmental immunity acts, and "Good Samaritan" laws.

To avoid the arbitrary and sometimes harsh results which often flow from a strict application of automobile guest statutes, premises liability rules, and the doctrine of contributory negligence, some courts have bent and stretched their definitions of wilful and wanton misconduct to the point that they are very close to ordinary negligence. For example, in Illinois wilful and wanton misconduct is the failure to exercise ordinary care after actual or constructive knowledge of an existing danger. Such liberal definitions probably do little harm in most cases, except that in jurisdictions which allow punitive damages in any case of reckless conduct, they may have the effect of authorizing punitive damages for conduct which amounts to little more than mere negligence.

CHAPTER 5

DEFENSES TO NEGLIGENCE LIABILITY

§ 5—1. Contributory Negligence

Since at least Butterfield v. Forrester (K.B. 1809), the general common law rule has been that a negligent tortfeasor is entirely excused from liability to a plaintiff who was himself negligent and whose negligence contributed proximately to cause plaintiff's harm. R. § 467.

The several justifications advanced for this rule do not withstand close scrutiny, at least by twentieth century standards, and thus its application as a complete bar to plaintiff's recovery has been increasingly criticized and narrowed in its application.

For example, it has been suggested that plaintiff is being punished for his own wrongdoing; but why should he bear the entire punishment when defendant was also at fault? Some have argued that courts will not aid those who do not come with clean hands. This is perhaps a variation of the old rule that courts will not apportion damages among joint tortfeasors. The weakness of this argument is that courts often do, in other contexts, grant relief to plaintiffs who were to some extent at fault; moreover, in most cases the refusal to apportion is simply arbitrary and unjust, and the rule against apportionment is generally on the wane.

It has also been suggested that the contributory negligence rule serves as a deterrent to negligent conduct. But common sense teaches that few of us will exercise greater care for our own safety than that which is motivated by the fear of personal injury; no additional incentive is added by the contemplation of the outcome of some future lawsuit. And since the negligence of many defendants (corporations, manufacturers, landowners, etc.) creates no corresponding risk of personal injury to them, any rule (such as contributory negligence) which reduces a defendant's liability exposure operates to reduce the sum total of the incentives toward safety which negligence law creates.

One of the most common justifications for the "all-or-nothing" rule of contributory negligence is that plaintiff's own negligence has become the direct, immediate and superseding cause of his own injury. The *Butterfield* case appears to be based on this idea, which perhaps reflects the early common law notion that there is but a single proximate cause of every injury. This often led to a search for the "last human wrongdoer" on whom the blame was fixed. In some (but not all) cases, this was the plaintiff, where his negligence occurred after that of the defendant. Of course, this "single cause" notion is simply not true. We now recognize that the negligence of several persons may combine to produce a single indivisible injury for which all are jointly and severally liable.

In light of the rule's shaky foundations, it is not surprising that it is often ignored. It is an open secret that juries frequently violate the court's instructions and award plaintiff some damages despite his contributory negligence, although less than he would have received if he were free from fault. In other words, juries commonly fashion and apply their own rule of comparative negligence.

Why then do American courts persistently refuse to abandon the rule? Probably because the preferable alternative—comparative negligence—is sufficiently complex to implement and administer (and the present rule so firmly established) that the courts perceive the problem as one for the legislature. See § 5—4, infra, for a discussion of this problem and developments.

In most jurisdictions, contributory negligence is an affirmative defense which must be pleaded and proved by the defendant. R. § 477. However, in a few states plaintiff must plead and prove freedom from contributory negligence as a part of his prima facie case. In most cases, the practical effect is the same. However, the latter rule may impose an impossible burden where the victim of defendant's negligence is deceased or incompetent. Thus, in such cases the courts usually relax the rules of evidence and permit proof that the victim was a person who habitually exercised ordinary care as evidence that he was reasonably careful on the occasion in question.

In general, the same standards apply for determining whether conduct is contributorily negligent as are used to determine whether conduct is negligent. R. §§ 463, 464, 466, 470. Plaintiff must act as a reasonably prudent person. However, the results of applying this standard are not necessarily the same for plaintiffs as for defendants. Reasonable care for one's *own* safety is not always the same as reasonable care for the safety of *others*. Generally speaking, courts and juries tend to be more lenient with plaintiffs, so that the same conduct which would have made a defendant negligent may be found to be reasonable as to a plaintiff. And courts more often find that questions of contributory negligence are for the jury.

The courts also apply more favorable rules of proximate cause on the issue of contributory negligence. This was not always so. Some courts once held that plaintiff's negligence barred his recovery if it made any contribution, "however slight," to his harm. Fortunately, this rule is now almost entirely abandoned, and the same "substantial factor" test is applied as in the case of defendant's negligence. R. § 465. In addition, the defense is usually strictly limited to the risk which made the conduct negligent. R. § 468. For example, a plaintiff who is negligent for standing on an unsafe platform is not contributorily negligent with respect to injuries sustained when an adjacent wall collapses upon him.

Contributory negligence is a defense to negligence, and therefore is ordinarily not available when plaintiff's action is based on some other theory of liability.   Thus, it is not a defense to an intentional tort, nor to wilful and wanton misconduct (although contributory wilful and wanton misconduct is).   R. §§ 481, 482.   And most courts have ruled that it is not a defense to liability for breach of warranty, strict liability for abnormally dangerous activities, or strict product liability. A few decisions have used the term (incorrectly) to describe a defense to strict liability which consists of plaintiff's voluntary exposure to a known danger, but the proper name for this defense is assumption of risk.

Nor is contributory negligence a defense to the tort liability created by certain types of statutes which are intended to protect a certain class of persons from dangers against which they are incapable of protecting themselves.   These include child labor laws, statutes prohibiting the sale of certain articles to minors, certain acts protecting intoxicated persons and their victims, and certain factory acts and other statutes for the protection of workmen.   R. § 483.

§ 5—2.   Imputed Contributory Negligence

Tort law includes the principle of vicarious liability, by which *A* is held liable for the wrongful act of *B* solely because of the existence of some prior relationship between *A* and *B*.   The most common examples of such relationships are employer-employee, partnership, joint venture or enterprise, and in some instances employer-independent contractor. Thus, if the requisite relationship exists, a third person (*C*) may sue *A* for injuries caused by the wrongful conduct of *B*, even though *A* was innocent of personal fault so far as *C*'s injuries are concerned. See §§ 8—16–8—18, infra. This vicarious liability may be thought of as a form of imputed negligence.

Given this principle, the question naturally arises, should imputed negligence work both ways, that is, when *A* is suing as well as when he is defending? In other words, if both *B* and *C* were concurrently negligent, resulting in injury to *A* or his property, should *B*'s negligence be imputed to *A* so as to bar his recovery from *C* under the contributory negligence rule?

The answer ought to be no. The policy considerations which justify vicarious *liability* simply do not apply in reverse. Nevertheless, despite this and the general hostility to contributory negligence, where the relationship is one of those which will support vicarious liability (such as employer-employee and joint venture or enterprise) most courts have applied a rule of imputed contributory negligence to bar plaintiff's recovery from a third person where plaintiff's agent was also negligent. This is still the majority view, and that of the Restatement. R. § 486.

Incredibly, at one time some courts went further and imputed contributory negligence on the basis of other relationships which do not even support vicarious liability. Thus, the negligence of the driver of a vehicle was imputed to his injured passenger, apparently on the theory that the passenger should have had better sense than to ride with one who might be negligent. The negligence of one spouse was imputed to the other. The negligence of a parent was imputed to the child, despite the fact that the child was innocent and incapable of negligence, thereby burdening the child with the parent's sins. The negligence of a bailee of a chattel was imputed to the bailor to bar the bailor's recovery from a third person for damage to the property. Happily, these decisions are now almost entirely overruled or obsolete. R. §§ 487, 488, 490, 494A.

A special case is created by the financial responsibility statutes enacted in about a dozen states (§ 8—16, infra) which make the owner of a motor vehicle liable for the negligence of its driver. A few courts have held that these statutes apply both ways and bar the owner's recovery from a negligent third person where the driver was also negligent. However, the better view refuses to interpret these statutes to impute contributory negligence, as they obviously were not intended to do so. Mills v. Gabriel (N.Y.1940).

Imputed contributory negligence, if applicable at all, does not apply to suits between those within the relationship (e.g. by an employer against his employee), except that a member of a joint enterprise cannot recover from another *non-negli-*

gent member (on a vicarious liability theory) for injuries caused by the negligence of a third member of the enterprise. R. § 491.

All of the foregoing assumes that plaintiff was not himself guilty of any *personal* contributory negligence. There are a number of cases in which the courts seem to talk in terms of imputed or vicarious contributory negligence, but in fact the negligence was that of the plaintiff himself, such as in failing to exercise care in the selection or control of his agent.

§ 5—3. Last Clear Chance

"Last clear chance" is a rule which in certain fact situations will excuse or negate the effect of plaintiff's contributory negligence and allow him to recover his full damages despite his own lack of ordinary care. As the name implies, it operates when plaintiff's negligence gets himself (or his property) into a zone of danger from which he cannot escape in time, leaving defendant as the person with the last opportunity to do something to prevent the harm which otherwise will occur. If defendant negligently botches this opportunity, he is not permitted to use plaintiff's prior negligence as a defense.

It is easy to understand why this rule has confused judges, lawyers and law students. Several different forms of the rule exist in the various jurisdictions, and the cases are often in conflict, even within a single jurisdiction. Its application requires complex multiple fact determinations, including the nature and time span of the negligence of two or more persons and often split-second time sequences of events and perceptions. The rule itself is complex and undoubtedly difficult for juries to understand—surely more difficult than comparative negligence rules for which it is an ersatz and incomplete substitute.

The doctrine is thought to have originated in Davies v. Mann (Exch.1842), where defendant's negligently driven wagon ran down plaintiff's donkey which he had negligently left in the roadway. At the time, the rule was probably simply another application of the common law's rules of proximate cause which searched for a single cause of every harm. Ordinarily the sole blame was placed on the last wrongdoer. Thus, if defendant's negligence was later in time than plaintiff's, defendant was liable. If plaintiff's was later, he was barred from recovery because the accident was his fault. Eventually, these rules became codified in the doctrines of last clear chance and contributory negligence. In the case of the latter, the time element was discarded, but not in the case of the former.

Since the law has long since abandoned the "single cause" idea, how do we account for the persistence of the doctrine of last clear chance? Several theories have been suggested, but the best justification is that it ameliorates the harsh effects of the doctrine of contributory negligence in circumstances where defendant's conduct is felt to be more culpable than plaintiff's. Plaintiff may have been wrong in getting himself into a position of danger, but at some point in time there was nothing more he could do to help himself. At that point, the situation was entirely in defendant's hands. Defendant alone had the power and duty to act to prevent the harm, and in most cases the instrumentality which created the danger was within defendant's control. Thus, defendant's failure to perform his duty from that point forward, given his superior opportunity to prevent the harm, is seen as the greater wrong which justifies liability.

Courts in different jurisdictions vary with respect to the fact situations in which they will permit the rule to be applied. The principal variables are (1) the nature of plaintiff's predicament, and (2) the state of defendant's attentiveness to plaintiff's peril. There are four different categories, which may be classified as *helpless plaintiffs, inattentive plaintiffs, observant defendants,* and *inattentive defendants.*

The *helpless plaintiff* is one who has negligently placed himself in a position of peril (e.g. in the path of defendant's moving vehicle or conveyance) from which he is now helpless to escape in time. For example, he may be caught or trapped, as where his foot is stuck in a railroad track; he may be unconscious or sick or in a drunken stupor; or he may have been previously injured by some one else and thereby rendered unable to move. This would also include the situation where plaintiff has negligently left his property in the zone of danger.

The *inattentive plaintiff* has negligently placed himself in a position of peril and has failed to observe the danger. For example, plaintiff is jogging down the middle of a road, oblivious to the approach of defendant's automobile from behind.

The *observant defendant* is one who actually sees the plaintiff in time to act so as to avoid the harm (assuming, of course, that he has a duty to act under the circumstances), and observes plaintiff's helpless or inattentive condition, but thereafter is negligent in failing to act so as to prevent the plaintiff's harm. In most cases, defendant's conduct is itself the source of plaintiff's danger, but this is not a requirement so long as a duty to act exists. For example, the rule should apply to a lifeguard who is negligent in failing to reach a drowning swimmer in time, even though the peril was created solely by the swimmer's own negligence.

Must plaintiff prove that defendant saw him *and* that defendant subjectively perceived his helplessness or inattentiveness, or is it enough to show that defendant actually saw him and that a reasonable person would have known that he was helpless or inattentive? Most courts have applied the latter, objective test. In reality, this is merely circumstantial proof of defendant's state of mind. Having seen the plaintiff in time, defendant will not be heard to say that he was unaware that plaintiff was helpless or inattentive when that fact would have been apparent to any observer.

The *inattentive defendant* is one who was under a duty to maintain a lookout such that he would have seen plaintiff in time to avoid the harm, and (had he been looking) would have been able to perceive his helpless or inattentive condition, and would have been able by the exercise of reasonable care to act in time to avoid the harm. However, due to defendant's negligence in failing to maintain the requisite lookout, he fails to see plaintiff in time and the injury occurs.

Thus, there are four possible cases in which the rule may be applied.

The classic "last clear chance" situation is *helpless plaintiff* against *observant defendant,* and all courts which accept the doctrine will apply it here. R. § 479. Even those few courts which do not recognize the rule will reach the same result under the doctrine of wilful and wanton misconduct.

In the *helpless plaintiff-inattentive defendant* and *inattentive plaintiff-observant defendant* situations, most jurisdictions which recognize the rule by name will permit it to be applied. R. §§ 479, 480.

However, where the facts are *inattentive plaintiff* versus *inattentive defendant* the justifications for the rule disappear, and thus all jurisdictions (save one) refuse to apply it. The lone exception is Missouri, where it is called the "humanitarian doctrine."

Note that defendant's negligence must occur *subsequent* to that point in time when he discovered (or should have discovered) plaintiff's peril. For example, where defendant's negligence is in failing to keep his automobile's brakes in repair, and the only reason he could not prevent the accident was because his brakes failed to work, the rule has no application.

All of this is, of course, a needless and confusing exercise. The doctrine may produce a rough but closer approximation of justice than would be the case without it. But it should be seen as an unsatisfactory intermediate stop on the road to comparative negligence, which no doubt will eventually entirely replace it.

§ 5—4. Comparative Negligence

As earlier noted (§ 5—1) there has long been dissatisfaction with the "all or nothing" contributory negligence rule, and it has recently come under increasing attack from judges and legal writers. The past decade has witnessed a strong trend in this country, following the lead of most other common law nations, to switch to the civil law and maritime doctrine of comparative negligence.

When applied, plaintiff's negligence is not a complete bar to his recovery. Instead, his damages are calculated and then reduced by the proportion which his fault bears to the total causative fault of his harm. For example, the trier of fact decides that defendant's negligence contributed 75% and plaintiff's negligence 25% to plaintiff's injury, and that plaintiff sustained $10,000 damages. Plaintiff will be awarded a judgment for $7,500.

The task of accomplishing the shift to comparative negligence has largely been delegated to the legislatures. The courts, having created and firmly established the contributory negligence rule, have been loath to abolish it. E.g., Maki v. Frelk (Ill.1968). They are reluctant to undertake (or to permit juries) to apportion damages without any hard criteria. Judicial adoption of comparative negligence would leave untouched various state statutes which are premised upon, or incorporate, the common law contributory negligence rule. And because of the drastic nature of any such change, and its effect upon insurance rate making, most favor the view that the comparative negligence rule must be adopted prospectively. This smacks of "judicial legislation," a practice which is seen by some as sinful if not unconstitutional. However, experience has shown that juries are not so inept as some have feared. Moreover, any approximate division is better than a rule which throws 100% of the loss on the plaintiff. And since tort law is traditionally created and revised by the courts, the "judicial legislation" charge is without merit. After all, the legislature is free to change any comparative negligence rules created by judicial decision if it is dissatisfied with them. Thus, several courts, impatient for legislative action, have abolished the contributory negligence rule and adopted comparative negligence. Hoffman v. Jones (Fla.1973); Li v. Yellow Cab Co. (Cal.1975); Kaatz v. State (Alaska 1975).

As of 1968, only seven states (and Puerto Rico) had comparative negligence statutes of general application. Then the flood of legislation began, and state after state converted. Well over half the states now have comparative negligence in some form, and it is safe to predict that the momentum will continue and soon it will be the universal rule.

There are two basic versions. A minority of jurisdictions (e.g., N.Y., Cal., Miss., Alaska, Fla., R.I., Wash.) and the F.E.L.A. and Jones Act have adopted the "pure" form in which plaintiff may recover no matter how great his fault in comparison to that of defendant. Thus, if plaintiff was 80% at fault and defendant 20%, plaintiff still recovers 20% of his damages. However, most comparative negligence statutes embody a "50%" rule by which plaintiff recovers nothing if his negligence was "as great as" (50%) or "greater than" (51%) that of defendant. Such provisions, representing a partial retention of contributory negligence, are not logically defensible, but probably reflect legislative compromise and the view that a plaintiff who is largely responsible for his own injury is unworthy of compensation. (Nebraska, South Dakota and Tennessee have different comparative negligence standards involving "slight," "gross," and "remote" negligence.)

The shift to comparative negligence has created a number of problems of adjustment. In most cases, the solutions depend in part on the wording of the particular statute, and thus vary from state to state. Many issues are as yet unresolved. Some of the principal problems include:

Multiple Parties. Suppose plaintiff's harm is caused in part by several joint tortfeasors, all of whom may or may not have been sued. Is plaintiff's fault compared to each, or to all jointly? What is the effect of a 50% statute in these cases? What about those unsued? How are the damages to be apportioned among the defendants?

Counterclaims. If one or more defendants are also injured, may they counterclaim against plaintiff? How is this to be handled procedurally?

Last Clear Chance. Does it survive? The better rule is no. Li v. Yellow Cab Co. (Cal.1975).

Assumption of Risk. Is it still a complete bar to plaintiff's recovery? Properly, only if and to the extent that it is not merely another form of contributory negligence. See § 5—5, infra.

Wilful and Wanton Misconduct. Even if defendant's conduct may be characterized as wilful and wanted misconduct, which would defeat the defense of contributory negligence (§ 4—7), comparative negligence is nevertheless applicable to reduce plaintiff's damages.

Punitive Damages. Where defendant's reckless misconduct is sufficient to justify punitive damages, are they to be reduced under the comparative negligence rule? Generally not.

Strict Liability. Where defendant is held strictly liable (see Chapter 3, supra, and § 8—9, infra), does the comparative negligence rule or statute apply? Much will depend on the statutory language, but it would seem that it should unless some statute requires otherwise.

Violation of Safety Statute. Where defendant's liability is based upon the violation of certain statutes intended to protect persons more or less unable to protect themselves against certain risks, some courts have held contributory negligence no defense. Does this rule apply to prohibit reduction of plaintiff's damages under comparative negligence? The prevailing view is that it does not, unless the statute requires otherwise.

Role of Court and Jury. The trier of fact allocates the parties' fault in percentages, and assesses plaintiff's total damages. Who then does the arithmetic and determines whether and how much plaintiff will recover? The statutory provisions, if any, control; and they vary. Where the question is open, it would seem preferable (and would reduce confusion and error) to use a special verdict procedure, asking the jury to decide only the fault percentages and total damages and permitting the court to make the computations.

For comprehensive treatment of this subject, see V. Schwartz, Comparative Negligence (1974).

§ 5—5. Assumption of Risk

Assumption of risk is another of those elusive concepts which has meant different things to different judges and legal writers. Much of the confusion arises from attempts to relate it to the duty concept. Thus, it is said that plaintiff's assumption of the risk of defendant's negligence operates to relieve defendant of his duty to exercise care for plaintiff's safety. Conversely, others maintain that the term really describes those areas where there is no duty in the first place, and that therefore plaintiff is required by law to accept those risks when he chooses to encounter them.

Such analyses, while perhaps technically accurate under some definitions of "duty," are of doubtful value and can be quite misleading. For almost all purposes, it is preferable to keep the two concepts separate. All persons are under a duty to exercise reasonable care for the safety of others, except as limited by the law's specific duty limitations (§ 4—5) and rules of proximate cause (§ 4—4). Assumption of risk is an affirmative defense, to be pleaded and proved by defendant, which will operate to defeat or excuse defendant's tort liability despite the fact that he owed plaintiff a duty of care and that he was negligent. Duty is a question of law for the court; assumption of risk is a question of fact for the jury. Analyses which commingle the two concepts—and there are many examples in the law books—can only lead to error.

Another fertile source of confusion is the failure to distinguish and eliminate from consideration those cases where defendant was not negligent at all. Absent negligence, we do not even reach the question of assumption of risk. Yet there are cases (and writers) which talk in terms of assumption of the risk of dangers which were not created by negligence in the first place. Bear in mind throughout this discussion that we are here concerned only with risks which were created by some negligent conduct on the part of the defendant.

Finally, much confusion is generated by the failure to distinguish between assumption of risk and contributory negligence. What is that distinction?

Fundamentally, assumption of risk is plaintiff's voluntary *consent* to encounter a known danger created by defendant's negligence. Contributory negligence is *unreasonable conduct*. Thus, the distinction is between *consent* and *conduct*. The same facts may give rise to one or both defenses. For example, assume that defendant offers plaintiff a seat in defendant's chair, which has a defective leg. Plaintiff accepts, the chair collapses and plaintiff is injured. If plaintiff knew that the leg was broken, he probably assumed the risk of that defect. In addition, his conduct may also have been negligent because the reasonably prudent person would not have used the chair. But if plaintiff did not actually know of the defect, then he did not consent to assume that risk, even though his conduct may or may not have been negligent depending on whether a reasonably prudent person would have noticed the defect or inspected the chair before using it.

The relation between the two defenses may thus be visualized:

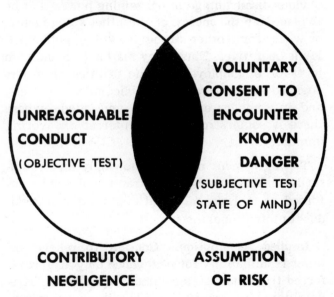

UNREASONABLE CONDUCT (OBJECTIVE TEST)

VOLUNTARY CONSENT TO ENCOUNTER KNOWN DANGER (SUBJECTIVE TEST STATE OF MIND)

CONTRIBUTORY NEGLIGENCE   **ASSUMPTION OF RISK**

[B5109]

Assumption of risk may be *express* or *implied*.

Express Assumption. In general, persons entering into a relationship may voluntarily agree that one will consent in advance to assume the risk of the other's negligence. R. § 496B. Ordinarily principles of contract law apply. These agreements sometimes take the form of releases or disclaimers.

However, courts have often refused to enforce such agreements where one party is at such an obvious disadvantage in bargaining power that he is placed at the mercy of the other's negligence, or where some other strong overriding public policy is operative. Thus, they may not be enforced in favor of employers, public utilities or others engaged in public callings, public bailees, carriers, and in some cases landlords and others where there is some strong public interest disfavoring immunity.

The agreement must be knowingly and voluntarily made. And such contracts will not be enforced as to risks of wilful and wanton misconduct or intentional torts.

Implied Assumption. Consent to relieve another from liability for negligence may also be inferred from plaintiff's conduct. R. § 496C. It is here that the principal difficulties have arisen. For purposes of this analysis, the cases will be divided into three general groups.

In the first group are the cases where plaintiff voluntarily enters into some relationship with defendant with knowledge that there are certain inherent but commonly accepted risks against which defendant will not protect him. This would include spectators and participants in sporting events, those who accept hazardous employment, and the like. It is these cases which are most often analytically unsound. What risks are assumed? In general, one assumes the ordinary foreseeable hazards of the activity; but as to these, there is *no negligence* on the part of defendant, and therefore no assumption of the risk of *negligent* harm. Used in this context, "assumption of risk" is a misleading misnomer. Some courts refer to this as the "primary sense" of the term, and the remaining cases (where defendant had a duty to exercise care for plaintiff's safety and was negligent) as its "secondary sense."

In the second group are the cases where plaintiff voluntarily enters into some relationship with defendant with knowledge that there is a substantial risk that defendant will act negligently. The passenger who consents to ride with an intoxicated driver is a typical example. It is sometimes said that one does not assume the risk of future negligence, but these cases constitute an exception and most courts will permit the defense to be asserted. While "assumption of risk" may properly be applied here, it will be seen that the true basis of the defense is the unreasonable conduct of the plaintiff in proceeding to enter into the relationship, and thus it would be preferable to restrict these cases to the defense of contributory negligence.

The third group are cases where plaintiff is fully aware of a risk which has already been created by the negligence of defendant and voluntarily proceeds to encounter it. For example, defendant furnishes plaintiff, a painter, a scaffold with a badly frayed rope. Plaintiff, fully aware of the rope's condition, proceeds to use the scaffold and is injured. Or defendant, owner of a baseball stadium, is under a duty to furnish a number of screened seats. None are provided. Plaintiff, a spectator, chooses to sit in an area which ought to have been screened and is injured by a foul ball. In both cases, plaintiff may be found to have assumed the risk.

Elements: Consent, Knowledge, Voluntariness. Three criteria must be met to support a finding of implied assumption of risk. The conduct must (1) manifest consent, and the risk must be encountered (2) voluntarily and (3) with full knowledge and appreciation of the danger.

(1) *Manifestation of Consent.* The essence of the defense is consent to relieve defendant of liability, and therefore plaintiff's conduct must implicitly manifest such consent. Not all conduct by which one voluntarily proceeds to encounter a known danger does. For example, a pedestrian who dashes into the path of a speeding car, fully

aware of the risk, does not thereby manifest his consent to relieve the driver of his obligation to exercise care for the pedestrian's safety, nor of his liability for failure to do so. Rather the opposite is true; he is demanding that care be taken for his safety. He may be contributorily negligent, but he does not assume the risk.

(2) *Knowledge.* To excuse defendant's liability, the consent must be an informed one, and therefore defendant must show that plaintiff actually knew, understood and appreciated the risk. R. § 496D. Unlike contributory negligence, the test is a subjective one—what did plaintiff actually know, not what should he have known.

At the same time, plaintiff's knowledge may be proved circumstantially, and where the risk ought to have been obvious to him, he will probably be unsuccessful if he tries to deny the import of what he saw. Similarly, he is ordinarily charged with matters of common knowledge, such as the slipperiness of ice, and those things which ordinary observation of his surroundings would reveal.

(3) *Voluntary Exposure.* No consent can be inferred unless plaintiff's exposure to the risk was free and voluntary. R. § 496E.

In many cases, voluntariness may be inferred from his conduct in entering or remaining in the zone of danger, albeit reluctantly or under protest. But there are cases, usually involving employees, where the danger is not imminent, plaintiff protests and defendant then promises to remedy the risk-creating condition. Plaintiff's consent is then vitiated until so long a time has passed that he can no longer reasonably rely on the promise.

Evidence that plaintiff exposed himself to the risk under duress or compulsion will, of course, negate this element. There is an analogy between the *voluntariness* of plaintiff's conduct here and the *reasonableness* of his conduct on the issue of contributory negligence. If plaintiff had no real or effective choice, or no better or safer alternative, his conduct in encountering the risk may be found not voluntary. Thus, a tenant does not assume the risk of his landlord's negligence in maintaining a common stairway which the tenant must use for access to his apartment. Nor is one required to surrender a valuable legal right (of which defendant has no right to deprive him) in order to avoid the zone of danger. For example, plaintiff is not required to forego use of a public railroad crossing because defendant railroad has failed to keep it in repair. And would-be rescuers do not assume the risk of their own injury by attempting the rescue, where the alternative is to permit the threatened harm to occur.

What about economic duress? Does an employee assume the risk of using negligently maintained equipment where the alternative is to be fired? Many courts have said yes, but the trend and better view is to permit such compulsion to be shown to defeat the defense.

Violation of Statute. As in the case of contributory negligence, assumption of risk is a defense to negligence based on violation of a statute, except for a limited group of statutes which are intended to protect a certain class of persons from dangers against which they are incapable of protecting themselves. R. § 496F. Some statutory torts (e.g. workmen's compensation, F.E.L.A., structural work acts) expressly exclude the defense.

Limitation to Particular Risk. The assumption is, of course, limited to the particular risk which plaintiff freely and knowingly encountered.

Abolition of the Defense. Misunderstood and thus misapplied, often confused with other tort concepts (such as duty and contributory negligence) and subject to some of the same criticisms which apply to contributory negligence, the defense of *implied* assumption of risk is in similar disfavor. Some jurisdictions refuse to recognize the doctrine separate from contributory negligence; others refuse to apply it in certain classes of cases. There appears to be a trend to abolish it as a defense (e. g., Williamson v. Smith, N.M. 1971; Rosenau v. City of Estherville, Iowa 1972) as applied in what the courts call its "secondary sense"—that is, where defendant had a duty to plaintiff and was negligent (see page 141, supra).

This has some merit. The courts have observed that there is a substantial overlap between implied assumption of risk and contributory negligence. The "voluntariness" requirement of the former has evolved to strongly resemble the "reasonable person" test of the latter. But in the remaining area of difference—where the assumption of risk was reasonable under the circumstances and therefore not negligent—there remains room for disagreement. It can be argued that if it was reasonable (and therefore not negligent) to encounter the risk, the negligent defendant should not be exonerated. Many legal writers support this view. On the other hand, as Prosser observes, there are cases where plaintiff may *reasonably* elect to consent voluntarily to accept the consequences of a negligently created risk—in other words, to deliberately, freely and knowingly "take a chance" and accept the consequences. Thus, the courts may be required to continue to recognize the defense, if only under another name.

Even where abolished as a defense in negligence cases, assumption of risk remains a defense in cases of strict liability.

As in the case of last clear chance, the implied assumption of risk defense has little justification in the law of a jurisdiction which has adopted comparative negligence, and the strong trend is to abolish it in those states. Farley v. M M Cattle Co. (Tex.1975); Lyons v. Redding Constr. Co. (Wash.1973); Hall v. Holton (Fla.App.1976).

CHAPTER 6

LIABILITY FOR INTENTIONAL MISCONDUCT

§ 6—1. Intent

As we have seen (§ 1—3), the early English law of wrongs was not much concerned with the wrongdoer's intent. If his act was voluntary and the resulting physical harm direct, liability usually followed.

Gradually, the actions of trespass and case evolved such that, so far as physical harm is concerned, the distinction between them was no longer whether the harm was direct or indirect, but rather whether the tort could be classified within the confines of the traditional trespass actions—battery, assault, false imprisonment, trespass to land and chattels—or whether the wrong involved mere negligence, for which case was the usual remedy. At the same time the courts came to require fault as a condition to trespass liability —that is, some sort of wrongful intent. Thus, the trespass actions became what we now call the intentional torts.

Morally, greater blame attaches to intentional misconduct than to lesser degrees of fault, and this is reflected in the law of intentional torts. In general, to establish a prima facie case, plaintiff need only prove that defendant intentionally invaded a protected interest. The burden then shifts to defendant to show some justification or excuse. And, unlike negligence actions, actual damages need not be proved. If plaintiff cannot establish any actual harm (tangible or intangible), nominal damages can be awarded.

Traditionally, the intentional torts are those named and discussed in the sections which follow. However, there has come to be recognized a general principle of intentional tort liability, analogous to the general principle of negligence liability (see § 3—1), sometimes called "prima facie tort," which may be invoked when no particular intentional tort applies. Section 870 of the Restatement (Second) as tentatively approved provides:

> One who intentionally causes injury to another is subject to liability to the other for the actual harm incurred, if his conduct is culpable and not justifiable. This liability may be imposed despite the fact that the actor's conduct does not come within one of the traditional categories of tort liability.

For a discussion of the elements and limits of this liability, see the Comments to this section; for authorities supporting it, see the Reporter's Notes. A recent case discussing this doctrine is Nees v. Hocks (Or.1975) (wrongful discharge). Of course, it must not be inferred from this that all unjustified intentional wrongs are actionable. But in a proper case, the courts need not and do not consider themselves bound by the traditional intentional tort pigeon-holes.

An intentional tort is an act committed (or omitted) with a particular state of mind. How is the actor's state of mind to be proved? Direct evidence—the actor's own statement of his actual intent—is rarely available. Indeed, after the fact he may claim to have had the best of intentions. Thus, as in all other cases where one's state of mind must be shown, it is usually proved by circumstantial evidence. His conduct, in the context of his surroundings and what he presumably knew and perceived, is evidence from which his intent may be inferred. The law presumes that one intends the natural and probable consequences of his acts in light of the surrounding circumstances of which he may be assumed to be aware.

Intent, in the sense required here, must be distinguished from motive. *Intent* is usually defined as the desire to cause certain immediate consequences. One who throws a rock with great force against a glass window obviously intends that it will be broken. One who points a loaded gun at another and pulls the trigger surely intends that the bullet will strike and injure him. The actor's *motive* for his conduct—revenge, protest, punishment, theft, self-defense, or even a desire to be of help (e.g. the surgeon who operates without consent)—may, in certain cases, aggravate, mitigate or excuse the wrong. For example, malice may permit assessment of punitive damages; self-defense may be a complete defense to tort liability. But to establish a prima facie case, all that need be shown is the defendant's conduct, the invasion of a legally protected interest of the plaintiff, and the requisite intent.

Since intent is a desire to cause certain immediate consequences, very young children may be held liable for intentional torts though so young as to be incapable of negligence.

Intent is a state of mind, a subjective matter. But the law's definition of intent is objective to this extent: an actor is deemed to intend the consequences of his act which he knows are substantially certain to result, irrespective of his actual intent. R. § 8A. Thus, *A* throws a bomb into a room in which *B* and *C* are present for the purpose of killing *B*. *A* knows that *C* is present, but has no desire to hurt *C,* and in fact fervently hopes that *C* will not be injured. Nevertheless, since he knew that physical harm to *C* was substantially certain, he is held to have intended that harm.

Thus, certainty of the harmful consequences is the basis on which we distinguish intentional torts from negligent or reckless ("wilful and wanton") ones. If the result is intended or substantially certain to occur, the tort is intentional. But if the actor's conduct merely creates a foreseeable *risk* of harm, which may or may not be realized, then the conduct is negligent or reckless depending upon the magnitude of the risk.

Unique to the intentional torts, borrowed from the criminal law, the doctrine of "transferred intent" reflects the greater blame which attaches to intentional misconduct. In effect, it is a broadened rule of proximate cause. Thus, where A acts with the intent to injure B, but at the same time or instead injures C, his intent to injure B "transfers" to C and A is deemed to have committed an intentional tort upon C, even though he was completely unaware of C's existence or of any risk of harm to C. For example, A shoots at B and wounds or misses him. The bullet strikes C who was hidden from view and not known to be in the vicinity. A may be liable to C in battery. In addition, the intent transfers among the five progeny of the parent trespass action—battery, assault, false imprisonment, trespass to land and trespass to chattels—so long as the harm is direct and immediate. For example, A's intent to commit only an assault upon B such as by shooting in his direction to frighten him may support liability for a battery to C who is unexpectedly struck by the bullet.

Often the same act is both a tort and a crime. This is especially true with respect to the intentional torts. But despite their common origins, tort and criminal law rules are now more different than similar, and analogies and comparisons between torts and crimes of the same name or having similar bases in conduct should be made only with the greatest caution.

Both a civil tort action and a criminal prosecution may be brought for the same wrongful conduct. The remedies are concurrent, and either a successful or an unsuccessful result in one is ordinarily not a bar to the other. However, since the most common intentional torts are more often committed by judgment-proof persons, and intentional torts are frequently uninsured and in some cases uninsurable, intentional tort litigation is of relatively minor significance in the day-to-day work of lawyers and courts.

§ 6—2. Battery

Battery is the remedy for an intentional and unpermitted physical contact with plaintiff's person by defendant or (now that the distinction be tween trespass and case has disappeared) by an agency defendant has set in motion. It reflects the basic right to have one's body left alone by others. Secondarily, it seeks to deter relatively minor but offensive contacts which can precipitate breaches of the peace.

Plaintiff's "person" is held to include his body and those things in contact or closely connected to it and identified with it, such as clothing, an object held in his hand, or an object so associated or identified with plaintiff that, considering the nature of the contact, a normal person would deem it an offense against his person.

The tort is the contact, and thus plaintiff need not have been aware of it at the time.

Two forms of contact are actionable. First and foremost are those which cause some *physical harm,* broadly defined to include any physical impairment of the condition of the body (such as a cut, a bruise, a burn, etc., however slight), even if beneficial; illness; and physical (but not emotional) pain. R. § 15. Second, battery also encompasses contacts which do not cause physical harm but are hostile, offensive, or insulting, such as poking with a finger in anger, angrily knocking off one's hat, dousing one with water, spitting in one's face, cutting hair, and even an unwanted kiss. R. §§ 18, 19. The gist of the action is contact without consent, resulting in harm to plaintiff's person or dignity.

The contact must have been intended (unless the doctrine of transferred intent applies); otherwise the action if any lies in negligence. But defendant need not have intended any harm. It is no defense that defendant intended only a joke or a compliment, or even to render assistance. Thus, where a doctor performs surgery without the patient's consent, a battery has been committed.

If plaintiff consents to the contact, defendant is privileged to make it and there is no tort. This is generally true of all torts. See § 7—2. So far as battery is concerned, consent may sometimes be assumed. In a crowded society, some unper-

mitted contact is inevitable, customary, and reasonably necessary. Consent to certain kinds of
contacts may also be assumed where there is
some prior relationship between the parties.
Thus, where reasonable and customary, given the
time, place and circumstances of the contact and
the relationship of the parties, a privilege will ordinarily exist, unless and until plaintiff gives
notice to the contrary.

§ 6—3. Assault

An assault is an act which arouses in plaintiff
a *reasonable* apprehension of an imminent battery. Like battery, the action (1) protects one's
right to his bodily integrity, in this case against
psychic harm, and (2) deters conduct which often
leads to disturbances of the peace.

Apprehension, but not fear, is required. The
tort is committed when plaintiff perceives the
threat, even though he is too courageous to be
frightened or intimidated. But since the essence
of the tort is the apprehension, plaintiff obviously
must be aware of defendant's threatening act at
the time. R. § 22.

The contact must be perceived as imminent.
R. § 24. There must be an apparent intent to
carry out the threat immediately. Thus, it is often said that mere words, however strong, do not
constitute an assault. R. § 31. There must be
some overt act. Ordinarily this is true. But
words may give character to an act. An other-

wise innocuous or inoffensive movement (e.g. reaching into one's pocket) or perhaps even a stance may become an assault when coupled with threatening words such that a reasonable person would apprehend a battery. Conversely, a threatening gesture accompanied by words which negate any present intent of a tortious contact may not be an assault if a reasonable person in plaintiff's position would perceive no immediate danger of a battery. For example, if defendant's words indicate that he jests, or that the threat is for the future ("The next time I see you I will hit you") or conditional or hypothetical ("If it were not assize-time, I would not take such language from you"), there is no assault.

Similarly, there must be an apparent present ability and opportunity to commit the threatened battery. For example, if defendant is located or confined or otherwise under some restriction or disability so as to be physically incapable of immediately carrying out the threat, and plaintiff is aware of this, then there can be no reasonable apprehension of contact and therefore no assault. Conversely, if plaintiff reasonably apprehends a battery, there is an assault even though defendant (unbeknown to plaintiff) is in fact incapable of it (such as when the gun he points at plaintiff is not loaded).

To be liable for assault, defendant must intend to commit an intentional tort but need not intend to commit battery. He may have intended only an assault. Or, under the doctrine of transferred intent (§ 6—1), his intent to commit one of the other trespassory torts will suffice, provided plaintiff reasonably apprehends an imminent battery.

Much confusion has arisen from the tendency of some to use the term "assault" as synonymous with battery, or as a shorthand expression encompassing both torts. While a battery and an assault are often parts of the same tortious event, either tort may be committed by itself and without committing the other. Be precise in the use of these two terms, and do not be misled by those who are not.

§ 6—4. False Imprisonment

The action for false imprisonment enforces another basic personal interest, the right to be free from wrongful confinement.

The essence of the tort is the mental harm caused by the knowledge that one is not free to move about at will. Thus, where there is no other harm caused by the confinement, plaintiff must of course be aware that he is confined at the time or there is no tort. But he may also recover damages for physical harm and any other consequential damages caused by the confinement; and where such damages are incurred there is a cause of action even though due to his mental incapacity or for some other reason he is then incapable of realizing that he is confined. R. § 42.

Prima facie, the tort occurs when defendant confines plaintiff, intending to confine him or another, within boundaries set by defendant. R. § 35. The place of confinement may be much broader than the term "imprisonment" implies. It is enough that plaintiff is prevented from leaving a given area, such as a room, an automobile, a building, or perhaps even a larger area. Within that area, however, the confinement must be total, and plaintiff must have no reasonable or safe avenue of escape known to him. Merely to block one's path in one direction is not sufficient. R. § 36.

Thus, the restraint may be by means of actual or apparent physical barriers, or by physical force or threats of force, express or implied. R. §§ 38–40. It may be by duress sufficient to vitiate consent, such as where defendant threatens to harm another or plaintiff's valuable property, or restrains such property. R. § 40A. However, merely moral or social pressure is not sufficient. Thus, where plaintiff remains confined to clear his name, or to avoid attracting attention or public humiliation, there may be some tort, but it is not false imprisonment.

Confinement may be imposed under color of legal authority, in which case it is sometimes called false arrest. R. § 41. If defendant has or asserts the legal power to detain the plaintiff and purports to exercise it, plaintiff believes that defendant has or may have such power, and plaintiff submits to it against his will, there is confinement. If the arrest is in fact without legal authority, it is a false arrest and therefore false imprisonment.

An actionable confinement may occur when plaintiff, once properly restrained, is now entitled to leave the premises, and defendant intentionally fails to perform his legal duty to release plaintiff or to provide or show him a means of egress. R. § 45.

In order to be liable for false imprisonment, defendant must be an active and knowing participant in procuring or instigating the confinement, including its wrongful aspect. R. § 45A. It is not sufficient that he merely gives information to others who independently decide whether and how to confine plaintiff. Nor is he liable where he requests a proper arrest and some one else performs an improper one.

The requisite intent, however, is merely the intent to confine plaintiff, or another where plaintiff is confined instead or in addition. A mistake of identity is no excuse. Similarly, a good faith belief that the confinement is justified is no defense. Of course, the presence or absence of malice will aggravate or mitigate the damages.

Once the fact of intentional confinement is shown, the burden is on defendant to prove legal justification.

Detention of a suspected shoplifter is a recurring case. Where defendant acted in good faith, the courts have struggled to deny liability, frequently by finding that plaintiff voluntarily consented to remain or by creating a special privilege to detain him on the premises, without arrest. See R. § 120A. Given the magnitude of this problem, most states have enacted statutes which give the shopkeeper a limited privilege to detain such persons for a reasonable time to investigate.

The torts of false arrest and malicious prosecution are sometimes confused. Basically, malicious prosecution is the remedy for the institution of groundless criminal proceedings against the plaintiff for an improper purpose. Thus, if defendant complies with the proper formal requirements in procuring plaintiff's arrest and confinement, he is liable if at all, only in malicious prosecution for misuse of legal process to effect a valid arrest for an improper purpose, and not for false imprisonment.

§ 6—5. Intentional or Reckless Infliction of Emotional Distress

The common law has been slow to accept plaintiff's interest in freedom from emotional distress as entitled to independent legal protection. Such reluctance is incongruous in view of the fact that damages for mental trauma and its physical effects have long been awarded as adjunct to damages for other kinds of harm, such as bodily injury. Moreover, equally intangible harms—pain and suffering, for example—are regularly valued and compensated. And harms to purely mental interests have long been recognized in the actions for assault, false imprisonment, and to a lesser extent battery (in cases where the contact is slight but offensive). Thus, any difficulties inherent in proving and measuring damages for emotional distress are insufficient to justify non-liability.

The principal bases of the reluctance to allow a separate action for causing emotional distress are probably the fear of false claims and a feeling that the courts should not redress mere wounds to the ego. But where defendant's conduct is sufficiently outrageous to be likely to produce a strong emotional response in a normal person, there is a sufficient assurance that the alleged harm is real together with a strong public interest in deterring such conduct. Thus, it is in such cases that many courts (and the Restatement) have recently come to recognize a separate and distinct cause of action, apart from any other tort, for the intentional or reckless infliction of mental anguish.

To qualify for liability, defendant's conduct must be "extreme and outrageous" (R. § 46), intolerable, and not merely insulting, profane, abusive, annoying or even threatening. It must go beyond all reasonable bounds of decency. Unless defendant knows of some special sensitivity of the plaintiff, mere verbal abuse, name-calling, rudeness, insolence, and threats to do that which defendant has a legal right to do are generally not actionable, absent circumstances of aggravation. The courts cannot provide a remedy for bad manners, rough laguage, and other such acts, merely inconsiderate and unkind, which are a regrettably common occurrence in human interaction. But where, by community standards, the conduct may be characterized as shocking and indecent there may be liability in tort.

(There is, however, an exception to the foregoing rule in the case of innkeepers, common carriers, and other public utilities, who may be liable for profane, grossly insulting, or indecent language or conduct by their employees acting within the scope of their employment. See R. § 48. It has been suggested, so far with little success, that this rule might be extended to all possessors of land whose premises are held open to the public. And cf. statutes in Virginia, West Virginia, and Mississippi making actionable insulting words likely to provoke violence.)

An increasingly common fact situation involves the abuse by defendant of some relation or status which gives him actual or apparent power to damage plaintiff's interests. For example, actionable conduct has been found in threats (and other indignities) by bill collectors, insurance adjustors, landlords, school officials, police and those posing as police, and officials of a trade association, where such threats go beyond the ordinary means of persuasion or demands which they have a right to make and become flagrant abuses of power in the nature of extortion.

Intentional or reckless mishandling of a corpse may give rise to a cause of action in the next of kin who are thereby emotionally distressed. R. § 868.

As previously noted, the courts are unwilling to redress minor psychic harm. Therefore, not only must defendant's conduct be extreme and outrageous, but plaintiff's emotional response must be severe. A plaintiff who merely becomes unhappy, humiliated, or mildly despondent for a short time and spends a sleepless night or two cannot recover. But if the emotional anguish is great, and especialy if it is prolonged, most courts (and the Restatement, § 46) will allow the action whether or not there is any physical manifestation of the mental suffering, or bodily harm (such as a physical illness, heart condition, miscarriage, and the like) caused by it. A few jurisdictions seem to require such resulting bodily harm as a condition to liability.

Special rules of proximate cause apply to this tort. Recall that the usual rule is that defendant takes his plaintiff as he finds him, and will be liable for all the physical consequences of his tort upon that plaintiff, however unforeseeable they are or specially sensitive that particular plaintiff may be. This is sometimes called the "thin-skulled" or "eggshell" plaintiff rule. See § 4—4, supra. However, in the case of the infliction of emotional distress, defendant is not liable to the extent that plaintiff's emotional response is not within the range of normal human reactions to that conduct. In other words, the distress must be such as a reasonable person of ordinary sensitivity would experience. And as a corollary rule, where defendant intended to inflict only severe emotional distress, he is not liable for greater harm (in the form of illness or other bodily harm) unless his conduct created a foreseeable risk of such aggravated harm. R. § 312.

Of course, if defendant has knowledge of a peculiar or special sensitivity of the plaintiff, he may be liable for conduct which is extreme and outrageous in light of that special vulnerability, even though the same conduct would not be expected to produce a severe response in a normal, healthy adult. The physically infirm, the mentally ill, children, and pregnant women are commonly held to be examples of such plaintiffs.

In most of the decided cases, the mental distress was inflicted intentionally—that is, defendant desired to cause it or knew that it was substantially certain to occur. However, some cases and the Restatement allow recovery where defendant is merely reckless ("wilful and wanton"), in that there is a high probability that emotional distress will follow from his conduct and he goes ahead in conscious disregard of that risk.

The intent required for this tort may *not* be supplied by the doctrine of transferred intent (§ 6—1), at least so far as defendant's intent was only to commit some *other tort*. R. § 47. For example, the intent to commit a battery, or to harm plaintiff's property, is not enough. Defendant must intend to cause emotional distress, or at least act in conscious disregard of a high probability of such harm. However, there would seem to be no good reason why the doctrine of transferred intent may not be applied as between different *persons*. Thus, where defendant intends to inflict emotional distress upon *A* and takes steps to do so, but due to unforeseen events *B* is traumatized instead, *B* should have a cause of action.

Moreover, defendant's *acts* need not be directed at plaintiff, so long as he intentionally or recklessly causes plaintiff's mental anguish. He will be liable to plaintiff for shocking conduct directed at some third person, *provided* plaintiff's mental harm was also intended or recklessly caused. The courts have generally required that plaintiff witness the conduct, and that defendant know or have reason to know of plaintiff's presence. And according to the Restatement (§ 46(2)), if the third person is *not* a member of plaintiff's immediate family, plaintiff may recover only if the distress reasonably results in some bodily harm. These requirements are intended as safeguards against questionable claims and excessively broad liability, such as to a large number of persons who witness a shocking event or to one who merely hears of it second- or third-hand. However, it would seem that liability may well be extended in favor of a close relative who was not present at the event when the circumstances of the case justify. See, e.g., Knierim v. Izzo (Ill. 1961) (defendant threatened to murder plaintiff's husband, and then did so).

§ 6—6. Invasion of Privacy: Intrusion

Protection against interference with the interest in privacy—the right to be "let alone"—is provided by what ought to be regarded as not one but several distinct tort actions. Prosser and the Restatement (Second) Torts (§ 652A) group the privacy cases into four major categories: (1) intrusion; (2) appropriation of one's name or likeness; (3) giving unreasonable publicity to private facts; and (4) placing plaintiff in a false light in the public eye. The latter three of these are founded upon improper publicity of the plaintiff, usually in the public press or electronic media. The harm caused is primarily to plaintiff's business and personal relations with others, similar to that caused by defamation, and these matters are beyond the scope of this book. Hence, (2)–(4) will not be treated here.

Intrusion, however, is an intentional tort closely related to the one discussed in the preceding section, infliction of emotional distress. Both protect plaintiff's interest in his mental tranquility and equilibrium—his "peace of mind"—against intentional interference by defendant's offensive conduct. In fact, not infrequently the same conduct may be tortious under either theory or both. But privacy encompasses something more—a basic right, founded upon the sanctity of each individual human being, to choose when and to what extent he will permit others to have knowledge of his personal affairs or to impinge upon his body, mind, and private activities against his will.

Essentially, intrusion is an intentional, improper, unreasonable, and offensive interference with the solitude, seclusion, or private life and affairs of another. See R. § 652B. It covers a broad spectrum. It may consist of an unprivileged entry into plaintiff's dwelling place or other premises of which he is entitled to exclusive possession. It includes an illegal search of his person or property. Unauthorized eavesdropping or spying upon plaintiff, with or without electronic or mechanical aids, is a common illustration of this tort. Another is persistent unwanted communication with plaintiff, as by a series of offensive telephone calls or by repeatedly and offensively interjecting one's presence into plaintiff's immediate surroundings—for example, where a photographer persisted in making a nuisance of himself in his efforts to photograph a president's

[*166*]

widow and children.   Galella v. Onassis (2d Cir. 1973).

It extends to unauthorized prying into one's private papers and records, such as his bank account, his mail, his safe or his wallet, or by inspection of his books and records pursuant to a forged or clearly invalid subpoena duces tecum. It has been held to include an improper physical examination or blood test made against plaintiff's wishes.

The tort is complete when the intrusion occurs; no publication or publicity of the information obtained is required.

It is, of course, essential that the intrusion be into that which is, and is entitled to remain, private.   Thus, it does not extend to recording public or formal testimony, or merely to following plaintiff around in public and observing him.   No tort is committed by the inspection or copying of records required by law to be kept and to which public access is available.   One who is arrested may be fingerprinted and photographed against his will.   And while one may not be photographed against his wishes in a private place, such as his home or hospital room, he may not complain if he is photographed in a public place since the photographer is merely recording on film what he had a right to observe.   However, it may be an invasion of plaintiff's privacy to photograph, even in public, private or personal parts of plaintiff's body unintentionally exposed.

In addition, the harm must be substantial. The intrusion must be seriously objectionable, offensive, or harassing to a reasonable person. Bad manners alone are not enough. Thus, no action will lie for a single solicitation of business, contributions, or other favors, absent circumstances of aggravation. A creditor who makes several phone calls asking for his money, or a landlord who comes to the door early on Sunday morning to ask for the overdue rent, commit no invasion of privacy.

As society becomes more crowded, and the ways and means of intrusion become more numerous and sophisticated, it may safely be predicted that remedies for invasion of privacy will be increasingly sought. Legislation at the state and federal level to protect various privacy interests is proliferating, and such statutes may either expressly create tort remedies or create a duty from which a common law remedy may be implied. For example, federal and state statutes prohibit or regulate electronic eavesdropping. And there are statutes which restrict the uses which may be made of personal information which has been collected and stored by business or government, despite the fact that the information was more or less voluntarily disclosed in the first place. See, e.g., the Privacy Act of 1974 (5 U.S.C.A. § 552a); 13 U.S.C.A. § 8(c) (census information); Greenawalt, Legal Protections of Privacy (1975).

A general constitutional right to freedom from unreasonable governmental intrusion into the private lives of its citizens is now recognized and is in the process of further development. At first it was based on the "liberty" or substantive due process guaranteed by the fifth and fourteenth amendments to the United States Constitution. But beginning with Griswold v. Connecticut (U. S.1965) there has evolved a general constitutional right of privacy found to be implicit in the Bill of Rights. This right of privacy has two aspects: (1) freedom from unreasonable governmental intrusion, and (2) freedom from unreasonable regulation of its citizens' private lives. Its full limits are yet to be charted. The Supreme Court has extended it to the right to an elective abortion, the right to use contraceptives, and the right to possess obscene materials. Lower courts have held that this constitutional right of privacy includes the right to possess and use small quantities of marijuana in one's home (Ravin v. State, Alaska 1975); the right to unmarried cohabitation with a member of the opposite sex (Atkisson v. Kern County Housing Auth., Cal.App.1976); and even the right to die or to permit an incompetent dependent to die (In re Quinlan, N.J.1976).

This right of privacy is, of course, in addition to specific constitutional protections against governmental intrusions, such as the fourth amendment's prohibition of unreasonable searches and seizures (which extends to electronic surveillance) and the first amendment right to refuse to disclose an organization's membership list.

Although this constitutional right of privacy is used mainly to invalidate state and federal laws and regulations, or as a defense to a criminal proceeding, it may also serve as a basis for a tort action against government personnel under the principles discussed in § 8—22, infra, and perhaps against other defendants.

§ 6—7. Trespass to Land

At common law every unauthorized and direct breach of the boundaries of another's land was an actionable trespass—trespass *quare clausum fregit* (wherefore he broke the close). For historical reasons already discussed (§ 1—3) no intent to commit a trespass (or other fault) was required. All that was necessary was that the act resulting in the trespass be volitional, and that the resulting trespass be direct and immediate. Nor did actual damage need to be shown. Any trespass justified at least nominal damages. The strictness of the common law trespass liability reflects the great importance in feudal times of the right to the possession of land and its incidents. It also reflects the fact that one of the chief functions of the action was to try the land's title, the technical trespass being merely a vehicle for doing so. (The action may also be a means to prevent the habitual trespasser from acquiring a prescriptive right.)

With the shift to fault as the principal basis of tort liability, almost all jurisdictions have come to require that the trespass be intentional, reckless or negligent to be actionable (R. § 166), excepting of course cases where the rules of strict liability for abnormally dangerous activities (§ 3—3) apply. (In such cases, it is inappropriate and perhaps misleading to use the term "trespass." Nevertheless, some do.) However, *nota bene*—defendant need not intend a *wrong;* he need only intend to (or negligently) cause the *entry*. It is no defense that defendant acted under a mistaken belief (not induced by the possessor) that he had a privilege to enter. Of course, some entries are privileged, as will be discussed in later sections.

At common law, the action of trespass could be maintained only if the invasion of plaintiff's land was direct, immediate, and by some tangible or visible agent. Otherwise, the remedy was in case. Thus, trespass was the proper form of action where defendant threw water directly on plaintiff's land, but not where he merely constructed a spout or erected a dam such that water of its own accord eventually flowed onto plaintiff's property. Or if defendant discharged water onto *B*'s land which then flowed across to the land of *C,* he was liable in trespass to *B* but not to *C*. And there was no trespass liability where the damage on plaintiff's land was caused by vibration of the ground, or by invisible fumes, gases or microscopic particles suspended in the air.

These distinctions have largely disappeared with the abolition of the forms of action, and today both direct and indirect entries are generally actionable under the rules applied to trespass to land. As to air-borne gases and particles, a number of courts have characterized them as a trespass, although most such cases seem to be brought under the alternative theory of nuisance (§ 8—18). Vibration or concussion waves, while still not technically a trespass, may cause damage which is actionable under principles of strict liability (§ 3—3) or nuisance.

It is still true that no actual harm need be shown where the trespass was intentional. However, where it was recklessly or negligently caused, there is no liability unless and to the extent that some damage results.

Once trespass liability is established, the damages recoverable include all harm directly resulting from the trespass and a broad range of consequential damage. Thus, defendant will usually be liable for any physical harm occurring on the land caused by or during the entry, no matter how carefully he acts while on the land. For example, a trespasser who builds a fire, digs a hole, or merely leaves a door or gate ajar may be liable for resulting physical harm, at least to the premises and to the possessor and members of his household and their property, without any showing of negligence. Physical harm includes emotional distress.

The interests protected are those incident to the right to possession of the land. Thus, only the person(s) then in actual possession of the land may bring a trespass action. As to unoccupied land, the owner is deemed to be in possession. If the interests of someone *not* in possession (such as the owner who has leased the premises to another) are damaged by the trespass, that person must sue under some other theory. However, it is no defense that the actual possessor has no legal right to be there. Even a wrongful possession carries with it rights superior to those of a trespasser.

Now that the distinction between trespass and case is abolished, a trespass may consist of entering upon the land, or causing some thing or third person to do so; remaining on the land after one's right to be there has terminated; or failing to remove from the land a thing which one is under a duty to remove.

Where the trespass consists of the failure to remove something from the land, it is a continuing trespass. May plaintiff bring successive actions, or must he recover in one action for all damages, past and prospective? Case law provides no clear answer; the Restatement (§ 161) would give the plaintiff an option to pursue either remedy.

The boundaries of land extend vertically as well as horizontally. Thus, it may be a trespass to cross the plaintiff's property line beneath the surface of the land or to penetrate his airspace, at least so far as the zone infringed is sufficiently close to the surface to potentially interfere with some conceivable use or enjoyment of the property. A bullet traversing the air above the surface, a mine shaft, utility wires, underground water, and the overhanging portion of a structure are illustrative.

Aircraft flights over private property present special problems. Several theories have evolved to balance the possessor's right to the peaceful use and enjoyment of his property against the needs of aviation. Under the "zone" theory, the landowner owns only so much of the airspace as is in his "effective possession," that is, the altitude up to which he might in the future make effective use of the airspace. The "actual use" theory denies any ownership of any airspace of which the owner of the land is not making some present use; there is no tort unless there is interference with the present enjoyment of the property. The first Restatement (§ 194) and a number of state statutes (based on the now-withdrawn Uniform Aeronautics Act) recognize unlimited ownership of upward space, subject to a privilege of flight similar to the public right to make use of a navigable stream which flows through private property. Finally, there is the "nuisance" theory, which is finding increasing support. It ignores arguments about ownership of the air, and gives a remedy in the form of an action for nuisance, or possibly negligence, only when the flight results in actual interference with the use of the land.

The full effect of federal aviation laws is yet to be determined, but clearly they will play a role. In United States v. Causby (U.S.1946), the Supreme Court held that continual low-altitude flights by military aircraft which ruined plaintiff's poultry business constituted a compensable "taking" of private property by the government. In doing so, it ruled that federal statutes and CAB regulations had the effect of making the airspace above the prescribed minimum altitudes a public, and a federal, domain and highway, so that it would appear that there can be no trespass (although there can be a "taking") in flights at or above such levels. This would appear to invalidate all state law to the contrary. Left unanswered are the questions, (1) whether federal law occupies the field, so that state law may be precluded from allowing recovery under any theory even for flights below the minimum, and (2) what remedies are now available for flights (a) above or (b) below the minimums which cause actual interference with possession or (c) below the minimums which do not interfere with the use of the land.

As to liability for falling aircraft or objects, or forced landings, see § 3—3.

§ 6—8. Chattels

Trespass to chattels and *conversion* are the two principal intentional torts against personal property.

Historically, the first remedy for interference with a chattel was the writ of trespass *de bonis asportatis* (for goods taken away). A direct descendant of the original trespass writ, it therefore required a direct, immediate and forcible interference with the chattel of another.

As the common law developed, case spawned the actions of detinue and trover. Detinue lay for the wrongful *detention* of a chattel where defendant's original possession was rightful. (In such cases, trespass was not the proper writ because trespass required that plaintiff have possession at the time of defendant's tort.) Trover, at first, was for the case where a finder of lost goods failed to return them to the person entitled to possession, and instead converted them to his own use or disposed of them to another. But trover had certain procedural advantages over the older forms of action, not the least of which was that defendant could not have trial by wager of law (oaths). Its popularity grew, and soon the necessary allegations of plaintiff's losing and defendant's finding of the chattel became mere formalities, fictions which could not be denied. Thus, trover came to be available for *any* intentional interference with another's chattel which was so substantial as to be inconsistent with own-

ership in another. In other words, defendant's
interference was the equivalent of a conversion,
and he could be forced to keep and pay for the
chattel. Detinue fell into complete disuse, and
trespass, while still a concurrent remedy with
trover, came to be used only for harm which was
not so substantial that defendant could be held to
have appropriated the chattel to himself and
therefore be compelled to pay plaintiff its full value and keep it. Thus, the main distinction between trespass and conversion is in the remedy.
Trespass is available for any intentional interference, but damages are limited to plaintiff's actual
harm. But if the interference is sufficiently substantial, plaintiff may bring an action for conversion and recover the full value of the chattel—in
effect, require defendant to buy it—even though
the actual damage to the chattel is less than total, or even nil. Hence, we see that virtually all
conversions are also trespasses, but all trespasses
are not conversions.

Conversion is the name of the tort for which
trover was the appropriate form of action. Now
that the forms of action are almost entirely abolished, the term "trover" is rarely used. Plaintiff
is said to bring a civil action for conversion.

Possession. In trespass to chattels and conversion, just as in trespass to land, the traditional
common law rule has been that the action must
be brought by the person who had actual possession of the property at the time of the tort, or at
least by the person entitled to immediate posses-

sion (such as a bailor at will). Indeed, so strong has been the law's protection of possessory rights that it is no defense that plaintiff's possession is wrongful, so long as he holds the property under some colorable claim of right superior to that of defendant. In other words, the defense of *jus tertii*—that some one other than plaintiff has title or a superior right to possession—is ordinarily not available unless defendant can connect himself with that third person's right. It is this emphasis on possessory rights which gave rise to the old maxim "possession is nine-tenths of the law." But the idea was carried to absurd lengths, and at one time *only* the possessor could bring these actions. Therefore, if defendant harmed the interests of some one *not* in possession, such as the owner who had leased the chattel or a chattel mortgagee, that person might have a cause of action but it was not trespass or trover. Obviously, any rule which bars the true owner of goods from the preferred remedies for damage to them merely because he is not in possession places far too great an emphasis on possessory rights, and a good many courts (and the Restatement) will now permit such an owner to sue for trespass or conversion for the damage to his reversion.

The fact remains, however, that the person in possession of the chattel—be he lessee, bailee, mortgagee, pledgee, finder, or whatever—is always a proper plaintiff. Thus, the true owner could wind up empty-handed. If the possessor sues and is successful, he may recover far more than the value of his interest in the chattel, and the owner must look to him to account for the owner's share of the recovery, no matter how irresponsible he may be. Or the possessor may mishandle the suit to the prejudice of the owner's interests. Nevertheless, it is the owner who has parted with possession, and the possessor who must account to the owner for the chattel's return, and therefore there is something to be said for the rule which permits the mere possessor to sue for conversion or for the full amount of the damage caused by the trespass.

Types of Chattels. Originally, trover and trespass were available only with respect to tangible personal property. By now, most courts have extended the action for conversion to include intangible personal property which is represented by or merged into a document, such as a promissory note or stock certificate, and even to intangibles represented by documents which do not embody the right but are merely important to its exercise, such as a bank deposit book or an insurance policy. Theoretically, there is no logical reason why intangible rights unrelated to a document cannot be converted, but as yet the cases have not gone that far.

Trespass to Chattels. One commits a trespass to another's chattel by intentionally interfering with it. Interference may consist of damage, alteration, destruction, unpermitted use or movement, or of depriving the possessor of his possession or control of it, however briefly. Since the abolition of the distinction between trespass and case, it is no longer necessary that the interference be inflicted directly and immediately.

As in the case of trespass to land, there is no longer liability without fault. But there is no such thing as a "negligent trespass" to a chattel. Unlike trespass to land, this is exclusively an intentional tort. If a chattel is harmed by defendant's negligence (such as in an automobile collision), the action is in negligence and the rules of negligence law apply.

Note, however, that as in the case of the other intentional torts, no wrongful motive is necessary. The intent required is merely to act upon the chattel. Thus, defendant's good faith but mistaken belief that he owns the chattel or for some other reason is privileged to deal with it is no excuse.

While there is not much law on this point, it appears that (unlike trespass to land) there is no trespass to a chattel in the absence of some actual damage. For example, a defendant who merely handles the chattel or moves it or perhaps even uses it, without harming or affecting it or impairing its usefulness, has committed no tort. But the foregoing must be qualified by the rule that *any* dispossession is a trespass, for which at least nominal damages may be awarded. If the possessor is deprived of the chattel for even a short time, there is nevertheless a dispossession even though it is returned to or found by the possessor before there is any significant injury.

Given a trespass, the same broad damage rules apply as in the case of trespass of land, and defendant will be liable for all resulting damages to the chattel and to the plaintiff, however innocently caused, including bodily harm (which encompasses emotional distress).

Conversion. The concept of conversion is sufficiently broad to defy accurate definition. For most purposes, it may be thought of as a trespass to a chattel which is so serious, aggravated, or of such magnitude, as to justify forcing defendant to buy it. It is often defined as intentional conduct which deprives another of his property permanently or for an indefinite time or the intentional exercise of dominion or control over a chattel which is inconsistent with another's property in it.

When is the interference with another's chattel so aggravated or serious as to constitute a conversion? There is no simple test. The Restatement (§ 222A) deems the following factors to be important:

(a) the *extent* and *duration* of the actor's exercise of *dominion* or *control;*

(b) the actor's *intent* to assert a right which is in fact inconsistent with the right of control of another;

(c) the actor's *good faith;*

(d) the extent and duration of the *interference;*

(e) the *harm* done to the chattel; and

(f) the *inconvenience* and *expense* caused thereby. It is a matter of degree, measured by the nature, extent and duration of the interference and defendant's motives and intentions.

As in the case of trespass, intent is required—there can be no negligent conversion—but again, no more is needed than an intent to act with respect to the chattel. Here, unlike trespass, defendant's motives may be *relevant* in determining whether the interference is sufficiently aggravated to constitute a conversion, but his good faith or honest mistake is no defense if the interference is otherwise sufficiently great. For example, one who steals my hat from a hat rack is liable for conversion even though he is immediately apprehended and the hat promptly tendered back. But so is one who by justifiable mistake takes my hat from a hat rack, promptly discovers his error, and is about to replace it when the wind catches it and blows it down the sewer.

Trespass and its damages are premised on the concept that title to the chattel remains in its owner, and the possessor retains possession or is entitled to the chattel's return. Conversion, on the other hand, is a forced sale to defendant. Thus, its measure of damages includes the full value of the chattel at the time of the conversion, plus interest. The traditional view has been that plaintiff is never required to (although he may) accept a tender of the chattel's return in mitigation of the damages, but some recent authorities would require him to do so where the conversion was by innocent mistake, the chattel is undiminished in value, and no special damage resulted from the detention.

The following are illustrative of the various ways in which a conversion may occur.

(1) *Acquiring Possession.* One who wrongfully acquires possession of a chattel, as by theft, illegal levy or attachment, duress or fraud, converts it. The same is true, in most jurisdictions, of a bona fide purchaser, lessee, pledgee or donee from a thief or one who had no power to transfer it. Not so, however, a b.f.p. from one who acquired the chattel by fraud or duress, who takes without notice of the wrong. And, of course, a b.f.p. who is a holder in due course of a negotiable instrument is ordinarily thereby protected.

Even acquiring possession under the mistaken belief that one has a privilege to do so may be a conversion, unless the interference with plaintiff's rights is relatively minor as where the duration is brief and no significant harm is done.

A bailee who merely receives possession of a chattel for storage, safekeeping or transportation is not liable for conversion unless he has knowledge that another is then entitled to immediate possession. The same is true of an agent or employee who receives the chattel on behalf of his principal or employer, except where he himself directly negotiates the transaction in which he takes possession on his principal's behalf.

(2) *Removal.* Moving a chattel from one location to another may constitute a conversion, but only if the interference with plaintiff's possession is significant or where defendant intends to exercise possessory rights or control over it inconsistent with those of plaintiff.

(3) *Transferring Possession.* The unauthorized transfer, delivery or disposal of a chattel to one not entitled to possession is normally a conversion, notwithstanding defendant's innocent mistake, unless the mistake is promptly rectified and no serious harm is done. Thus, an auctioneer who innocently sells stolen goods, or a carrier who by justifiable mistake misdelivers a chattel, are converters. Even involuntary bailees, such as a finder or one who acquires possession of the chattel by accident or mistake, are so liable.

Some protection is given to bailees, agents and employees, who may redeliver the chattel to their bailor, principal or employer or deliver it pursuant to his instructions without liability, provided they have no knowledge of plaintiff's right to possession. But even an innocent agent will be liable for conversion where he himself negotiates on his principal's behalf the transaction by which the chattel is transferred to a third person.

(4) *Withholding Possession.* Refusal to surrender possession of a chattel to one entitled to it

is a conversion, again unless the tort was relatively insignificant as where the delay was short, the chattel was not harmed, and there was no intent to deprive the plaintiff of his right of control.

Where defendant came into possession of the chattel rightfully, there is no tort unless and until there is a demand and refusal to surrender. Moreover, not every failure to deliver the chattel upon demand is a conversion. Defendant is not liable in conversion where he no longer has the chattel, even though it was lost or destroyed through his own fault (in which case the remedy, if any, is in negligence), unless he converted it in some other way.

There is no conversion if the refusal is reasonably qualified. Defendant may insist on a reasonable time, place and manner of delivery, or upon a reasonable delay for a proper purpose (such as to verify title, charges, agency or other facts). Of course, the delay must be sought in good faith and for the reason stated.

(5) *Destruction or Alteration.* Obviously, there is a conversion when a chattel is intentionally destroyed; and also when, intentionally, its condition is materially altered or substantially damaged such that to repair or restore it would be impossible or unduly burdensome, or whereby plaintiff is thereby denied the use of it for a substantial period of time.

[*185*]

(6) *Use.* The casual and harmless use of a chattel, involving no intent to usurp the owner's right to dominion and control, is not a conversion. On the other hand, mere use may be a conversion where it is so substantial as to amount to the exercise of dominion and control over the chattel; or where the use, however brief, was with the intent to usurp dominion and control (e.g. a short joy ride in a stolen car); or where the chattel is seriously damaged by or during its use.

Similar rules apply in the case of agents or bailees who are authorized to make some use of a chattel and exceed or deviate from the scope of their permission.

(7) *Asserting Ownership.* Merely to assert ownership of a chattel, without more, is not a conversion. But little else is required. Coupled with any interference with the owner's rights of possession or control, the tort is complete.

CHAPTER 7

DEFENSES TO LIABILITY FOR INTENTIONAL MISCONDUCT

§ 7—1. In General

"Privilege" is the general term applied to certain rules of law by which particular circumstances justify conduct which otherwise would be tortious, and thereby defeat the tort liability (or defense) which, in the absence of such circumstances, ordinarily would follow from that conduct. In other words, even if all of the facts necessary to a prima facie case of tort liability can be proved, there are additional facts present sufficient to establish some privilege, and therefore defendant has committed no tort. Privileges thus differ from other defenses, such as contributory negligence, which operate to bar plaintiff's recovery but do not negate the tortious nature of defendant's conduct. Conversely, plaintiff's privilege may defeat a defense which defendant otherwise might have had.

The term and concept of privilege apply primarily to the intentional torts, but also appear in other areas, such as defamation.

Privileges may be divided into two general categories: (1) consent, and (2) privileges created by law irrespective of consent. In general, the latter arise where there is some important and overriding social value in sanctioning defendant's conduct, despite the fact that it causes plaintiff harm.

Consent will be treated in the next section, and the remaining intentional tort privileges in the sections which follow.

Strictly speaking, consent is technically not a privilege in the case of the intentional torts which are invasions of plaintiff's interests in his person (assault, battery, false imprisonment) as opposed to his property interests, since lack of consent is an element of the tort and ordinarily plaintiff must establish it as a part of his prima facie case. However, the consent rules are similar as to all torts and for convenience are customarily treated as part of the law of privilege.

Except as noted in the last paragraph, privilege is an affirmative defense which must be pleaded and proved by defendant.

A word about mistake. As we saw in Chapter 6, defendant's mistake, in and of itself—even a nonnegligent one—is per se no defense to an intentional tort, nor does it negate the requisite intent. One who intentionally (and without a privilege) enters upon plaintiff's land, or confines plaintiff, or uses plaintiff's chattel, or performs unauthorized surgery, is no less a tortfeasor merely because he quite reasonably (but erroneously) believed that he was entitled to do so. But as will be seen, mistake is often relevant in determining the existence of a privilege. Certain privileges are based on defendant's reasonable belief concerning some fact(s), even though it later turns out that he was mistaken. Generally, a mistake is privileged where it appears necessary for defendant to act quickly to protect some important interest which does in fact exist, or when defendant is under a duty to act for the protection of the public interest. In addition, it is a general rule that where plaintiff himself induced defendant's mistake, defendant is absolved of liability for that mistake so long as he did not act unreasonably.

§ 7—2. Consent

Consent is a defense to virtually any tort. The law ordinarily has no interest in compensating one who validly, knowingly and freely consents in advance to the invasion of the interest which the law would otherwise have protected. In the law of negligence and strict liability, consent goes by the name "assumption of risk," and a separate body of law has grown up around that concept which is described elsewhere (§ 5—5). While consent will be treated here in relation to the intentional torts, similar or analogous rules apply in other areas of tort law.

There is consent when one is, in fact, willing for conduct to occur. It is a matter of plaintiff's subjective state of mind, and assuming it can be proven, the fact that he failed to communicate his secret consent to anyone does not make it any less valid.

At the same time, people must rely on the overt words and acts of others, rather than their undisclosed thoughts. Thus, plaintiff's words or conduct manifesting consent are sufficient to create a privilege for defendant to act in light of the apparent consent, notwithstanding the fact that plaintiff's actual but undisclosed state of mind was to the contrary. R. § 50.

Consent, may, of course, be communicated by affirmative conduct as well as words, such as by beckoning defendant onto one's land or by holding up one's arm to be vaccinated without protest. Even silence and inaction may indicate consent, provided such conduct would ordinarily be so interpreted, as where a reasonable person would be expected to speak or move if he objected.

Consent may be inferred from custom and usage, from prior dealings between the parties, or from the existence between them of some relationship. For example, where there is a general custom to embrace friends upon meeting, and plaintiff and defendant are friends, consent to an embrace may be assumed, at least until defendant is given notice to the contrary. Participants in sporting events thereby consent to the physical contacts consistent with the understood rules of the game.

The consent must be given by one having the capacity to do so, or one authorized to consent for him. Infancy, intoxication, or mental incapacity, known or obvious to defendant, ordinarily will vitiate effective consent. Consent in such cases, if required (as for medical treatment), must first be obtained from some person empowered to give it on plaintiff's behalf, such as his next of kin.

Where an emergency actually or apparently threatens death or serious bodily harm and there is no time or opportunity to obtain consent, it is said that consent is "implied," which is to say that defendant is privileged because he has no reason to believe that plaintiff or some one acting for him would not consent if given the chance.

The consent is to defendant's conduct, and therefore plaintiff cannot complain of the consequences of that particular conduct even though unforeseen. One who plays football consents to ordinary tackles, even if one renders him quadriplegic. But defendant's privilege is limited to the conduct consented to or acts substantially similar. Consent to right ear surgery (if, indeed, such consents are ever so limited in medicine today) does not authorize surgery on the left (absent an unforeseen emergency). And consent to an operation does not create a privilege to perform it negligently. In addition, the consent may properly be conditioned or limited as to time, place, duration, area and extent, and defendant will be liable to the extent that he fails to conform to the conditions or limitations.

Even though plaintiff's consent is given pursuant to his material mistake, misunderstanding or ignorance as to the nature or character of defendant's proposed conduct or the extent of the harm to be expected from it, the consent is effective as manifested unless defendant knows of the mistake or induced it by his misrepresentation. Even here, the mistake must go to the essential character of the act or its consequences, and not merely some collateral inducement, in order for the privilege to be lost. Suppose plaintiff consents to permit defendant to punch him in the nose in return for fifty dollars. The consent is still effective even though the money is counterfeit and defendant knows it, but not if defendant is secretly wearing brass knuckles. In the former case there may be an action for deceit or upon the contract, but not for battery.

The doctrine of informed consent, applicable in professional malpractice cases, is derived from these rules. For example, if a physician misrepresents or fails to disclose the proposed treatment or consequences which he knows are certain to follow from it, knowing of the patient's ignorance of these matters, the patient's consent is ineffective. Some cases have gone beyond this and vitiated the consent, and thus found a battery, where the doctor merely failed to disclose known *risks* inherent in the treatment. The prevailing view is to treat the failure to disclose mere risks as collateral, and thus a matter of negligence only, which permits inquiry into the proper professional standards of disclosure, instead of making full disclosure mandatory in all cases.

Consent is not effective if it is given under duress, which of course includes actual physical force, but it is not entirely clear what kinds of threats are sufficient.   Threats of immediate harm directed against plaintiff, his family, or his valuable property are usually enough, depending upon the nature of the tort.   But it has been held that threats of future harm, such as arrest, or "economic" duress such as loss of employment, did not render the consent ineffective (although some other tort may have been committed).

There is a division of authority as to whether plaintiff's consent is effective if the conduct consented to is a crime.   At least in battery cases, the prevailing view seems to be that it is not, apparently on the theory that to hold otherwise would condone violence and lawlessness.   However, a strong minority and the Restatement (§§ 60, 61, 892C) reject the notion that the spectre of tort liability has any effect whatsoever on the parties' decision to engage in the conduct and hold that the consent in such cases is nevertheless effective, *except* in the case of statutes making conduct criminal in order to protect a certain class of persons irrespective of their consent—for example, statutes fixing the age of consent to sexual intercourse or prohibiting boxing matches because of the danger to the participants.   The cases involving criminal abortions are divided, some denying recovery on the ground that the statute is for the benefit of the unborn child and the public and not the woman. Incredibly, a few courts have even denied the woman recovery for negligence in the performance of the operation in order to punish her for her participation in the wrong.

§ 7—3. Defense of Self and Others

Self-Defense. The basic instinct to defend oneself against the threat of harm together with the fundamental ethic that one has a right to do so justify the law's privilege to commit in self-defense an act which otherwise would be a tort. "Self-preservation is the first law of nature." It is a kind of self-help remedy, where there is no time to resort to the law. Most often the threatened harm is battery, but there is also a privilege to use appropriate and reasonable force to defend against an unlawful confinement or arrest, and even against the threat of negligently-caused harm. The defensive conduct may take the form of an assault, a battery, or a confinement, as appropriate to the situation.

The privilege exists not only where the danger to defendant is real, but also where defendant reasonably (but mistakenly) believes that self-defense is necessary. Thus, where plaintiff reaches into his pocket for the apparent purpose of retrieving a weapon, defendant may be privileged to act accordingly even though no weapon in fact existed. The reasonableness of defendant's belief, frequently a jury question, is judged by the objective standard of the reasonable person of average courage, and will depend, in part, on the circumstances of the event and the past history of the relationship, if any, between the parties.

Defendant may use only as much force as is or reasonably appears to be immediately necessary to protect himself. When he becomes the aggressor he exceeds the scope of the privilege, which does not encompass retaliation or revenge, and will be liable to the extent of the damage caused by the excessive force. Thus, he may not use violence after plaintiff is subdued, disarmed or helpless, or has clearly withdrawn from the fray or terminated the immediate threat. Nor may defendant use violence in response to verbal abuse, insults, threats for the future, or other mere provocation. Only defensive force is permitted.

Defendant may use force likely to inflict death or serious bodily harm *only* where (1) he reasonably believes that he is in danger of similar harm, and (2) it is not required that he retreat or escape. As to the latter, there is a division of authority. Some jurisdictions *never* require retreat, permitting defendant to defiantly stand his ground. However, others and the Restatement (§ 65) hold that defendant is not privileged to cause death or serious bodily harm, even in defense of a threat of similar harm, if he has some reasonable means of escape. Of course, retreat will be required only when it is obviously safe and expedient to do so, and if there is any reasonable doubt he need not flee. Moreover, there is an exception to the rule requiring flight, which is that one need not retreat if he is attacked within his own dwelling place, based apparently on the traditional sanctity of the home.

When in the course of defending himself defendant *accidentally* injures a third person, ordinary principles of negligence law apply and liability will depend on the reasonableness of defendant's conduct under the circumstances. However, if he *intentionally* causes harm to another (whose conduct was not the cause of defendant's jeopardy) because to do so is or seems necessary to save himself from harm, there is no privilege and defendant will be liable for at least compensatory damages for the harm he caused, unless it was relatively minor compared to the harm with which he was threatened. For example, where defendant kills an innocent person to save his own life, or uses another person as a shield to absorb a bullet meant for him, or intentionally runs down another and seriously injures him in order to escape his peril, he is liable; but not where the harm to the innocent bystander is merely offensive or slight, such as knocking him down or confining him against his will for a short time.

Defense of Others. In general, consistent with the Good Samaritan principle, the modern view seems to be that one is privileged to come to the defense of any third person. Absent mistake, he stands in that person's shoes and acquires that person's privilege of self-defense with the same rights and limitations.

Here, there is disagreement as to the effect of a mistake as to the actual necessity of intervention or the extent of the force required. The prevailing view seems to be that in such cases defendant assumes the risk that he is mistaken, and is privileged only if and to the extent that the third person was. However, some courts and the Restatement (§ 76) hold that a reasonable mistake does not negate the privilege.

§ 7—4. Defense and Recovery of Property

Defense of Property. One's interest in the peaceful possession and enjoyment of his property justifies a limited self-help privilege to defend it against imminent intrusions. However, the social value of property is considerably less than that of the safety and bodily integrity of human beings, and therefore the privilege is more limited than that of self-defense.

A possessor is privileged to use *reasonable* force to expel another or a chattel or to prevent another's intrusion upon his land or chattels, even though such conduct would otherwise be an assault, battery, false imprisonment, or trespass to the chattel.

There must be an actual intrusion or a threat of an immediate interference with defendant's possession.

Unless it would clearly be in vain or there is no time or opportunity, the possessor must first request that the intruder desist. If he does not, defendant may use a threat of force or reasonable force itself, but it must be such as is minimally required to prevent or terminate the intrusion. Force or the threat of force calculated to cause death or great bodily harm is not permitted. But if the intruder persists, greater force may be used. The intruder, of course, has no privilege of self-defense, and if the intruder threatens bodily harm to defendant, ordinary principles of self-defense apply, and defendant may use any force required to defend his person, including the infliction of death or serious bodily harm if he is threatened with similar harm. But such force is never justified solely in defense of the property. Even the traditional notion that one may kill in defense of his dwelling house has been replaced in most jurisdictions by the more humane rule that such force is not permitted unless the intrusion threatens the personal safety of the occupants or the commission of a felony.

Clearly, defendant may not do indirectly what he himself could not do. Spring guns, concealed traps and other mechanical devices, and vicious animals, calculated to cause death or great bodily harm, are used at the possessor's risk. He will be liable to the intruder for any harm which he would not have been privileged to inflict if he were personally present, in most cases notwithstanding posted warnings of the device or animal. R. § 85.

The same rules of apparent necessity apply here as in the case of self-defense. Note, however, that a mistake concerning the intruder's actual status is not privileged. Thus, where the intruder in fact has a privilege to intrude upon the land or chattel, the possessor's ignorance or mistake concerning the existence of that privilege is no defense to the tort he commits upon the intruder, unless the intruder himself was responsible for that mistake. Conversely, the intruder's mistake does not defeat the possessor's privilege unless the mistake was caused by the possessor's fault.

There are a number of rules which govern privileges to enter upon land and to invade interests in chattels. See R. §§ 167–215, 252–278. Except as discussed in the remainder of this section, or mentioned collaterally elsewhere, they are beyond the scope of this book.

Forcible Retaking of Chattels. Where plaintiff has wrongfully and forcibly taken defendant's chattel from his possession, even under claim of right, or obtained it by fraud or duress, the law recognizes a limited self-help privilege to recapture it by the use of force or threats of force.

Defendant must begin his recapture efforts promptly after his dispossession, or at least immediately upon learning of it, and must continue his efforts without interruption. He must be in "fresh pursuit." Where the chattel rightfully came into plaintiff's possession and he merely wrongfully detains it, or though wrongfully acquired defendant acquiesces in his possession for any period of time, defendant has no privilege and must resort to his legal remedies.

Ordinarily, where feasible, defendant must first demand return of the property. If plaintiff refuses, necessary and reasonable force may be used. Again, force calculated to cause serious bodily harm is not privileged. Of course, plaintiff is not privileged to resist, and if he does and thereby threatens defendant's person, defendant may use any force required to defend himself.

Unlike self-defense, defendant's mistake as to the existence of the privilege is no defense, unless knowingly induced by plaintiff.

Under certain circumstances, the privilege includes a privilege to enter upon another's land in pursuit of the chattel without liability for trespass, such as where the land is plaintiff's or the possessor is aware of the facts and still refuses defendant reasonable entry, or is otherwise at fault. In other cases there may be a right to enter the land but liability for any damage caused thereby. But where the chattel is on the land with defendant's consent or through his fault, he must resort to legal process. A conditional seller of goods, by a clause in the contract, may acquire an irrevocable license to enter the buyer's premises upon his default and remove the property, but even this permits him only to enter peaceably, at a reasonable time and in a reasonable manner, and he will be liable if he uses any force to break in. A clause in the contract authorizing him to use force is probably void as contrary to public policy.

A special application of this principle of recapture is found in court decisions and statutes authorizing a shopkeeper to detain a suspected shoplifter for a reasonable time to investigate the suspected crime without liability for false imprisonment. See § 6—4.

Forcible Repossession of Land. One who as owner is entitled to the immediate possession of land may, if he can, peaceably enter the land and retake possession without liability for trespass, and may thereafter maintain his possession as discussed in the first part of this section.

The next question is, when is he privileged to use force to enter and evict the occupant without liability for assault, battery or some other tort.

If the occupant qualifies, he may be entitled, even as against the owner, to the protection of a forcible entry and detainer statute. These statutes are designed to prevent just such self-help remedies.

Assuming no such statute applies, defendant may use reasonable force to enter and take possession where:

(1) He (or his predecessor in title) was tortiously dispossessed, either without claim of right or under claim of right but by fraud, duress, or breaking and entering; or the occupant holds the land for the defendant.

(2) Plaintiff was the one who tortiously dispossessed defendant, or else plaintiff acquired custody or possession from someone who he knows or should know so dispossessed him.

(3) Defendant is in fact entitled to immediate possession.

(4) Defendant enters promptly after his dispossession or after he learns or should know of it.

Unless it would be useless, dangerous, or counterproductive to do so, defendant must first demand that plaintiff surrender possession. If he refuses, defendant may then use such reasonable force (short of that likely to cause serious bodily harm) as he reasonably believes necessary to effect the entry.

Here, as in the case of recapture of chattels, defendant's mistake as to the existence of his privilege is no defense unless knowingly induced by plaintiff.

§ 7—5. Necessity

The privilege of necessity may be invoked when defendant, in the course of defending himself or his property or others or their property from some threat of imminent harm for which plaintiff is *not* responsible, intentionally does some act reasonably deemed necessary toward that end which results in injury to plaintiff's property and which would otherwise be a trespass or a conversion.

Thus, it is analogous to the privileges of self-defense and defense of property, with the important difference that here plaintiff did not put defendant or his property in jeopardy and therefore plaintiff is entitled to greater protection. Hence, this privilege is more limited. In essence, an innocent plaintiff's property interest is necessarily sacrificed for a worthy cause. This may excuse the tort, but in some cases at least defendant will still be required to compensate plaintiff for his loss.

Frequently the decided cases have involved threats of harm from forces of nature, such as fires, floods, storms, disease, and the like. But the potential sources of harm are not so limited; all that is required is that the necessity arise from some independent cause not connected with the plaintiff.

The law distinguishes between "public" and "private" necessity. Where the danger affects the entire community, or so many people that the public interest is involved, most cases have held that the privilege is complete and defendant is entirely excused from liability. Thus one who dy-

namites a house to stop the spread of a fire
which threatens the entire town, or destroys animals having an infectious disease to prevent its
spread, or in time of war destroys property to
prevent it from falling into enemy hands, is completely privileged and is not liable to the owner,
provided the emergency is sufficiently great and
defendant acted reasonably under the circumstances. This seems fair enough where defendant
is a private individual, who ought not to have to
pay out of his own pocket for acts which benefit
the public. But most courts have held that the
privilege is complete even where defendant is a
governmental unit and the act was done by its
employee or under its specific direction for the
benefit of its citizens. (Moreover, the destruction of private property under such circumstances
is generally construed not to be a "taking" under
constitutional provisions requiring compensation
where private property is taken for public use.)
Such decisions would appear to be open to question.

Where no public interest is involved and defendant acts only to protect a private one, his
own or that of another, it is deemed a "private
necessity" and the privilege is properly more limited. Again, the emergency must be sufficiently
great, and defendant must have acted reasonably
under the circumstances. Defendant will not be
liable for mere technical torts, such as a trespass
on private land to escape a danger, and the possessor is not privileged to resist or expel him. But

where the act causes actual damage, as where a boat is saved by being kept moored to a dock during a storm causing damage to the dock, defendant is required to compensate plaintiff for the injury. Vincent v. Lake Erie Transp. Co. (Minn.1910); R. § 263.

As in the case of self-defense and defense of property, defendant's reasonable mistake as to the existence of the privilege does not negate it.

It would seem that a similar, although perhaps more restricted, privilege should apply to torts against plaintiff's person committed under the duress of necessity, but so far there is little law on this. See § 7—3, supra.

§ 7—6. Authority of Law

There is, of course, a privilege to do that which is authorized or required by the law. The difficult problems here are in determining (1) what is the law, and whether it is valid, questions which often vex the best of lawyers, and (2) the effect of the actor's good faith mistake as to his legal authority. The execution of legal process by a public official is a common situation in which this privilege may be invoked.

The law commonly distinguishes between "discretionary" and "ministerial" acts. Where the law is such that a measure of judgment or discretion is required to be exercised in order to determine whether or how to act, such as to seek an indictment or to close a public street, the act is privileged so long as done honestly and in good faith. Ministerial acts (those requiring little or no personal judgment as to whether or how they shall be done—for example to close an office at five o'clock or to record a deed) are not privileged if done improperly, regardless of the actor's good faith. As might be expected, it has been found exceedingly difficult to distinguish one from the other, and the cases are in hopeless confusion.

Another such distinction is between acts done without jurisdiction, which are not privileged because not official acts at all, and acts which are merely "in excess of" the official's jurisdiction—that is, within the scope of the general subject-matter of his power but outside his authority on the particular facts—which are privileged if done in good faith. Here also the distinction has been hard to make, and where the officer takes action under a law which later is declared unconstitutional, there is a tendency to hold that the act if done in good faith is privileged.

Arrest. Arrest of the person is one of the more common acts under authority of law. It may be with or without a warrant, which is simply a court order directing the arrest.

An arrest under a warrant, or the seizure of goods under civil process (to which the same rules apply), is generally regarded as a ministerial act, which means that the officer is not privileged unless his acts in fact conform to law. As noted above, there is no privilege if the warrant was issued by a court without jurisdiction to issue such warrants. But if the court has the general power to issue arrest warrants, the arrest is privileged if the warrant appears valid and proper on its face, even though there were errors or irregularities in its issuance which would be regarded as divesting the court of jurisdiction of this particular case.

In addition, the officer must properly carry out the order given him in the proper manner, and if he does not there is no privilege even where his act is based on an entirely reasonable good faith mistake. For example, if the warrant commands the arrest of *A*, but the officer arrests *B* instead, there is no privilege even though he reasonably believed that *B* was *A*.

Under certain circumstances, either a police officer or a private citizen may make a lawful arrest without a warrant. The common law developed an elaborate set of rules governing such arrests, which have now been largely superseded by statute. Again, such arrests are privileged, but only when in actual conformity to law.

Trespass ab Initio. The common law developed a fiction that where an act or series of acts was properly commenced under authority of law, and subsequently that authority was exceeded and a tort thereby committed, defendant's abuse of his authority "related back" and he was deemed to be a wrongdoer, without privilege, from the very beginning—ab initio. The result was that he was liable not merely for the subsequent tort, but as though his entire course of conduct, including the initial entry, seizure or arrest, had been tortious.

Since the turn of this century, the doctrine has been thoroughly discredited and disapproved, and has rarely been invoked except occasionally in cases of arrest. The Restatement (§§ 136, 214(2), 278(2)) has rejected it entirely, and most writers consider it doubtful that it will ever again be applied.

Immunity. In addition to the foregoing, one must remember that public officials and governmental entities are sometimes immune from tort liability for certain of their official acts. See § 11—1, infra.

§ 7—7. Discipline

Within certain relationships, as a matter of custom and necessity, one party is privileged to discipline the other by the intentional use of threats, physical coercion, corporal punishment, and restraint, which would otherwise constitute assault, battery, false imprisonment, and perhaps even the infliction of emotional distress.

The privilege of a parent, or one standing in the place of a parent, to use force and restraint in the control, training and education of his child, is the most common example. The privilege also extends to a school teacher, to the extent necessary to maintain order in and about the school, and when necessary for this purpose may even extend to discipline for the pupil's conduct away from the school premises.

Only the force reasonably necessary to accomplish the permissible purpose is privileged, and the teacher or the parent (if not otherwise immune; see § 11—3) may be liable to the extent that the force used is excessive. The reasonableness of the force used is a question of fact which depends upon a variety of factors, such as the nature of the offense and its apparent motive, the age, sex and physical and mental condition of the child, his past behavior, and the like. An external standard applies; the parent or teacher cannot be permitted to judge for himself what is reasonable. It must be administered in good faith for a proper purpose and without malice, and may not be unnecessarily degrading nor calculated to cause serious or permanent harm.

Military officers have a privilege of discipline over their subordinates which is governed largely by military law. And the master of a ship may exercise reasonable discipline over his crew and passengers.

CHAPTER 8

SPECIAL LIABILITY RULES FOR PARTICULAR ACTIVITIES

§ 8—1. Introduction

To the general rules of tort liability for physical harm discussed in Chapters 3 through 7 there must be added a number of special liability rules which apply in particular fact situations. Chief among these are the rules discussed in this Chapter 8 which govern the liability of (and to) those engaged in certain activities with respect to those activities: owners and occupiers of land; sellers of products; employers, employees and contractors; owners and drivers of vehicles; and others.

In some cases, these special rules are merely specific applications of (and are consistent with) the general rules of tort liability previously discussed; they have evolved as separately-stated rules because the recurrence of common fact situations has led the courts to generalize about them. In many cases, however, these special rules contract or expand the duty which would otherwise exist in response to felt considerations of social policy.

The trend of American tort law during the twentieth century has been to expand the scope of potential tort liability, especially as to business and property owners, mainly by: (1) abolishing duty limitations and immunities in negligence cases and moving toward a general duty of ordinary care under the circumstances for all activities; (2) abolishing special limitations on the class of persons to whom defendant's duty is owed (i.e., privity limitations) and applying ordinary rules of proximate cause to all; (3) making sellers of products strictly liable in tort for product defects; and (4) creating new liability rules by statute (e.g., workmen's compensation, F.E.L. A., and auto compensation acts).

This chapter will provide an overview of the most important of these special liability rules.

A.   OWNERS AND OCCUPIERS OF LAND

§ 8—2.   Liability to Persons Off the Premises

Until the late nineteenth century, real property was of dominant importance in the economies of England and America. Important social values included individualism and the sanctity of private property. Thus, predictably, the value of the rights to ownership, possession and use of land weighed heavily in the law's balance of competing interests, and special tort liability rules emerged which reflect this balance. So strong has been the land ethic that it is only within the last decade that the special duty limitations favoring land owners and occupiers have begun to be abolished by the courts.

The term "owners and occupiers" reflects the fact that in general these special rules may be invoked only by (or against) the possessor of the land—the person who occupies it or, if it is not occupied, its owner who is then deemed to be in possession. The benefits and burdens of the rules stated in this Subchapter A ordinarily extend (1) to activities carried on by members of the possessor's household (R. § 382) and (2) to activities conducted and conditions created on the land by another who is acting for the possessor (R. §§ 383, 384). If one who conducts an activity or creates a condition on land does not fit one of these categories, then the special liability rules discussed in this subchapter do not apply to him and he is liable or not according to the usual rules of tort law (R. § 386).

In the main, the special liability rules applicable to possessors of land take the form of limitations on the duty of land owners and occupiers to take affirmative precautions for the safety of persons who enter upon the land for nonbusiness purposes, with or without permission. These are discussed in the sections which follow.

As to persons *outside* the premises, however, no social policy operates in favor of a limited duty rule. Even under the view that a possessor of land ought to be free to do as he pleases within the confines of his own property, it is agreed that his special domain ends at its boundaries and he must exercise reasonable care to see that activities and possessor-created conditions on his premises do not harm his neighbors or passers-by on adjacent ways.   R. §§ 364, 365, 366, 370, 371.

Liability to persons off the premises is, of course, not limited to negligence. It may be based upon principles of intent, negligence, or strict liability as discussed in the preceding chapters, or in accordance with the law of nuisance discussed in § 8—18, infra. But where the theory of the action is the possessor's negligence, the courts have articulated a number of rules. For the most part, these are but special applications of the general principles of negligence in fact situations which frequently recur.

Adjacent Public Ways. Many cases have involved dangers to persons traveling on public ways (highways, streets, alleys, sidewalks) adjacent to defendant's land. The possessor's duty to them is one of reasonable care, and thus he may be liable where he obstructs a public way, allows a sign or structure to fall upon it, or conducts an activity upon his land so as to create a foreseeable and unreasonable risk of harm to travelers. R. § 368.

His duty may require him to foresee slight deviations from the public way upon his land, and so to exercise reasonable care not to cause or allow unsafe artificial conditions (e.g. an excavation) so close to the public way as to create an unreasonable risk of harm to those who so deviate. This includes both inadvertent deviations (e.g. where a pedestrian slips and falls off the sidewalk and onto defendant's land) and even in a proper case one who deviates intentionally for some purpose connected with his travel (e.g. a pedestrian who stops momentarily in defendant's doorway to tie his shoelace). Intentional deviations by children may be quite foreseeable (see § 8—4, infra). R. § 369. But where the adult traveler leaves the public way, enters upon defendant's land, and temporarily ceases his journey (e.g. to rest or to chat with a friend), he ceases to be a traveler and becomes a trespasser with all the consequences of that status (see § 8—3, infra).

While most cases have involved deviations of only a few feet, what is important is not so much the distance as the foreseeability that a normal user will deviate so as to encounter the danger. Cf. R. § 367 (possessor maintains a part of his land so that it appears to be a public highway).

Natural Conditions. The traditional rule has been that reasonable care does not require the possessor of land to alter its natural condition so as to prevent harm—however foreseeable—to persons outside the premises or to adjoining land. R. § 363(1). Typically, these cases involve harm caused by (1) the natural flow of surface water off the land, (2) natural accumulations of ice and snow on adjacent public sidewalks, and (3) trees which die and fall upon adjacent ways.

This principle is strictly limited. If the possessor or anyone else has ever altered the natural condition of the land so as to create or aggravate the risk, the possessor is subject to liability—for example, where he or another erects or maintains a structure such that water, snow or ice is discharged or unnaturally accumulates on a public way, or plants a row of trees next to a highway, or landscapes so as to change the natural flow of water, or dams a stream, or piles sand where it will blow. And, of course, the occupier may be liable if he undertakes to remove snow or ice from his premises or an adjoining public way and does so negligently.

Moreover, it must be remembered that the "natural conditions" rule developed in a predominantly rural society where tracts of land were large and it might indeed be an unreasonable burden to require the possessor to take affirmative action to alter the natural state of his property when he was making no use of the land which would itself require him to do so. There are indications that the courts may be willing to modify the rule with respect to land in urban areas when ordinary principles of negligence compel a different result. For example, it is now generally agreed that an urban property owner may be liable for his negligence in failing to inspect and maintain his trees so as to prevent an unreasonable risk of harm to passers-by on adjoining public ways. R. § 363(2).

§ 8—3. Trespassing Adults

When plaintiff's injury occurs *on* premises occupied by defendant, a different situation is presented. Except in the rare case where the visitor enters under a privilege conferred by law, a possessor of private property may, of course, determine whom he will allow to enter upon it, and the conditions of the visit. Therefore, the amount of care which the possessor may *reasonably* be required to exercise to make the premises safe for plaintiff's visit (or to discover dangers and warn of them) depends on (1) the extent to which his entry is foreseeable, (2) the scope and other conditions of his privilege to enter, if any, and (3) the purpose of his visit. The latter is relevant on the theory that the greater the benefit or potential benefit of the visit to the possessor, the greater should be his obligation to take precautions for the visitor's safety.

The common law might have simply left the question whether the possessor exercised reasonable care with respect to each plaintiff—that is, acted as a reasonably prudent occupier of land under the same or similar circumstances—to a case-by-case determination, as in other negligence cases, using the foregoing factors as guides to the trier of fact or as standards by which to review its decision. It did not. Very likely, the courts did not trust juries to give adequate protection to land owners. Instead, it divided entrants upon land into three rigid categories—(1) trespassers, (2) licensees, and (3) invitees—and then established fixed limitations on the possessor's duty with respect to trespassers and licensees.

As in the case of other duty limitations, these arbitrary classifications have proved increasingly unsatisfactory, and the courts have been required to change the definitions and to create exceptions to the duty limitations in order to do justice in the infinite variety of fact situations which occur. Dissatisfaction with this approach has now reached the point that courts have begun to overthrow it completely and impose instead the prevailing general duty of ordinary care under the circumstances—one of those circumstances being the status of the entrant. This movement will be noted in § 8—6.

Nevertheless, the traditional common law system of classifications and duty limitations is still the law in most jurisdictions. What, then, are these classifications and limitations?

Adult Trespassers. The law subdivides trespassers into (1) adults and (2) children, recognizing that the latter sometimes require special protection (§ 8—4, infra). Thus, the rules discussed in this section apply only to (1) trespassers who are of legal age and (2) trespassing children who do not meet the qualifications for special treatment.

A trespasser is a person who enters or remains upon land in possession of another without a privilege to do so. R. § 329. In the usual case, the privilege, if any, arises from the possessor's consent. See §§ 6—7 and Chapter 7, supra, and R. §§ 10 and 167–215 for discussions of such privileges.   (While there are few cases, these same principles apply to one who trespasses upon a chattel (e.g. a motor vehicle).)

The general rule is that with respect to a trespasser, a possessor of land is under no duty to exercise reasonable care (1) to make the premises reasonably safe for him (or to warn him of hidden dangers) or (2) to carry on activities on the premises so as not to endanger him.   R. § 333. So far as the possessor is concerned, one who is wrongfully on the premises must watch out for himself and take the premises as he finds them, concealed dangers and all.   He has no right to expect ordinary care for his safety.

As to portions of the premises where *no* visitor is permitted to go, this rule is perhaps justifiable on the ground that in the usual case it leads to the same result as if general principles of negligence were applied.   Generally a reasonably prudent possessor can safely ignore portions of the premises where visitors are prohibited.   But the rule is not so limited.   It applies, for example, to a portion of the premises as to which there is an open invitation to the public or which is otherwise frequently used by invitees (to whom the possessor would owe a duty of ordinary care), and despite the fact that there is an equally strong probability that either trespassers or invitees may be present.   And it bars recovery by a technical trespasser who was on the premises in the good faith (but erroneous) belief that he had a privilege to be there and who meant no harm. One can even imagine a trespasser and an invitee standing side by side, both injured by the same negligent act of the possessor, the former being barred and the latter recovering a judgment. In other words, the possessor's limited duty to trespassers may sometimes prevent recovery where ordinary principles of negligence would not.

One might suppose that the rule could be justified in part on the ground that a trespasser is a wrongdoer whom the law will not assist. Not so; a trespasser injured while on the land by the negligence of anyone other than the possessor is not barred. R. § 386. The rule can only be understood as a special privilege possessed by the occupier of land solely by reason of his right to exclusive possession and control of the premises.

As in the case of other duty limitations, the law has been forced to recognize exceptions in situations where the equities favoring plaintiff outweigh the policies underlying the rule. Generally, these are cases where (1) the foreseeable probability of trespassers and (2) the nature and extent of the foreseeable harm to such trespassers outweigh (3) the burden to the possessor of taking precautions and (4) the value of his right to exclude others at will.

Intentional and Reckless Misconduct. Naturally enough, the possessor's privilege does not extend to intentional torts. Trespassers may not be shot merely for trespassing.

In addition, most jurisdictions have adopted the blanket rule that a possessor of land is subject to liability to a trespasser for harm caused by the possessor's "wilful and wanton" or reckless misconduct. (This concept is discussed in § 4—7, supra. Some jurisdictions have rather generous interpretations of this concept in premises liability cases.) On the other hand, some courts (and the Restatement) do not recognize a general rule of liability for reckless misconduct; but almost all jurisdictions have embraced the rules discussed in the remainder of this section protecting (1) discovered trespassers and (2) frequent trespassers on a limited area. These special rules cover the most common fact situations in which reckless misconduct may be committed by a possessor against a trespasser, and in addition go further and subject the possessor in such situations to liability for ordinary negligence.

Frequent Trespassers Upon a Limited Area. When the possessor knows (or from facts within his knowledge ought to be aware) that trespassers constantly intrude upon a limited area of his premises, he is subject to liability for ordinary negligence with respect to them in two situations: (1) in the conduct of active operations on the premises which create a risk of harm to them (R. § 334); and (2) when he has created or maintains a dangerous artificial condition which he has reason to believe they will not discover, and he fails to warn them of the condition and the risk (R. § 335). For example, a railroad which knows that the public habitually crosses its tracks at a particular spot, albeit as trespassers, must exercise reasonable care for their safety in the operation of its trains at that point, and would have a duty to exercise reasonable care to warn them if it decided to electrify one of the rails. (In fact, most of the decided cases have involved railroad defendants.) Liability is justified on the ground that the frequency of the trespasses makes the presence of intruders highly foreseeable, and the limited area reduces the burden to defendant of protecting them. Although the cases mostly have involved activities or conditions which created risks of serious bodily harm or death, which would further justify liability, the rule need not be limited to such activities or conditions. R. §§ 334, Comment *b.*, and 335, Comment *b.*; Prosser, § 58.

Discovered Trespassers. From the rule that a possessor will be liable for intentional harm to a trespasser there evolved the rule that he will also be liable for wilful and wanton misconduct with respect to a discovered trespasser. A few courts have still not yet gone beyond this point. Some have broadened the rule to include *all* reckless conduct, whether the trespasser's presence is known or not. But almost all courts now go further and hold that once the possessor discovers the presence of the plaintiff-trespasser on his premises, the possessor's duty to him is similar to that stated in the preceding paragraph, with equal or greater justification. If he has reason to believe that a discovered trespasser is unaware of a danger arising from active operations on the premises, he must exercise reasonable care to warn him of that danger, or if it is apparent that a warning is not enough, he must exercise reasonable care to conduct or control these activities so as not to injure him (R. §§ 336, 338). And while there is older authority to the contrary, the trend of recent decisions is that he must exercise reasonable care to warn the known trespasser of a dangerous artificial condition to which the trespasser is in dangerous proximity if the possessor has reason to believe that the trespasser will not discover the danger or appreciate the extent of the risk (R. § 337). In these cases, the presence of a trespasser is no longer merely foreseeable, it is a known fact; and the burden of protecting him is less than the burden of protecting merely foreseeable trespassers because it is now focused on a particular person in a particular situation. Therefore the equities justify a duty of ordinary care. Again, the cases have mainly involved risks of serious bodily harm, but the principle need not be so limited. R. §§ 336, Comment *b.*, and 337, Comment *b.*

A corollary rule is that the possessor may have a duty to exercise reasonable care to rescue or aid a trespasser who is injured or in peril on his premises even though the possessor is not legally liable for the trespasser's condition. Pridgen v. Boston Housing Auth. (Mass.1974).

Note that the possessor's duty to even a discovered trespasser is *not* a general duty of reasonable care; he is not obligated to make the premises reasonably safe for the trespasser, but merely in the first instance to exercise reasonable care to warn him of proximate dangerous conditions and activities, and as to active operations to conduct or control them for the trespasser's protection only when it is apparent that a warning is insufficient.

§ 8—4. Trespassing Children

By custom and tradition, all adults have a special responsibility for the physical safety of children, and this is no less true of owners of land. Children at play instinctively wander and explore, more or less oblivious to property lines. It is neither customary nor practical for their parents to confine them or to supervise them closely at all times. And by reason of their immaturity, lack of judgment, and inexperience, they often do not recognize nor fully appreciate the dangers in their surroundings.

Thus, it is generally agreed that the arbitrary and rigid limitations on the possessor's duty to trespassers would lead to especially unjust results in many cases if they were applied across the board to trespassing children. Accordingly, most courts have held that these considerations alter the balance of competing interests in such cases, and have adopted special liability rules which impose on land owners and occupiers a greater duty of care as to children.

These special liability rules are equally applicable to children who are trespassers, licensees, and even invitees (R. § 343B). But the cases almost always involve youngsters who are trespassing and so the doctrine is invariably discussed as to them.

The doctrine is sometimes called the "turntable doctrine" because it originated in two cases, both of which involved a trespassing child injured while playing on a railroad turntable. Sioux City & P. Ry. v. Stout (U.S.1873); Keffe v. Milwaukee & St. P. Ry. (Minn.1875). In *Keffe*, the court rationalized its result on the theory that the turntable had attracted the child onto the defendant's land and thus defendant, having induced the trespass, would not be permitted to set it up as a defense. This theme was picked up in subsequent cases, and from this idea the doctrine acquired the unfortunate misnomer "attractive nuisance," a label which persists to this day. It cannot be taken literally, since the courts have now largely rejected the notion that the child must be attracted by that which injures him, and whether or not the condition is in fact a "nuisance" (see § 8—18) has nothing at all to do with defendant's liability to the child.

Despite its apparent equity, the doctrine has not had universal acceptance. A number of jurisdictions initially rejected it as too soft on trespassers, and while most of these have since reversed themselves and adopted it in some form, there are still about half a dozen states where it is not recognized as such.

Among the jurisdictions which do accept the concept, there are important differences in its component liability rules. However, the courts have increasingly relied upon the Restatement's formulation of the doctrine in § 339, and it now represents the most widely held version. Under § 339, "A possessor of land is subject to liability for physical harm to children trespassing thereon caused by an artificial condition upon the land" if the following requirements are met.

(a) [T]he place where the condition exists is one upon which the possessor knows or has reason to know that children are likely to trespass . . . .

It is not enough that trespasses by children are merely foreseeable. But neither does the possessor have to have actual knowledge that children are entering upon his premises. This requirement is met if he has such knowledge, or if he has actual knowledge of facts from which he ought to infer that such trespasses are likely to occur. In other words, he need not inspect the premises to determine whether children are present or whether the conditions are conducive to their trespasses, but he is held to what he actually knows about his premises and what he can reasonably anticipate based upon that knowledge.

In most jurisdictions, it is not necessary that the child be attracted onto the premises by the condition which injures him. This was once a fairly common requirement, derived from the "attraction" justification for the rule which originated in the *Keffe* case and given impetus by a much-criticized opinion by Mr. Justice Holmes in United Zinc & Chemical Co. v. Britt (U.S.1921); but this limitation has now been largely abandoned. It is enough that children who do trespass for whatever reason can be expected to encounter the condition. Thus, it is not necessary that the condition be an open and obvious one, or that the child intermeddle with it or even discover it prior to his injury.

(b) [T]he condition is one of which the possessor knows or has reason to know and which he realizes or should realize will involve an unreasonable risk of death or serious bodily harm to such children . . . .

The doctrine applies only to *conditions* on the land, not to activities. Of course, as to the latter the child has the same protection given to all other trespassers (see § 8—3, R. §§ 334, 336).

The possessor need not have created the condition; it is sufficient that he maintains it or permits it to exist. However, it is generally held that the doctrine applies only to "artificial" (i.e., man-made) conditions (e.g., structures, excavations, swimming pools, machinery and equipment) and not to natural conditions such as trees, land formations, and bodies of water (including, however, man-made lakes and ponds which resemble those which exist in nature).

This limitation is derived from the broader rule that the hazard must be an unusually dangerous one. The key phrase is "unreasonable risk." Some critics of this doctrine have failed to observe that it is not every condition on the land which presents a foreseeable risk of harm to a child which will subject the possessor to liability. The condition must create a risk of serious bodily harm to a child which is unreasonable in light of the utility of the condition and the burden to the possessor of reducing or eliminating the danger to the child. In addition, the risk is not unreasonable if the child whose trespass is to be anticipated can be expected to observe and fully appreciate the danger and avoid it. There are a number of cases denying liability where a child trespasser injures himself or another while engaged in recklessly making some hazardous use of an object or condition which, in and of itself, presents no unusual danger. Quite apart from any issue of contributory negligence, the possessor is not liable because the risk was not unreasonable, provided the possessor could expect the child to perceive and appreciate the consequences of his reckless misuse. The possessor is not required to make his premises "child-proof."

Fears that this doctrine will be abused have led some courts to create arbitrary categories of con-

ditions for which there is no liability. It is sometimes said that a possessor is not liable for "common hazards," or is liable only for "dangerous instrumentalities." Thus, some courts have held
that any child old enough to be allowed to wander about will be held as a matter of law to be capable of appreciating such dangers as fire, falling
from a height, drowning in water, ordinary visible machinery in motion, piles of lumber, and so
forth. But like all such rigid rules, they have
tended to break down in particular cases, as
where the possessor knows or has reason to know
that the children who are likely to trespass are so
extremely young that they cannot appreciate the
danger, or where there is some unusual or enhanced danger associated with the condition
which is *not* apparent to the child. The trend is
to abandon such arbitrary rules.

Here lies the true basis for the rule excluding
liability for natural conditions of the land. In
the typical case the hazards presented by such
conditions do not create *unreasonable* risks, because almost all children may be expected to appreciate them and the burden of altering or
guarding them usually is disproportionately
great. Cases may arise, however, in which the
risk even of a natural condition might be an unreasonable one under the circumstances, and
hence the Restatement leaves open the possibility
of liability in such cases. R. § 339, Caveat and
Comment *p.*

In addition, the risk must be one of serious bodily harm or death to the child; but if it is, the possessor will of course be liable for any lesser injury which the child in fact sustains.

The possessor must know, or have reason to know, (1) of the existence of the condition and (2) that the condition presents an unreasonable risk of serious harm to a child of the class whose trespass he knows or should know is likely. Here, also, there is no duty to inspect the premises, but the possessor is charged with the facts he actually knows and logical inferences from those facts.

(c) [T]he children because of their youth do not discover the condition or realize the risk involved in intermeddling with it or in coming within the area made dangerous by it . . . ..

It must be proved that the child did not recognize and fully appreciate the risk—that is, did not assume the risk (§ 5—5)—by reason of his age and inexperience. This is, of course, to be distinguished from contributory negligence, which is unreasonable conduct. The child may have been too young to be capable of contributory negligence, or may have acted reasonably for a child of his age, but he cannot recover if he knew of the condition and fully understood the danger and proceeded to encounter it anyway. And plaintiff has the burden of proof on this.

As might be expected, most of the cases have involved rather young children, usually under twelve. A few courts have established an arbitrary age limit for the doctrine, such as fourteen. In theory, however, there is no reason why it should not apply to children as old as sixteen or seventeen if the hazard is a particularly sophisticated one, and the Restatement no longer limits the doctrine to "young" children. But obviously, the older the child the fewer the dangers which it may be found he did not understand and appreciate.

(d) [T]he utility to the possessor of maintaining the condition and the burden of eliminating the danger are slight as compared with the risk to children involved, and

(e) the possessor fails to exercise reasonable care to eliminate the danger or otherwise to protect the children.

Clauses (d) and (e) are somewhat duplicative of each other, since (d) is essentially Learned Hand's classic test for negligence and (e) merely reiterates that the possessor must have been negligent. It would appear that the purpose of clause (d) is to give the court an additional opportunity to rule that the risk was not unreasonable as a matter of law since the question whether defendant was negligent (clause (e)) is ordinarily one of fact for the jury. The term "slight" in clause (d) could be interpreted as imposing a greater burden upon plaintiff than in other negli-

gence cases, where plaintiff need only establish
that the utility and burden to defendant were
"less than" the risk, but there is no indication in
the authorities that any such greater proof is required. Nor is there anything to suggest that
the term "eliminating the danger" should not include *warning* of the danger, as it would in other
cases, assuming of course that a warning would
have been a reasonable and effective means of
protecting the child against the risk.

It will be seen that the duty created by § 339 is
not very far removed from the one which would
be imposed if we simply said that a possessor of
land must exercise reasonable care for the safety
of foreseeable child trespassers. But the practical difference is that questions of negligence are
for the jury but questions of duty are for the
court, and thus by stating these rules as duty limitations, the courts retain greater control over
the outcome of these cases. There are indications, however, that the courts may now be willing to surrender that function, abolish such special duty rules, and apply a general standard of
reasonable care under the circumstances. See, e.
g., Kahn v. James Burton Co. (Ill.1955); § 8—6,
infra.

§ 8—5. Licensees and Invitees

One who enters upon the premises of another
with a privilege to do so is either a licensee or an
invitee. Actually, the term "licensee," strictly

speaking, encompasses *all* such entrants, including invitees. However, in this branch of the law it is customary to use "licensee" in a narrower sense to mean those who enter with a privilege but not as invitees.

Much controversy and confusion has surrounded the classification of particular entrants upon land, especially as between licensees and invitees, a subject which will be discussed later in this section. At the outset, however, it must be noted that the term "invitee" can be confusing unless it is remembered that not all persons who come upon the premises at the invitation of the possessor are invitees. In a nutshell, the distinction is this. An invitee is one *invited* by the possessor to enter or remain upon his land *for a particular purpose*. Traditionally, that purpose had to be one which involved some *economic benefit* to the possessor, and thus the term "business invitee" was often used to describe the entire class of invitees. The typical example is a customer in a store. Most courts today have broadened invitee status to include persons on land as a member of the *public* for a purpose for which the land is held open to the public—for example, a visitor to a public park or beach. R. § 332. Absent one of these purposes, however, one who is invited and even encouraged to come or remain upon another's land is in most states merely a licensee. A typical example is a social guest in one's home. Licensee status also includes those who enter merely with the possessor's express or implied consent, and usually also those who enter pursuant to some other privilege. Compare R. §§ 330, 345.

Duty to Licensees. The duty owed to a licensee is very close to the duty owed to a trespasser. The possessor is under no general duty to exercise reasonable care for his safety. It is agreed that the possessor must not injure him intentionally or by reckless or "wilful and wanton" misconduct. He must conduct active operations on the premises with due care for his safety once his presence is discovered, and if the presence of licensees at a particular place is to be expected he must conduct such operations with a view toward the possibility of their presence. R. § 341. As to such operations, however, he may assume that the licensee will watch out for himself to the extent that he can and that the licensee will not expect the possessor to alter his customary activities for the licensee's benefit.

As to static conditions, the licensee, like the trespasser, must take the premises as he finds them. He is not entitled to have the premises made safe for his visit, nor is the possessor required to inspect the premises for the benefit of the licensee.

The principal difference between the duties to licensees and trespassers is that the licensee is entitled to be *warned* of *concealed* dangerous conditions of which the possessor has *"actual knowledge"* and the licensee does not, and which the licensee is not likely to discover. R. § 342. (The Restatement says "knows or has reason to know," but the cases generally have required something very close to actual knowledge.) The duty here is to exercise reasonable care to *warn,* and hence whether a warning is required and when and how it should be given will be judged by what a reasonably prudent possessor would have done under the same or similar circumstances, knowing what he actually knew about the condition, the foreseeability of the licensee's presence, and the likelihood that the licensee would encounter it without discovering it first.

Duty to Invitees. The duty owed to an invitee can be stated very simply; it is to exercise reasonable care for his safety. R. §§ 341A, 343. The possessor must take the precautions which a reasonably prudent possessor of land would take under the circumstances to make the premises reasonably safe for his invitees. This may, in a given case, require that he inspect the premises to discover dangerous conditions, keep the premises in safe repair, remove hazards where invitees are likely to walk, obviate slippery conditions, anticipate foreseeable activities and uses by invitees and others (R. § 344), and, of course, conduct active operations on the premises with reasonable care for their safety. And when a hazard cannot reasonably be reduced or eliminated, he must exercise reasonable care to warn invitees of the danger. Of course, the possessor is not a guarantor of his invitees' safety; his duty is only to exercise *reasonable* care. For example, he may reasonably expect that invitees will avoid known or obvious dangers if they can, and he will not be liable unless the patent danger is such that injuries to invitees exercising proper care for their own safety can be anticipated. R. §§ 343(b), 343A. As in all other negligence cases, the question whether the possessor has exercised reasonable care is ordinarily for the jury.

The possessor's duty to invitees is, of course, nondelegable, and he will be liable if his employee or an independent contractor whom he has hired to perform it for him fails to perform it properly.

An interesting question which arises from time to time is the extent of the possessor's duty to a business invitee to protect him against criminal violence by third persons on the premises. The authorities are divided. Some courts have held on particular facts that there is no duty, for example, to accede to criminal demands even at the risk of harm to an invitee (e.g. Boyd v. Racine Currency Exch., Inc., Ill.1973); but in other cases the possessor's negligence has been held a question of fact for the jury. See, e.g., 72 A.L. R.3d 1269 (1976); 51 A.L.R.3d 711 (1973).

Classifications of Entrants. The most difficult and controversial problems in this area involve attempts to define the categories of entrants and to apply the definitions in particular cases.

As between licensees and trespassers, the line is
not unduly obscure. In the usual case the issue is
whether the entrant had a privilege to enter arising from the possessor's manifestation of consent
that he do so. Such consent may be express, or
implied from words or conduct. A recurring
question is whether the possessor's mere failure
to object to entry may be interpreted as a manifestation of consent; the answer is that it may or
may not, depending upon all the facts. The test
is whether, in light of all the surrounding circumstances, a reasonable person would interpret the
possessor's words or conduct as manifesting that
he is in fact willing for another to enter or remain upon his land. For example, when the possessor constructs or maintains a path or roadway
across his premises, or permits another to do so,
he may have manifested consent to entry, especially if he then tolerates some public use of it;
but not if he erects a gate or barrier or posts a
"no trespassing" sign. But when discouraging or
prohibiting trespassers would be unduly burdensome (e.g. pedestrians who walk along defendant's railroad tracks), mere tolerance of such
entries ordinarily may not reasonably be interpreted as manifesting permission for them.
Consent may also be implied from customs of the
community, at least in the absence of a locked
gate or posted notice to the contrary. Thus, a
traveler in need of assistance, solicitors and canvassers, and friends paying a social call may ordinarily infer consent at least to enter and knock

upon the occupier's door unless otherwise informed.

Typical licensees include persons on the land solely for their own purposes, members of the occupier's household, and social guests. (Servants and paying lodgers are invitees.) Classifying social guests as licensees has been justified on the ground that they should stand in no better position than members of the possessor's own household and must take the premises on the same terms. However, there is a good deal of dissatisfaction in placing the possessor's friends, who usually have been expressly invited and even urged to visit, in the same class as canvassers and bill collectors and only slightly ahead of trespassers, and in preferring the possessor's business visitors (who may be strangers) to his friends who provide him the important benefits of friendship and companionship. Nevertheless, the courts remain generally committed to this classification (several states to the contrary).

Incidental services performed by the guest do not transform him into an invitee. The visitor's gratuitous services must be sufficiently substantial that he could reasonably expect additional protection in return for them before he can be deemed an invitee. Nor does the existence of a business motive lurking in the invitation (as where the boss is invited to dinner) transform a social guest into an invitee.

By analogy to social guests, some jurisdictions have treated guest passengers in automobiles as the equivalent of licensees upon real property. See § 8—16, infra.

As previously noted, invitees traditionally have included at least persons invited to enter the premises for a purpose which involves some economic benefit to the possessor. His greater duty is justified as the quid pro quo for that benefit. Customers of stores and patrons of theaters, banks, places of amusement, and the like are all invitees. So are persons making or receiving deliveries of goods, and employees and independent contractors of the possessor doing work on the premises. The list is, of course, endless.

At one time, the "economic benefit" test was the sole test in most jurisdictions. So confined, the courts displayed considerable ingenuity in finding the requisite economic benefit when required to reach a just result. Thus, persons entering a place of business merely to browse or use a public telephone or public rest room or entering a bank to change a bill, and friends or children accompanying a customer to the store or other place of business all have been held to be invitees on the somewhat specious ground that the economic benefit may be merely potential, indirect, or remote in time.

The fact that the courts have had to stretch the economic benefit test past the logical limits of its underlying rationale is a good sign that there

is something wrong with the test. It is too narrow to encompass the entire spectrum of cases in
which invitee status is justified. Accordingly,
the courts have gradually developed a second test,
called the "public invitation" test, which supplements and expands it, and is now recognized in
most jurisdictions. It extends invitee status to
members of the public where (1) defendant invites the public (or a segment thereof) to enter
his premises and (2) plaintiff enters for a purpose for which the invitation was extended. Under this test, invitees include persons attending
free public meetings, lectures, church services,
and college reunions, spectators at free public
amusements, and those using public or private
land held open to the public for a recreational or
social purpose, absent any economic benefit whatsoever to the possessor. (Statutes in most states
have modified this rule as to recreational land.
See page 243, infra.)

The Restatement codifies both tests in § 332:

(1) An invitee is either a public invitee or a
business visitor.

(2) A public invitee is a person who is invited to enter or remain on land as a member of
the public for a purpose for which the land is
held open to the public.

(3) A business visitor is a person who is invited to enter or remain on land for a purpose
directly or indirectly connected with business
dealings with the possessor of the land.

What is the element common to all these persons which justifies their classification as invitees? Such entrants are entitled to expect that the premises have been made reasonably safe for them. In these circumstances, the invitation may be construed as carrying with it an implied representation by the possessor that reasonable care has been exercised for their safety during their visit, upon which representation they are entitled to rely. The courts have now come to recognize that this reliance is justified, and ought to be protected, not only where the possessor derives some economic benefit from the visit, but also where the premises are opened to the public for whatever purpose.

Thus, consistent with this rationale, a person is an invitee only when the possessor expressly or impliedly invites or encourages his entry, and not when his presence is merely tolerated or permitted. This is true even though he enters for a purpose of mutual economic benefit. Thus, a salesman who calls at a private home or place of business without an invitation or appointment is ordinarily a licensee unless and until he is invited to remain and discuss his business, unless custom would imply the invitation. And a property owner who merely permits neighborhood children to play on his vacant lot does not make them invitees unless he somehow encourages such use, as by improving the premises for them.

By the same token, a visitor is an invitee only when he is upon the area of the premises within the scope of the invitation, which in turn depends upon the physical character of the premises and the purpose which makes him an invitee. It extends, of course, to any portion of the premises to which the purpose of his visit may be expected to take him and which gives the appearance of being open to him, including entrances and exits, public rest rooms and telephones, and other common areas. As to portions of the premises normally maintained for the private use of the possessor and his employees (e.g., storerooms, private rest rooms and private telephones), plaintiff may be an invitee, licensee, or trespasser, depending on whether he was invited or encouraged to go there for a purpose consistent with the purpose of his visit, or goes there as a social guest or on his own initiative and with the possessor's mere consent, or goes there without permission. Similarly, a visitor's status as an invitee may be limited in time, either expressly or by the purpose of the visit.

Public Employees. Persons who enter upon defendant's premises without invitation or even consent but pursuant to some other privilege, such as to recapture a chattel or in pursuit of a felon (see R. §§ 191–211 as to such privileges) are ordinarily classified as licensees. R. § 345 (1). But the courts have had considerable difficulty with one group of such persons: public employees who enter on official business involving the occupier.

Publicly-employed sanitary and safety inspectors, garbage collectors, meter readers, postmen, and even revenue collectors are generally held to be invitees on the theory that their visits, while not always an economic benefit, are at least an economic necessity. A better rationale is that such visits are required by law and definitely foreseeable, and the visitor may reasonably rely on the fact that the portion of the premises where he is to be expected has been made reasonably safe for him.

Firemen and policemen present the greatest problem. Traditionally they have been classified as licensees, the best justification being that they arrive at unexpected times and go to unexpected places and thus it might be an inordinate burden on the landowner to provide for their safety. Nevertheless, this is not invariably true; and even when it is true, ordinary principles of negligence and proximate cause arguably would provide adequate protection to the occupier when the time or place of entry is unforeseeable.

Accordingly, there is something of a trend to broaden the landowner's duty to them. Some courts treat them as a special separate category, more than licensees but less than invitees; for example, some hold that they are invitees in certain situations, as when a policeman routinely and thus foreseeably makes an after-hours security check of defendant's business premises (Cameron v. Abatiell, Vt.1968) or when a fireman or policeman is injured by an unsafe condition on a portion of the premises held open to the public (R. § 345(2)). At least one court has held that they are always invitees. Dini v. Naiditch (Ill. 1960). And other courts are beginning to reach the same result by abolition of the classifications and substituting a general duty of reasonable care under the circumstances, either as to public employees (Spencer v. B. P. John Furniture Co., Or.1970) or generally, as discussed in the next section.

Note that even if he owes the fireman a duty of reasonable care, the possessor is not liable to him for injuries caused by the fire itself notwithstanding the fact that the fire resulted from the possessor's negligence.

Recreational Entrants. All but a few states now have statutes, most of them recently enacted, which limit the liability of a landowner or possessor to visitors whom he invites or permits to come upon his land for recreational purposes, provided he makes no charge to, or receives no "consideration" from, the visitor. The occupier's duty varies and the individual statute must be consulted, but in general the visitor's status is similar to that of a licensee or trespasser. See J. Page, The Law of Premises Liability §§ 5.13–5.22 (1976).

§ 8—6. Rejection of Categories

There has long been an undercurrent of dissatisfaction with the rigid categories of trespasser, licensee, and invitee, and increasingly with the proliferation of rules and subrules and exceptions necessary to administer them. In addition, there is strong sentiment to the effect that in our increasingly urban and crowded society, land owners no longer need or deserve special protection. Many legal writers have urged that the categories be abolished and replaced with a single duty applicable to possessors in all premises liability cases: a duty to exercise reasonable care under the circumstances, one of those circumstances being the status of the plaintiff. Premises liability cases would thus be treated the same as other negligence cases, and the foreseeability of the entrant's presence, the purpose of his visit, and the extent to which he could reasonably expect the premises to be made safe for him would be subsumed under the general principles of negligence, proximate cause, contributory negligence, and assumption of risk.

England abolished the distinction between licensees and invitees by statute in 1957, substituting a single duty of care owed to all lawful visitors (i.e. all those other than trespassers) and enumerating various factors to be considered. In 1959, the U.S. Supreme Court did the same for purposes of admiralty jurisdiction, holding that the ship owes a duty of reasonable care to all persons lawfully on board. Kermarec v. Compagnie Generale Transatlantique.

The first state to abolish the categories was California. In the oft-cited Rowland v. Christian (Cal.1968), the court held that whether plaintiff was an invitee, licensee or even trespasser makes no difference as to the duty owed to him—henceforth the general duty of reasonable care—but may be considered on the issue of what was reasonable care under the circumstances. As of the end of 1976, seven more states have followed suit. In chronological order, they are Hawaii (1969) (status irrelevant), Colorado (1971), Minnesota (1972), Massachusetts (1973), Rhode Island (1975), Wisconsin (1975), and New York (1976). So has the U.S. Court of Appeals for the District of Columbia Circuit (Smith v. Arbaugh's Restaurant, Inc., 1972), but this decision is not binding on the local District courts, from which no response has yet been heard. And New Hampshire probably must be included in this group in light of Sargent v. Ross (N.H.1973), which imposes a general duty of reasonable care upon lessors. All except Minnesota, Massachusetts and Wisconsin include trespassers among those to whom the duty of reasonable care is owed.

It may safely be predicted that a number of additional states will join this group, especially now that New York has done so. It is doubtful, however, that the states will ever be unanimous on this, although we can expect to see a further expansion of the possessor's duty to lawful visitors in almost all jurisdictions. The decisions following *Rowland* usually include dissenting opinions, and about a dozen cases expressly disapprove it, even while imposing a greater duty on the possessor. For example, Florida has expanded the invitee category to include *all* persons invited upon the premises, regardless of the purpose of the visit, but at the same time expressly refused to abandon the remaining licensee and trespasser categories and the rules traditionally applicable to them. Wood v. Camp (Fla.1973). And several states have made social guests invitees.

The reasons advanced for retaining the categories include: (1) they make sense; (2) they have been painstakingly developed and should not be discarded without compelling justification; (3) they work sufficiently well; (4) in general, they have evolved to keep pace with changing social policy, and can continue to do so; (5) they reflect judgments on matters of social policy, which are for the courts and not for the jury; and (6) juries are notoriously sympathetic to plaintiffs and cannot be trusted to give proper weight to the interests of the landowner. See e.g. Breitel, C.J., concurring in Basso v. Miller (N.Y.1976).

Developments in this area will have to be closely watched for some time to come.

§ 8—7. Lessors

The general rule is that a lessor of real property is not liable to his lessee or anyone else for physical harm sustained by such persons during the term of the lease as a result of a condition of the premises, even though that condition existed at and before the time the lessee took possession. R. §§ 355, 356. Traditionally, as a matter of property law a lease is the equivalent of a sale of the premises for a term. During that period of time the lessee becomes the owner and occupier and he is entitled to exclusive possession of the premises, even against the lessor (unless the lease provides otherwise). Absent a contrary provision in the lease, he alone has the right and the responsibility to keep the leased premises in repair and otherwise to determine how they shall be maintained and used.

However, to this general rule there are several important exceptions. The trend has been to enlarge the number and scope of these exceptions, mainly in recognition of the changing nature of the landlord-tenant relationship and the economic realities of life. In today's society, the typical lease is not a demise of a plot of ground but a contract for the use of space in the lessor's building. Especially in the case of residential leases, the landlord often has the superior bargaining power and can virtually dictate the terms of the lease. And it is he who receives the rent and who has the greater incentive, opportunities and resources to maintain the premises; he is the one who can allocate and distribute maintenance costs and best insure against the risks inherent in the condition of those parts of the premises which are there when the tenant takes possession and will be there when he leaves. Thus, his tort liability increasingly tends to reflect these factors. The exceptions also cover cases where he retains actual control over the premises or some aspect of them or fails to disclose a latent hazard.

Exception: Latent Hazards. When the lessor knows or has reason to know of a concealed unreasonably dangerous condition (artificial or natural) existing on the premises at the time the lessee takes possession under the lease, but says nothing to the lessee about it, he has committed a species of fraud which subjects him to liability for physical harm sustained prior to the time the lessee discovers or should have discovered the danger. R. § 358.

Jurisdictions vary as to the extent of the lessor's knowledge of the condition required for liability.

Almost all agree that there is no duty to inspect the premises to discover such conditions, but neither does the lessor have to have actual knowledge of the danger. Most require that he have knowledge of facts which would put a reasonable person on notice that a dangerous condition may exist—in the words of the Restatement, that he "know or have reason to know of the condition," and that he "realizes or should realize the risk involved."

In addition, the condition must create a latent danger, in the sense that it may be expected that the lessee will not discover the condition or the extent of the risk. The duty is only to disclose the existence of the condition, and therefore there is no liability for open and obvious hazards, however dangerous.

Liability extends to the lessee and all persons on the premises with his consent or by his right, since the lessor's concealment of the danger from the lessee has deprived them of the opportunity to have the lessee protect them from it.

Exception: Persons Outside the Premises. If there is a condition on the land which the lessor realizes or should realize unreasonably endangers persons outside the premises, the lessor's liability to such persons survives the transfer of possession to the lessee just as though the lessor remained in possession. R. § 379. He cannot escape liability for such hazards by leasing the premises. Thus, as to such persons it is immaterial that the lessee is aware of the condition or even that he has promised to alter or repair it, or that there is a clause in the lease exonerating the lessor from liability for such conditions, although this may affect rights as between the lessor and lessee. Of course, the lessor's liability is not exclusive; the lessee may in certain cases be jointly liable.

Generally, the lessor is not liable for conditions on the premises which come into existence after the lessee takes possession (R. § 377) or for the lessee's activities on the premises. But if the lessor knows at the time the lease is executed that the lessee intends to conduct an activity on the premises which will necessarily subject persons off the premises to actionable harm, and nevertheless consents to this activity or fails to require proper precautions, the lessor is subject to liability for foreseeable harm which results to those persons. R. §§ 379A, 837.

Exception: Public Admission. When the lessor leases his premises for a purpose which involves the admission of the public, he has a duty to them to exercise reasonable care to inspect for and remedy unreasonably dangerous conditions which exist when possession is transferred. R. § 359. Here, too, the lessee's agreement to alter or repair the dangerous condition does not absolve the lessor of liability unless the lessee agreed not to admit the public until this was done, and the lessor could reasonably expect him to keep that promise.

The first cases recognizing this exception involved the admission of large numbers of persons, but it is now well established that the rule is not so limited and encompasses any place, however small, where the public may enter. And it is not necessary that admission be charged or that the visitor be a business invitee of the lessee or the lessor; any purpose involving public admission is sufficient. But, of course, the lessor's liability is limited to those parts of the premises which, under the express or implied terms of the lease, are to be open to the public, and to visitors entering for the contemplated purpose. And the lessor is

[*250*]

not liable for the lessee's negligence after possession has been transferred, as to conditions which
were not unreasonably dangerous at that time.

Exception: Retained Control. Most leases today involve the rental of an apartment, suite of
offices, or similar space within a building such
that the lessor retains control over portions of
the premises not exclusively possessed by any tenant. These portions include (1) common areas
for use by the tenants and their visitors, such as
approaches, entrances, hallways, common stair-
ways, elevators, yards, garages, common rooms,
and basements, (2) appliances and other appurtenances necessary to the use of the premises, such
as heating and air conditioning systems, water
and water heating systems, electrical systems,
and common laundry facilities, and (3) structural
components, such as foundations. Since he retains control over these portions of the premises,
the lessor must exercise reasonable care to keep
them in a reasonably safe condition. R. §§ 360,
361.

Liability extends to the lessee, members of his
family, his employees, and to all lawful visitors
on the premises, even though as to a tenant a
particular visitor may be only a licensee. The
landlord is in the business of providing these facilities for the benefit of all such persons, and
therefore as to him they may be regarded as invitees. But his liability does not extend to areas of
the premises where tenants and their guests are

forbidden, nor to visitors of a tenant who intrude upon areas which have nothing to do with the proper purpose of their visit.

His duty is one of reasonable care, and he must inspect, repair or warn as circumstances and that duty require. The fact that the danger is apparent does not affect his duty, but of course may be relevant on plaintiff's contributory negligence or assumption of risk. And most courts extend liability to unreasonably dangerous natural, as well as artificial, conditions.

A clause in the lease exonerating the lessor from this liability may or may not be effective as to the tenant (see § 5—5) but of course it is always ineffective as to third persons not parties to the lease.

An interesting issue which is currently being litigated with regularity is the nature and extent of the lessor's liability to residents in his building for criminal violence by third persons occurring in common areas by reason of his failure to provide security devices or personnel. The cases so far are divided, some holding that there is no duty as a matter of law and others finding an issue of negligence for the jury. See 62 Va.L.Rev. 383 (1976).

Exception: Agreement to Repair. Where the lessor has contracted, in the lease or otherwise, to repair certain defective conditions or to keep the premises in safe repair generally, may he be held liable in tort if he fails to perform his promise with the result that a tenant or another is injured?

The law here is in a state of transition. At one time the general rule was that there was no tort liability for the mere failure to perform a contractual promise. See Chapter 10, infra. This limitation is in the process of being abandoned, and by now a majority of jurisdictions follow the Restatement § 357 (which represented a distinctly minority position when it was first adopted) and hold that such a promise by a lessor creates a duty which runs not only to the tenant but to others on the premises with the tenant's consent. Reliance by the lessee upon the promise is reasonable and ordinarily will induce him to forego undertaking the repairs himself, to the detriment of himself and all others who enter with his consent. However, there are still a substantial number of courts which have not yet embraced this rule.

The promise to repair must be enforceable; liability may not be based on the failure to perform a gratuitous promise to repair. Hence, if not a part of the lease agreement, as where it is made after the lease has been executed, there must be a separate or new consideration for it.

The lessor's duty is, of course, defined by the contract. And ordinarily his duty is only to exercise reasonable care to make the repairs after he has notice of the need for them. He need not inspect the premises unless he is required to do so by the lease.

By analogy, there may be liability for failure to provide a service required by the lease (e.g. heat, light) where the premises cannot be safely used without it.

Exception: Negligent Repairs. As a general rule, one who undertakes to perform a task, even gratuitously, must perform it with reasonable care. See § 4—5, supra. Logically this principle can be applied to a lessor who undertakes to repair the premises. However, the majority rule is that the lessor is not liable when he negligently makes gratuitous repairs unless (1) he increases the danger which existed before he undertook the repairs or (2) a concealed danger remains and his repairs create a deceptive appearance of safety or (3) the danger is a latent one and the lessor assures the lessee that the repairs have been made when in fact they have not been. R. § 362. The lessor is liable only if the danger (or enhanced danger) is such that the lessee neither knows nor should know that the repairs were not made or were made negligently. Thus, the lessor's liability is based on a theory of deceit.

Independent Contractors. In general, the lessor cannot escape his responsibilities by delegating the work to an independent contractor, and he is liable for the contractor's negligence to the same extent as if the contractor were his employee. R. §§ 419–421.

General Duty of Reasonable Care. Here, as elsewhere, we see the courts beginning to reject this system of classifications and duty limitations in favor of imposing upon the lessor a general duty of reasonable care under the circumstances. Sargent v. Ross (N.H.1973); Brennan v. Cockrell Investments, Inc. (Cal.App.1973); Old Town Development Co. v. Langford (Ind.App.1976); cf. Presson v. Mountain States Properties, Inc. (Ariz.App.1972).

About half the states now recognize an implied warranty of habitability in short-term residential leases, but so far the damages for breach of that warranty have not included damages for physical harm.

Statutes. All of the foregoing are common law rules. Statutes and ordinances in many jurisdictions impose duties on certain lessors which may have the effect of expanding their tort liability, typically with respect to their duty to keep the premises in repair.

§ 8—8. Vendors and Vendees

Vendors. When a landowner transfers title and possession of his property to another, unlike the lessor he has no continuing or reversionary interest in the premises. Thus, as would be expected, the general rule is that his responsibility for the condition of the premises and the tort liability accompanying it pass to the buyer upon completion of the transfer. However, there are two exceptions.

Exception: Latent Hazards. At one time, consistent with the principle of caveat emptor, the vendor was not even liable for injuries resulting from concealed dangers of which he was actually aware and which he failed to disclose to his buyer. However, most states now impose liability in this situation in favor of the vendee and others upon the land with his consent, provided (1) the vendee did not know or have reason to know of the condition or the risk involved; (2) the vendor knew or should have known of the condition, realized or should have realized the risk it created, and could anticipate that the vendee would not discover the condition or appreciate the risk; and (3) the risk is an unreasonable one. R. § 353. As in the case of the similar liability of a lessor, it is based upon the vendor's deceit under circumstances where the burden of imposing a duty to speak is small compared to the risk of harm created by his failure to do so.

The vendor's liability continues until the vendee has had a reasonable opportunity to discover the condition (or if the vendor actively concealed the condition, until actual discovery) and a reasonable time thereafter to correct it.

Exception: Persons Outside the Premises. When a vendor transfers land which has on it an artificial condition unreasonably dangerous to persons outside the premises such that he would have been liable as possessor for harm caused by it (see § 8—2, supra), his liability for the actionable consequences of that condition continues for a reasonable time after the transfer, until the vendee has had a reasonable opportunity to discover the condition (or actually discovers it, if it was actively concealed by the vendor) and a reasonable time to correct it.

According to the Restatement (§ 373), this liability is limited to conditions created or negligently permitted to remain on the land by the vendor. This limitation would seem to have little justification.

Builder-Vendors. As to buildings sold new by the person who built them, the courts are increasingly basing liability for injuries caused by defects in them upon ordinary principles of negligence, by analogy to manufacturers of chattels, or upon principles of strict liability for breach of warranty by creating an implied warranty of habitability. And a few courts have even imposed strict liability for unreasonably dangerous defects by analogy to principles of strict product liability (see § 8—9, infra), at least where the builder-vendor is a mass-producer of homes.

Vendees. When a transferee of real property acquires possession, he of course will have a reasonable time to discover and remedy actionable conditions on the premises before he will be held liable for them, although undoubtedly he must exercise reasonable care to warn of them or take such other temporary precautions as he reasonably can (where his duty is one of reasonable care) until that time.

Where the condition is one which creates an unreasonable risk of harm to persons or property *outside* the premises (typically a private or public nuisance, see § 8—18, infra), the rule is no different, except that where the condition constitutes a private nuisance he may in certain circumstances be entitled to assume that it exists with the consent of the adjoining landowners (or that compensation has been paid for it) and so he will not be liable until he is on notice that it is in fact an actionable nuisance. However, if the condition constitutes a public nuisance, no such notice is required, since the vendee is required to know that the public cannot consent to it, and therefore he must take immediate steps to abate it. R. § 366.

B. PRODUCTS LIABILITY

§ 8—9. An Overview of Products Liability

In recent years the law governing liability for injuries caused by defective products has undergone rapid growth and dramatic changes. "Products liability" law has moved from caveat emptor to strict liability, and at present is one of tort law's most important areas. It is estimated that over one million claims for product-caused injuries were made in 1976, half involving litigation.

Products liability law has become so specialized and complex that it is properly the subject of a separate Nutshell (D. Noel & J. Phillips, Products Liability in a Nutshell (1974)). Therefore, this section will be confined to a brief overview of this area, merely to place product-caused injuries in perspective in the general scheme of the law of liability for physical harm.

Theories of Liability.   When physical harm to plaintiff or his property is causally related to the unsafe condition of a "product," he may have a cause of action against the person(s) who designed, manufactured, sold, or furnished that product.   (The scope of the concept "product" is a separate and interesting issue.   It is not confined to manufactured goods purchased by consumers;   but for simplicity's sake that is the sense in which it is used herein.)

In most jurisdictions, plaintiff's cause of action may be based on one or more of three different theories: (1) negligence; (2) breach of warranty and (3) strict tort liability.

Negligence.   There are many ways in which the manufacturer of a product (or of one of its component parts) may have negligently created an unsafe condition.   For example, he may have chosen an unnecessarily dangerous *design.*   Some one may have been negligent during the *manufacturing* process, as by using defective materials, or omitting a part or a step.   Perhaps there was negligence in the testing and inspection of the product. Sometimes the product's container or packaging is inadequate. Or he may have failed to furnish adequate *warnings* and directions for use with the product.

Moreover, after the product has left the manufacturer's hands, subsequent sellers or furnishers (e.g. a wholesaler, distributor, retailer, or lessor) may also have been negligent in failing to discover or failing to warn of the unsafe condition.

The usual principles of negligence apply. Thus, the issue is whether the burden of conduct which would have prevented the harm is greater or less than the foreseeable probability and gravity of that harm, and this is a question of fact.

Breach of Warranty. "Warranty" is a general concept. The law recognizes a variety of warranties besides those with which we are concerned here. Basically, warranties are certain kinds of express or implied promissory representations of fact which the law will enforce against the warrantor. Most warranties arise in transactions involving transfers of real or personal property.

Products liability law is concerned primarily with three of these warranties, as they concern the product's quality or fitness for use: (1) *express* warranties; and the *implied* warranties of (2) merchantability and (3) fitness for a particular purpose. While these warranties are now regarded as a branch of sales or commercial (i.e. contract) law, their roots are in the old law of wrongs (see § 1—3) and for a long time the remedy for their breach was in tort. These warranties are of interest to us because the remedies for their breach include damages for physical harm. These and other warranties are now codified in the Uniform Commercial Code; comparable warranties existed under the Uniform Sales Act and common law.

An *express warranty* (U.C.C. § 2—313), as the term implies, is simply a promissory assertion of fact about the product which the seller made as a part of the sales transaction and which was a "basis of the bargain"—for example, that "this widget is guaranteed to be free from defects for one year from date of purchase."

The *implied warranties* are those created and imposed by law, and accompany the transfer of title to goods unless expressly and clearly limited or excluded by the contract. (With respect to damages for personal injury, any such contractual limitations or exclusions are "prima facie unconscionable." U.C.C. § 2–719(3).)

The implied warranty of *merchantability* (U. C.C. § 2—314) requires that the product (and its container) meet certain minimum standards of quality, chiefly that it be fit for the ordinary purposes for which such goods are sold. This includes a standard of reasonable safety.

The implied warranty of *fitness for a particular purpose* (U.C.C. § 2—315) imposes a similar requirement in cases where the seller knows or has reason to know of a particular purpose for which

the goods are required and that the buyer is relying on him to select or furnish suitable goods; he
then warrants that the goods are fit for that particular purpose.

The action for breach of one of these warranties has aspects of both tort and contract law.
Its greatest value to the injured product user lies
in the fact that liability for breach is *strict;* no
negligence or other fault need be shown.   However, in addition to the privity limitation (to be
discussed), certain contract-type defenses have
impaired the remedy's usefulness.   These include:
(1) the requirement that the seller receive reasonably prompt *notice* of the breach as a condition to his liability; (2) the requirement that the
buyer have *relied* upon the warranty; and (3)
the ability of the seller to *limit* or *disclaim entirely* the implied warranties.   Obviously, these
defenses are most appropriate in cases of commercial loss (economic loss caused by the product's
failure to perform as expected), and there has
been a trend away from strict enforcement of
these defenses in personal injury cases where the
action has more of a tort flavor.

Privity Limitations.   The history of the law of
products liability is largely a history of the erosion of the privity limitation which severely limited the seller's liability in both negligence and
breach of warranty actions.

In negligence, the seminal case is Winterbottom v. Wright (Exch.1842), which established

the rule that liability for injuries caused by a
negligently made or maintained product is limited
to the parties to the contract (see Chapter 11, infra). In other words, defendant's duty of reasonable care arose only from the contract and only a
party to that contract could sue for its breach.
This meant that a negligent manufacturer who
sold his product to a retailer, who in turn sold it
to plaintiff, was effectively insulated from liability; and the plaintiff was usually without a remedy in tort, since it was the manufacturer and not
the retailer whose negligence caused the harm.

Gradually exceptions to the *Winterbottom* rule
emerged. Soon privity of contract was not required (1) where the defect was fraudulently concealed by the seller (based on a deceit theory)
and (2) for products "inherently" or "imminently" dangerous to human life or health, such as
poisons and guns. The decisions then began to
expand these exceptions. Some courts dropped
the fraud requirement; a concealed defect coupled
with some sort of "invitation" by defendant to
use the product was enough. And a few cases
construed the term "imminently dangerous" to
mean especially dangerous by reason of the defect itself, and not necessarily dangerous per
se—for example, products intended for human
consumption, a defective scaffold, and a coffee
urn which exploded.

Finally, MacPherson v. Buick Motor Co. (N.Y.
1916) (Cardozo, J.) broadened the category of

"inherently" or "imminently" dangerous products so as effectively to abolish the privity requirement in negligence cases. It held that lack of privity is not a defense if it is foreseeable that the product, if negligently made, is likely to cause injury to a class of persons which includes the plaintiff. Since this is essentially the test for negligence anyway, the exception swallowed the rule. The *MacPherson* case quickly became a leading authority, and the privity rule in negligence cases soon was history.

In warranty, a similar privity limitation was imposed, in part because warranties were thought to be an integral part of the contract of sale. Beginning in 1913, an exception developed for cases involving products intended for human consumption (food, beverages, drugs, etc.) and eventually also for products intended for "intimate bodily use" (e.g., cosmetics), so that the warranty in these cases ran all the way to the ultimate consumer. In the case of *express* warranties which could be said to be made to the public generally, such as a statement by a manufacturer in literature distributed with an automobile that the windshield was "shatterproof," the privity requirement was quickly abandoned following Baxter v. Ford Motor Co. (Wash.1932). But with respect to *implied* warranties, there was almost no extention beyond food, drink and similar products until Henningsen v. Bloomfield Motors, Inc. (N.J. 1960) abolished the privity limitation generally and held that the implied warranties run to the foreseeable ultimate user or consumer of the product. (*Heningsen* also invalidated the manufacturer's attempted disclaimer of implied warranty liability.) *Heningsen* has been followed in almost all jurisdictions.

Strict Tort Liability. During the 1930's, '40's, and '50's various legal writers and an occasional judge proposed the creation of strict liability in tort for defective products. The best known judicial exposition of this view was Justice Traynor's concurring opinion in Escola v. Coca Cola Bottling Co. (Cal.1944). The principal justifications advanced for strict product liability are: (1) negligence is often too difficult to prove; (2) res ipsa loquitur has been stretched to nearly this point anyway; (3) strict liability can be accomplished already through a series of actions for breach of warranty; (4) strict liability provides needed safety incentives; (5) the manufacturer is the one best able to either prevent the harm or insure or spread the cost of the risk; and (6) the manufacturer of a product by placing it on the market induces justifiable consumer reliance on the expectation of the product's safety, and since reputable manufacturers do in fact stand behind their products all should do so. In addition, after *Heningsen,* the last major barrier to direct strict liability was removed, leaving only the remaining contract defenses to warranty liability which many felt were inappropriate to personal injury cases.

Finally, in Greenman v. Yuba Power Products, Inc. (Cal.1963), California became the first jurisdiction to adopt strict tort liability for defective products. At about the same time, work was underway on the Restatement (Second) of Torts, and its Reporter was Dean Prosser, an advocate of strict product liability. Relying only on *Greenman* and a New York warranty case (Goldberg v. Kollsman Instrument Corp., N.Y.1963), the American Law Institute approved § 402A which embodied strict liability as follows:

(1) One who sells any product in a defective condition unreasonably dangerous to the user or consumer or to his property is subject to liability for physical harm thereby caused to the ultimate user or consumer, or to his property, if

(a) the seller is engaged in the business of selling such a product, and

(b) it is expected to and does reach the user or consumer without substantial change in the condition in which it is sold.

(2) The rule stated in Subsection (1) applies although

(a) the seller has exercised all possible care in the preparation and sale of his product, and

(b) the user or consumer has not bought the product from or entered into any contractual relation with the seller.

Strict product liability, almost always in the form provided in § 402A, has swept the country and is now the law in at least forty states. At the same time, negligence and breach of warranty remain alternative or concurrent theories of recovery. In fact, some writers and a few judges have been unable to understand how the courts could simply bypass the warranty provisions of the U.C.C. (which purport to legislate liability rules for exactly the same fact situations) and adopt common law tort rules different from the Code. But the simple answer is that the courts have regarded the U.C.C. as contract or sales law which does not affect their traditional role as makers of the common law rules of tort law. As a practical matter, the differences between strict tort liability and liability for breach of warranty are now slight; but differences do exist in certain cases.

Other Issues. The emergence of strict product liability has raised a host of new issues which the courts are now in the process of resolving. The principal questions are as follows.

Defect. What is a "defective condition unreasonably dangerous"? In negligence cases, the focus is upon defendant's conduct. In strict liability (whether warranty or tort) the focus shifts to the condition of the product; but there is still an element of fault, in the sense of placing on the market an unsafe product. Many cases have had to deal with this question. As in negligence cases, the defect may be in the design (in which case a balancing test similar to that used in negligence cases must be used), in manufacture, or in the failure to warn or to provide adequate directions for use.

Type of Harm. What kinds of harm are compensable under § 402A? The authorities are divided. The majority, of which Seely v. White Motor Co. (Cal.1965) is the leading example, limit § 402A damages to physical harm (personal injury and property damage to other than the product itself) on the ground that warranty law is better suited to govern merely economic or commercial loss. But others, such as Santor v. A & M Karagheusian, Inc. (N.J.1965), have allowed recovery for such losses under § 402A.

Plaintiffs. Who may be a plaintiff? Section 402A speaks of the "user or consumer" of the product, but in a Caveat the Institute leaves open the possibility that liability may be extended in favor of others. The courts have generally allowed recovery by "bystanders" (i.e. persons other than the purchaser, user or consumer) whose exposure to the risk of injury was foreseeable (e. g. a third person injured in a crash caused by a defect in the vehicle).

In contrast, the U.C.C. (§ 2—318) provides three alternative provisions; each state is free to choose the one it likes best. Alternative A includes personal injuries to members of the purchaser's family or household and household guests. B covers personal injuries to all those who foreseeably may be expected to be users, consumers, or "affected by" the goods; and C covers *all* compensable harm (personal injury, property damage and economic loss) to those in group B.

Defenses. What defenses are available? It is generally agreed that plaintiff's contributory negligence is not a defense to strict liability (§ 5—1, supra), but assumption of risk (§ 5—5) is. In addition, the courts have recognized plaintiff's "misuse" of the product as a defense. It would appear that this is merely another way of saying that the product was not defective (or if it was that the defect was not a cause in fact of the injury), since the manufacturer need only make the product reasonably safe for foreseeable uses. At the same time, if plaintiff's use, while not an *intended* use, is a *foreseeable* and not an uncommon one (e.g., standing on a chair, an infant drinking furniture polish), the manufacturer may have a duty to design his product in light of the foreseeable misuse. On this basis, the trend of authority is to hold manufacturers of automobiles strictly liable if the vehicle is unnecessarily dangerous to the occupants in the event of an accident (the so-called "crashworthiness" doctrine), since motor vehicle accidents are a rather common and foreseeable "misuse" of the product.

Defendants. Finally, who may be a defendant? Strict liability under § 402A extends to the manufacturer of the product, and in most jurisdictions to the supplier of the component part which was defective.   It also encompasses all those in the distribution chain—wholesalers, distributors, retailers, and commercial lessors and bailors.   Defendant must be "engaged in the business" of dealing in that product, but such products need not be his principal business; it is no defense that furnishing the product was merely an incidental part of his business (see R. § 402A, Comment *f*).   But if defendant is primarily engaged in rendering services, some (but not all) courts have refused to impose strict liability for defective products incidentally supplied.   And the courts have so far refused to impose strict liability on dealers in used products.

Recent cases have extended strict liability for personal injury to mass developer-builder-vendors of new homes (e.g. Schipper v. Levitt & Sons, Inc., N.J.1965).

C.   EMPLOYERS, EMPLOYEES AND CONTRACTORS

§ 8—10.   Vicarious Liability

Vicarious liability is a form of strict liability by which *A* is held liable to another for the tort of *B* for no other reason than that there exists some relationship between *A* and *B* and *B* was acting within the scope of that relationship when he committed the tort.   The overwhelming majority of vicarious liability cases arise from the employer-employee[1] relationship, but the principle extends to other relationships such as partnership, joint venture or enterprise, and in some instances principal-agent and employer-independent contractor.

Basically, if the requisite relationship exists, a third person (*C*) may sue *A* for injuries caused by the tort of *B*, even though *A* was entirely innocent of personal fault so far as *C*'s injuries are concerned.

Often this is characterized as an instance of *imputed negligence*. That term is inaccurate for two reasons. First, there is vicarious liability for many torts besides negligence. It applies to all forms of strict liability, and as a general rule to intentional torts committed by *B* in the scope and furtherance of *A*'s business. Second, it is not the negligence or other fault which is imputed, but the *liability*.

Various justifications have been advanced for the vicarious liability of an employer, and by analogy of others. These include: (1) he has a measure of control over the conduct of his employee; (2) it is he who initiated the activity out of which the tort arose; (3) he selected the em-

---

[1] Traditionally, the terms "master" and "servant" have been used to designate the parties to an employment relationship, and these terms still appear in the cases and other authorities, and particularly in digests and indexes. "Employer" and "employee" are more modern and descriptive, and will be used instead herein.

ployee; (4) vicarious liability is the price of the privilege to employ others; and (5) he is, frankly, more likely to have the means to compensate the plaintiff than is his employee.

Obviously, none of these standing alone is a sufficient reason. Perhaps the best justification is that torts are a more or less inevitable byproduct of the conduct of such activities, and thus tort liability should be treated as a cost of the enterprise as a whole. It is a cost of doing business (using that term in a broad sense). The enterprise functions through its employees; their acts may be said to be the acts of the enterprise. In addition, the enterprise is better able than either the innocent plaintiff or the employee to absorb the loss, plan for it, insure against it, and allocate the cost in the last instance to those who do business with it and partake of its benefits. Further, there is some merit to the argument concerning control. Employer liability does provide an incentive to exercise care in the selection of employees and the conduct of the activity, and thereby promotes the injury-prevention function of tort law.

For these and other reasons, the principle of vicarious liability is well-established and there is no tendency at all to retreat from it.

§ 8—11. Employees

Let us first clarify some terms—principal, agent, employer, employee, independent contractor. The following are not intended as definitions, and must not be relied upon as such.

The terms *principal* and *agent* encompass a variety of relationships, some of which may be subclassified as *employer-employee* and some as *employer-independent contractor.*

An *agent* is one who, by mutual consent, has undertaken to represent or act for another, the *principal,* subject to the latter's right to exercise some degree of direction and control over the former.

An *employee* is a particular kind of agent. Unfortunately, there is no one satisfactory definition of that term. Instead, the status question is resolved by considering the combined effect of all of the facts surrounding the actor's relationship to the other for whom he acts. By far the most important factor is the degree of *control* possessed or exercised by the latter. As a general rule, if the principal controls, or by custom or agreement has the right to control, the physical details (time, place, method, etc.) of the performance of the work, then the agent is very likely an employee and therefore his principal is his employer. If this degree of control does not exist, the relationship is very likely something else, but not necessarily. There are other relevant factors, and where they point strongly enough in the direction of an employment relationship, such may be found to exist notwithstanding the absence of control over the manner of performance

of the work.   These factors include (1) the skill
required of the worker;   (2) the term of the employment;   (3) whether the work is part of the
principal's regular business;   (4) whether the
worker has a separate business of his own;   (5)
who supplies the tools and other requisites of the
job;   (6) where the work is performed;   (7) the
method of payment;   (8) the intent of the parties;   and (9) so on.   See Restatement (Second)
Agency § 220.

Note that since all employer-employee relationships necessarily involve *some* degree of control
by the employer over the employee, all employers
are also principals and all employees are also
agents;   but of course the converse is not true.

As the term implies, an *independent contractor*
is one who is engaged to perform services for another (who in this instance is also termed an *employer*) but remains independent of the employer's own work force.   It is a looser relationship;
he retains a separate identity.   It is commonly
said that an independent contractor is one who is
paid primarily to accomplish certain results (as
opposed to an employee, who is paid for his
time), with the manner of performance being left
to the contractor's own discretion.   This is usually true, but not always;   one may be an independent contractor when the factors mentioned
above so indicate, even though the employer possesses or exercises some significant control over
how and when the work shall be done.   If the

employer retains some degree of control (as opposed to contracting solely for the result), he is also deemed to be a *principal* and the independent contractor is also his *agent* to that extent. If not, then no principal-agent relationship exists, but merely employer-independent contractor.

By way of illustration, a lawyer may be any of the three. A salaried associate of a law firm, or one who is on the payroll of a corporation or governmental unit, is ordinarily an employee (even though he is highly skilled and performs his work autonomously.) An attorney in private practice who is retained by a client to perform legal services on his behalf is customarily an independent contractor, and also the client's agent. But a lawyer who merely contracts to write a law book is an independent contractor, but not the publisher's agent.

It must be remembered that status is always a question of fact, and while the parties' own characterization of their relationship is one factor to be considered it is never determinative.

Given the absence of definitive tests and clearly visible lines, the courts have had difficulty with these status questions, and the cases are not always consistent. Perhaps after all is said and done, the customs, common sense and experience of the community are as reliable a guide as any.

The rules alluded to above are a part of the law of agency, to which reference must be made for further guidance. But these issues have important tort law consequences. As noted in the preceding section, an employer is liable to third persons for torts committed by his employee while acting within the scope of the employment. However the general rule (subject to a number of exceptions) is that an employer is *not* vicariously liable for the torts of his independent contractor. (And deciding whether or not one is an employee will be necessary to determine whether he is entitled to certain other remedies, such as workmen's compensation.)

Once it is determined that the tortfeasor was an employee at the time he committed the tort, his employer is vicariously liable if his conduct was within the "scope" (or sometimes the "course" or "course and scope") of his employment. This is also a question of fact for which no very useful test has been devised. All of the surrounding circumstances must be considered, including (1) the employee's job description or assigned duties, (2) the time, place and purpose of the employee's act, (3) the similarity of his conduct to the things he was hired or authorized to do, or which are commonly done by such employees, and (4) the foreseeability of his act. In general, "course" and "scope" have not been narrowly construed. Acts not strictly necessary to the work or authorized by the employer are included, so long as they bear a reasonable relation to the employment.

The employee was not necessarily beyond the scope of his employment merely because he did some act which his employer had expressly prohibited him to do, or did a permitted act in a forbidden way. For example, a gun salesman is within the scope of his employment when he inserts a live cartridge into a gun which he is demonstrating to a prospective purchaser, despite the fact that his employer expressly told him never to do this. An employer cannot limit his own liability merely by instructing his employee to act carefully. The forbidden act is within the scope of the employment if it is reasonably necessary in order to accomplish the assigned tasks, or if it is naturally to be expected that the employee will do such an act in performing the assigned work. On the other hand, an employer may limit an employee's duties as he sees fit, and thus one employed exclusively as an airplane pilot *may* be outside the scope of his employment when, contrary to specific instructions, he undertakes to make repairs on the airplane. (In such a case, there could be vicarious liability, but on some other ground.)

Relatively minor deviations from the acts necessary to accomplish the assigned work usually will not take the employee outside the scope of his employment. Personal acts of an incidental nature, such as going to the toilet, lighting a fire to keep warm, smoking, and even taking a coffee break are ordinarily held to be within the scope, even though such acts are not among those the

employee was hired to do. But he goes beyond
the scope where the deviation is more substantial
—constituting, to use the classic phrase, a "frolic
and detour" for the employee's own purposes.
The distinction is between major and minor de-
partures from the tasks and methods authorized
or reasonably foreseeable by the employer, and
the principal variables are (1) the length of time
of the departure, (2) the physical distance of the
departure from the place or route assigned or expected to be used, and (3) the extent to which
the employee was, at the same time, secondarily
accomplishing a purpose of his employment.
Thus, a deviation of a relatively short time and
distance for a purely personal errand is not beyond the scope. A greater deviation is permissible if there is an employment purpose incidental
to the personal one, as where a deliveryman varies from his assigned route in order to favor a
customer who gives him presents. But a deliveryman with hours from eight to five who is assigned a delivery at four p.m. but goes home instead for personal reasons does not reenter the
scope of his employment when he makes the delivery at 10 p.m.

An employer's vicarious liability includes torts
negligently or recklessly committed. It even extends to intentional torts committed in the scope
of the employment and at least in part in furtherance of the employer's business. For example, a
bill collector who commits assault, battery, false
imprisonment, or intentionally inflicts emotional

distress or maliciously prosecutes or defames the plaintiff in an effort to extract payment of a bill subjects his employer to liability for the intentional tort. Going a step further, some courts (a growing minority) will visit vicarious liability on an employer for intentional torts committed during a fight which ensued when the employee lost his temper during an argument which arose out of the employment. And it is generally agreed that where there is some special relationship between plaintiff and the employer such that the employer owes plaintiff a duty of protection (such as in the case of a carrier, an innkeeper, or a hospital) the employer is subject to vicarious liability to plaintiff for his employee's intentional tort even though the tort is committed for entirely personal reasons.

Ordinarily, an employer is not vicariously liable for harm caused by the employee's use of an instrumentality (such as an automobile) entrusted by him to the custody of the employee, when not then being used in the scope of the employment. However, a few courts have held otherwise where the instrumentality is a particularly dangerous one.

Bear in mind that all of the foregoing applies only to the employer's *vicarious* liability. There are many situations in which an employer may be held responsible for harm caused by the acts of his employee on the basis of the employer's *own* conduct, in which case the liability is direct and not vicarious and the foregoing limitations do not apply. Thus, an employer may be liable for his own negligence in the selection or instruction of the employee, or for failure to properly supervise him. Or he may be held liable under usual principles of agency law where he has commanded, authorized or ratified the employee's tortious act.

For purposes of tort liability to third persons, partners can be regarded as employees of the partnership, or of each other, and therefore all partners are jointly and severally liable for the tort of one, committed while acting within the scope of the partnership business. The same is true of the principals in a joint venture, which for almost all purposes is the legal equivalent of a partnership, the main difference being that a joint venture is more limited in its scope.

§ 8—12. Independent Contractors

As to agents who are *not* employees, the general rule is that the principal is *not* vicariously liable for their torts, even where committed within the scope of the agency, since such agents are not a part of the principal's enterprise, and therefore the most important justifications for vicarious liability (§ 8—10) do not apply. There are, however, exceptions, chiefly involving wrongful statements or representations which the agent has actual or apparent authority to make and the institution of legal proceedings which the agent was authorized to bring. (Here, too, the principal may be *personally,* not vicariously, liable where he commanded, authorized or ratified the agent's tortious act, or for his personal negligence in the selection, instruction or supervision of the agent.)

The same general rule of non-(vicarious) liability applies, for the same reasons, as to torts committed by those classified as independent contractors. (Recall that there may or may not be an agency relationship between an employer and his independent contractor. See § 8—11, supra.) But as to independent contractors, the general rule has been ravaged by exceptions, to the point that it "is now primarily important as a preamble to the catalog of its exceptions." The Restatement states the general rule in one section (§ 409) followed by twenty-four sections which set forth the exceptions (§§ 410–429). Seven of those (§§ 410–415) involve liability based on the employer's own fault, and therefore are not, strictly speaking, exceptions to any *vicarious* liability rule; however, they are exceptions to the rule of nonliability for harm caused by the acts of the independent contractor, and all such exceptions may conveniently be treated together.

The various exceptions may be grouped into three general categories:

(1) The employer was negligent in selecting, instructing, or supervising the contractor;

(2) Out of some special relation to the public or the plaintiff, there arises a duty which is of

sufficient importance that defendant cannot escape responsibility for the proper performance of that duty by hiring an independent contractor to perform it;

(3) Work which is particularly or inherently dangerous.

(1) Employer's Own Negligence. Apart from any rule of vicarious liability, the employer of an independent contractor will be liable under ordinary principles of negligence for his own negligence in dealing with the contractor. Thus, he must exercise reasonable care to select a reasonably competent, experienced, careful, and properly equipped contractor. If the work will create a foreseeable danger to third persons, ordinary care may encompass a requirement that the employer insist (in the contract or otherwise) that the contractor take the necessary safety precautions, and then see that he does so. Reasonable care may also require inspections of completed work.

To the extent that the employer retains, by contract or in fact, authority to supervise and control the contractor's work, he will be liable for physical harm to others caused by his failure to exercise such supervision and control with reasonable care. This principle is important, since it is a common practice for employers to retain some such authority. Of course, his authority must be such that he could have acted with respect to the danger. A mere general right to supervise, receive reports, make suggestions, or alter the plans and specifications is usually not sufficient where such powers relate solely to the quality of the work and compliance with the plans. The control must involve the right to influence the manner of performance of the details of the work or otherwise to affect its safety.

(2) Nondelegable Duties. Where the safe performance of some duty is of sufficient importance to the community, the law will not permit the obligor to delegate his responsibility to an independent contractor and thereby insulate himself from tort liability for physical harm caused by its misperformance. Thus, one who does employ an independent contractor to perform such a duty will be vicariously liable for physical harm resulting from his contractor's negligence, even though the employer was himself entirely without fault.

The list of such duties is long, and there is as yet no general definition or test. They may be imposed by law (statutory or common), contract, franchise or charter. What such duties seem to have in common is a substantial safety purpose underlying them. Examples include the duties owed by a common carrier to its passengers, the duty of a municipality to keep its streets in repair, the various duties owed by the owner or possessor of land to lessees and business visitors, the duty of an employer to provide his employees a safe place to work, the duty of the lessor or bailor of a chattel to maintain it in a reasonably safe condition, the duty of an auto owner to maintain adequate brakes, and the duty of one who deals with highly dangerous instrumentalities to construct and maintain them with care (e.g. a power company's duty to maintain its wires). Duties imposed by a statute or regulation requiring specific safeguards or precautions for the safety of others are nondelegable.

(3) Inherently Dangerous Work. Another important exception to the general rule is that there may be vicarious liability for the tort of an independent contractor where the work contracted to be performed involves some special, out-of-the-ordinary danger.

If the activity is one which may be classified "abnormally dangerous" such that one who engages in it will be subject to strict liability (e.g. blasting; see § 3—3), this exception clearly applies and the employer will be vicariously liable. But it is not so limited; "inherently dangerous" is much broader than "abnormally dangerous." A typical case involves the construction, repair or maintenance of a structure, which often will create special dangers to those in the vicinity. An independent contractor who hauls potatoes creates no *special* danger by the operation of his truck, and therefore there is no vicarious liability when he does so negligently; but one hired to transport explosives or huge logs which will be unusually dangerous if not securely fastened may subject his employer to vicarious liability under

[284]

this exception when he is negligent with respect to the unusual risk.

While the risk must be a special or unusual one, it need not be an inevitable or unavoidable one. It is enough that the danger is one which is likely to arise in the normal course of the activity as that work is customarily done. Perhaps it is not strictly necessary to stack bricks on a public sidewalk in order to construct an adjoining building, but if it is to be anticipated then it is sufficiently inherent and this exception may be applied.

It will be observed that there is substantial overlap between the "nondelegable duty" and "inherently dangerous work" exceptions, since the employer's nondelegable duty is often based on the existence of some special danger to others. Many cases apply more than one of these exceptions.

Collateral Negligence. As a general rule, the employer's vicarious liability is limited to the particular risk or risks which give rise to the exception. In other words, the employer is *not* liable where the contractor's negligence pertains to or creates a risk which is collateral—not one of those inherent and foreseeable in the dangerous activity which creates the employer's liability. For example, there may be vicarious liability for physical harm caused when a bricklayer negligently drops a brick onto a passerby or negligently constructs a wall, but not where he negligently drives a truck en route to the brickyard.

Liability to Contractor's Employees. While the general rule seems to be that the employer's liability under these exceptions extends to injured employees of the contractor, there is a view which holds that the employer is not liable for injuries to the contractor's employees where the injuries arose out of those risks created by the conditions upon which the contractor was hired to work. In other words, suppose a contractor is hired to demolish an antiquated building (inherently dangerous work) and due to his failure to furnish certain safety equipment one of his employees is injured. There are those who would say that since the contractor is hired because of his (and his employee's) expertise in handling these risks, an owner, while perhaps liable to third persons who are strangers to the work, ought not to be liable to the contractor's own employees for injuries resulting from the very risks for which the contractor's expertise was sought.

Where the employer's liability is solely vicarious (as under the "nondelegable duty" and "inherently dangerous work" exceptions), an interesting and unresolved question is whether the contractor's immunity from tort liability to his own employee under the workmen's compensation act would inure to the benefit of the employer of the contractor.

§ 8—13. Employer's Liability to Employee; Workmen's Compensation

As commerce and industry flourished during the late nineteenth and early twentieth centuries, injuries to workers proliferated and became a major social problem.

In theory, if the accident was due to the employer's fault, the employee had his common law negligence action against his employer. But in practice, only a minor fraction of industrial injuries were compensated; limitations on the employer's duty and potent defenses often created insurmountable barriers to the employee's recovery.

In essence, the employer's basic common law duty is to exercise reasonable care to provide his employee with reasonably safe working conditions, and to warn of unsafe conditions which he should anticipate will not be discovered by the employee. It is analogous to the duty of a land owner or occupier to business invitees. Broken down into more specific components, this duty would include (1) a duty to provide safe premises, tools, equipment, structures, appliances and instrumentalities for the work; (2) a duty to provide a sufficient number of competent fellow servants so as not to create an unreasonable danger; (3) a duty to promulgate and enforce plans and rules for the conduct of the work and of the employees so as to make the work safe; (4) a duty to provide adequate supervision; (5) a duty

[*287*]

to properly instruct the employee and to give him suitable work; and (6) so on. See Restatement (Second) Agency §§ 492–520.

But even if it can be proved that the employer breached this duty (and such proof is often not easy, since ordinarily the other witnesses to the occurrence will be co-employees), the employer must circumvent the so-called "unholy trinity" of defenses—the fellow servant rule, contributory negligence, and assumption of risk.

The scope of the employer's liability is greatly constricted by the so-called "fellow servant" rule, which is both a duty limitation and a defense. Generally, the employer is not vicariously liable for an injury to an employee caused solely by the negligence of a fellow servant in the performance of the operative details of the work. The distinction is this. To the extent that a fellow servant is charged with responsibility to perform some part of the employer's duty to provide a safe place to work, the employer will be vicariously liable for that servant's negligence in executing that responsibility. It is sometimes said that the employer's duty to provide a safe place to work is nondelegable, and therefore he is vicariously liable for the negligence of anyone—employee or independent contractor—engaged to perform that duty on his behalf. Such an employee is sometimes called a "vice-principal," but this term is a little misleading since it does not matter whether the employee is superior or subordinate to the plaintiff. But when the fellow servant is doing work which is *not* in furtherance of the employer's duty to provide a safe place to work but rather is engaged in performing the "operative details" of the work of the enterprise (the ordinary tasks of production), the employer is not vicariously liable for his negligence which results in injury to plaintiff, a fellow employee. Thus, an employer may be liable for the negligent repair of a machine but not for its negligent operation.

In addition, the employer's defenses include contributory negligence and assumption of the risk. The usual rules of contributory negligence apply, even though they are especially inappropriate to a work environment, so that the employee's momentary lapse of care will bar or mitigate the employee's recovery despite the employer's continuing and greater negligence. And the employee is held to assume the risk of even negligently-created unsafe conditions of which he is (or is presumed to be) aware when he enters upon or continues his employment, even though under protest or economic duress. See § 5—5. It was once even held in some states that the employee could assume the risk of his employer's violation of safety statutes passed for his protection.

Decisions in some states limited or abolished these defenses in certain cases. But in general, until recently, these defenses were rather vigorously applied in favor of the employer. The result was that, absent legislation, most victims of

[*289*]

industrial accidents bore the loss themselves as best they could, which was not very well.

During the latter half of the nineteenth century, as industrialization proceeded apace, the pressure to provide compensation for injured workmen grew. In response, a number of states enacted a variety of employer liability statutes. Most retained common law tort principles of liability but limited or abolished some or all of the employer's defenses. Many of these applied exclusively to railroads. Other statutes created safety standards for particular kinds of work (e. g., structural work, mining) and provided the employee with a civil remedy for their violation. Most of these have now been rendered obsolete or have been superseded by workmen's compensation, but occasionally such remedies survive (e.g., the New York and Illinois structural work acts).

Still, at the turn of the century the statutory and common law remedies available to workmen and their survivors were far from adequate, and interest mounted in the enactment of workmen's compensation legislation along the lines of that then being adopted in Europe. It was urged on both humanitarian and economic grounds, as witnessed by the slogan, "the cost of the product should bear the blood of the workman." And it was correctly assumed that such legislation would create much-needed incentives to make greater provision for the safety of workers.

A workmen's compensation act for federal employees was enacted in 1908, followed by the first state statute in New York in 1910. By 1921, most states had such a law, and today all do.

While there are important differences among the various statutes, the basic pattern is similar. Liability is strict. No employer negligence need be shown, and the "unholy trinity" of common law defenses are not available. If a covered employee is injured in a work-related accident, his injury or his death is compensated according to a fixed schedule of benefits, irrespective of anyone's fault or lack thereof. Ordinarily benefits are payable weekly for a fixed number of weeks, and are computed as a percentage of the employee's weekly wages subject to a maximum limit. Compensable injuries usually include temporary and permanent disability (partial or total), fractures, total or partial loss of use of various specified parts of the body, disfigurement, and sometimes other permanent injuries. Death benefits are payable to designated dependents. And the employee is entitled to all necessary medical care. Many occupational diseases are compensated under the act or a related statute.

To obtain compensation, the employee must file his claim with the appropriate administrative agency. Usually an arbitrator initially determines whether the injury is compensable and what the award should be. An administrative board reviews or rehears the case and makes the award, approving, disapproving or modifying the arbitrator's recommendation. Judicial review similar to that afforded other administrative rulings is then available.

Although the overwhelming majority of all employee injuries are compensable under some act, certain coverage issues remain. Due to early doubts about the constitutionality of such legislation (which were reinforced when the first New York act was held unconstitutional in 1911 because it imposed liability without fault), most acts were made wholly or partly elective, the latter making coverage mandatory only in the case of certain specified "hazardous" occupations. Often coverage was not required as to farm or domestic servants, or as to businesses employing less than a certain number of employees. However, no act since New York's first has been held invalid, and today there is little doubt that virtually any required coverage is permissible. Thus, there has been a strong trend to broaden coverage in most states. (Of course, as will be seen in the next two sections, most railroad and maritime employees are beyond the jurisdiction of state compensation legislation.) Even where coverage remains elective, most such employers in fact elect it.

Nearly all statutes require that the injury occur "by accident"; sometimes this is held to exclude damage which develops gradually over a period of time. However, the tendency has been to

give this requirement the broadest possible inter-
pretation, if indeed such injuries are not otherwise compensable under the occupational diseases
act.

The injury must occur "in the course of" the
employment, a concept similar to that discussed
in § 8—11, supra. And the injury must also be
one "arising out of" the employment, which
roughly means that it must have at least some
minimal connection with the risks of the employment.

If for some reason an injured employee is not
within the coverage of a compensation act, then
he may pursue any remedies otherwise available
to him, including his common law negligence action against his employer. But if he is within the
coverage of an act (whether or not his injury is
compensable), workmen's compensation is made
his exclusive remedy against his own employer.
His right to the full common law measure of
damages for his injury has been exchanged for a
reduced but relatively quick and certain compensation. However, he retains the right to bring
any and all actions otherwise available to him
against third persons who may have some common law or statutory liability for his injury. (In
some states this does not include fellow servants,
and in a few jurisdictions any third party who
also happens to be covered by the compensation
act is also immune.) For example, if he is injured by a defective punch press, he may collect

compensation from his employer and then sue the press manufacturer in a products liability action. Of course, if his third party action is successful, his employer is entitled to reimbursement for his compensation payments, and in fact may bring such a third party suit if the employee fails to do so.

§ 8—14. Railroad Employees

If at the time of his work-related injury, an employee is lucky enough to be in the employment of a common carrier by rail, and if his work has a sufficient nexus with interstate commerce (i.e. directly or closely and substantially affects it), he is under the benign protection of a special federal statute: the Federal Employers' Liability Act (45 U.S.C.A. § 51 et seq.).

The Act, adopted in 1908 (a 1906 version was invalid), is based upon the same considerations which were simultaneously generating the pressure which would lead to the widespread enactment of workmen's compensation legislation. But railroading was then a dominant and vital national enterprise, largely interstate in character, and uniquely dangerous and notorious for the carnage visited upon its workers. Thus, there was thought to be a special need for federal legislation directed solely at this industry, and since it predated the general movement to workmen's compensation, the remedy was fashioned by modifying traditional tort law doctrine. (Note that a number of states had enacted employers' liability acts of various types during the preceding fifty years; many of them applied only to railroads.)

In essence, the F.E.L.A. preserves the railroad employee's common law negligence action against his employer while abolishing assumption of risk and the fellow servant rule as defenses. His contributory negligence is not a complete bar to his recovery; the pure form of comparative negligence is applied. Damages are computed in accordance with the usual common law rules.

One might speculate that the burden of proving the railroad's negligence would reduce the remedy's effectiveness and leave a number of injured workers uncompensated. But, in keeping with the strong trend of the courts (particularly during recent years) to favor a compensation-oriented approach to the law of work-related injuries, special negligence rules have evolved. Following a series of cases in which the plaintiff's case was allowed to go to the jury even though evidence of negligence was weak, the Supreme Court in Rogers v. Missouri Pac. R. R. (1957) declared that:

> Under this statute the test of a jury case is simply whether the proofs justify with reason the conclusion that employer negligence played *any part, even the slightest,* in producing the injury or death for which damages are sought. [Emphasis added.]

Thus, proof of only a very slight departure from ordinary care, or entirely circumstantial and somewhat speculative evidence of causation, will support a jury's verdict for plaintiff, even though in an ordinary (non-F.E.L.A.) negligence case the same evidence would require a directed verdict for defendant.

The Act preempts the employee's resort to any state law remedies which he might otherwise have had *against his employer*.

Certain statutes, notably the Federal Safety Appliance Act and the Boiler Inspection Act, impose absolute requirements with respect to certain parts of the train—locomotive tender, brakes, automatic couplers, grab irons, sill steps, ladders, running boards, etc. See 45 U.S.C.A. §§ 1–34. If the employee (or for that matter anyone else) is injured as a result of a violation of one of these statutory requirements, the railroad is strictly liable. Plaintiff need not prove that the violation was negligent, and his contributory negligence is no defense and does not mitigate his damages.

There has been a good deal of discussion, pro and con, as to whether F.E.L.A. is an effective remedy and whether railroaders and seamen (see § 8—15, infra) should be singled out to receive its benefits (or be burdened with it, depending on one's viewpoint). However, such workers have generally resisted any efforts to shift them to a system of workmen's compensation and thus appear reasonably satisfied with the present system.

§ 8—15. Maritime Employees

The maritime employee is in a class by himself because he is usually subject to the federal law of admiralty, a separate body of law with roots deep in the history and tradition of the law of the sea.

In general, if the employee is within federal maritime jurisdiction, the remedies for his work-related injuries or death are provided for by federal maritime law (including common law and statutory rules) which preempts pro tanto all state tort law. For this purpose, federal maritime jurisdiction includes all injuries or deaths occurring on board a vessel or caused by a vessel in navigable waters, as well as injuries occurring ashore which have some appropriate nexus to a vessel in navigable waters.

"Navigable waters" is a term of art which roughly means all waterways, including those inland, navigable in fact, which will support interstate or foreign commerce, either themselves or by connection with other waters.

A "vessel" is any floating structure capable of transporting something over the water.

There are two principal classes of maritime employees.

(1) *Seamen.* A seaman is a more or less permanent member of the ship's company (master, officer, or crewman) of a ship which is "in navigation," that is, capable of operation as a vessel (as opposed, e.g., to a floating restaurant which cannot leave the pier by itself).

(2) *Harbor workers* are all those (excluding seamen) who service the ship, such as longshoremen and maintenance and repair personnel, whether on board or dockside, and whether employed by the ship or by an independent contractor.

Very briefly, the principal remedies available to maritime workers include:

Maintenance and Cure. Any seaman who falls ill or is injured while in the service of his ship (whether on board or ashore and whether or not then actively engaged in the performance of his duties) is entitled to "maintenance and cure," an ancient form of workmen's compensation which consists of wages to the end of the voyage (or other period of time for which he signed on) and subsistence, lodging and care until he reaches the maximum cure attainable. Liability is absolute, irrespective of anyone's fault or lack thereof, except that he may not recover for certain injuries caused by his own wilful misconduct.

Seaworthiness. A *seaman* has a common law tort action against the ship or its owner for injuries caused by its being "unseaworthy." Traditionally, this form of strict liability involved a nondelegable duty to keep the ship and its appurtenances in good working order, and to supply sufficient proper and non-defective tools and equipment. But the concept has been broadened to include a duty to employ a sufficient and reasonably competent crew, and even to transitory unsafe conditions, such as an oil slick on the deck or the misfeasance of other ship personnel. Thus, it now amounts to a warranty of the fitness of the ship, its appurtenances and crew, irrespective of anyone's negligence and of the exercise of reasonable care by the other seamen on board. It is, therefore, a very potent remedy, particularly since the usual common law measure of damages applies.

Until Congress took it away from them in 1972, this remedy had been judicially extended to most harbor workers on the ingenious theory that they were doing work which seamen had historically done.

Jones Act (Negligence). The seaman's common law negligence action against his own employer was subject to the same limitations and inadequacies that had prompted workmen's compensation legislation and F.E.L.A. The seamen persuaded Congress to give them the latter, and in 1920 the Jones Act (46 U.S.C.A. § 688) extended the benefits of F.E.L.A. to seamen by merely incorporating most of its operative provisions by reference.

Defenses. The obligation for maintenance and cure is absolute (except for certain injuries caused by the seaman's own wilful misconduct). As to unseaworthiness and the Jones Act, the traditional maritime rule of pure comparative negligence is applied, and assumption of the risk is no defense except to the extent that it also constitutes contributory negligence and accordingly mitigates the award; the fellow servant defense is also unavailable.

Concurrence of Remedies. Maintenance and cure, unseaworthiness and the Jones Act are concurrent remedies, and the seaman (depending on which court he selects) may sue his employer for all three in the same lawsuit. Of course, these remedies are not cumulative; there is considerable overlap in the measure of damages and no double recovery is permitted. In addition, if his injury was caused in whole or in part by the fault of some third person, he may bring any tort action otherwise available to him against that third person, often in the same lawsuit, again with the proviso against double recovery.

Harbor Workers. If a harbor worker's work brings him within the scope of federal maritime jurisdiction, he is for that reason beyond the reach of state workmen's compensation laws. Not being a seaman, he does not receive maintenance and cure. And his common law negligence action against his own employer is subject to the same difficulties previously discussed (§ 8—13).

However, for some reason the harbor workers never persuaded Congress to bring them under the Jones Act, although clearly it could have done so. It opted instead for workmen's compensation and twice attempted to bestow upon the harbor worker the benefits of the appropriate state compensation law. The Supreme Court scotched both attempts as unlawful delegations of federal power to the states. When the Court in 1926 held that a harbor worker could be a "seaman" under the Jones Act, Congress got busy and in 1927 enacted the Longshoremen's and Harbor Workers' Compensation Act (33 U.S.C.A. §§ 901 et seq.). It is similar to the state compensation acts, and in fact was patterned after the then New York Act. It compensates work-related injuries or deaths of most harbor workers within the scope of maritime jurisdiction, *except* where the work is deemed "local" in nature—that is, only incidental to navigation and commerce. In such cases, the appropriate state's compensation act applies, if the worker is otherwise covered by such an act. If the work falls within what is called the "twilight zone" where it cannot be determined in advance of trial whether or not the work is local in nature, the worker may choose either state or federal compensation.

Compensation under the Act is the exclusive remedy against the harbor worker's employer (be he ship owner or independent contractor), but does not bar any tort actions otherwise available against third persons, such as a common law negligence (but *not,* recall, Jones Act or unseaworthiness) action against a ship owner not his employer, or a products liability case. In such actions, if the harbor worker is within the scope of maritime jurisdiction, any appropriate admiralty law rules (e.g. comparative negligence) will apply to such third party suits.

Limitation of Liability. By statute (46 U.S.C.A. §§ 181–189), a shipowner may in certain cases limit his maximum *personal* liability for injury or death to the value of the vessel after the occurrence (but not less than $60 per ton), if he was without "privity or knowledge" of the cause of the loss. Generally, this means that he was without personal fault in the matter and had no prior knowledge of the situation or condition which caused the injury.

D. AUTOMOBILES

§ 8—16. Special Automobile Liability Rules

Automobile accidents are another important social problem, and it is not surprising that there are some special tort law rules applicable to this activity. For the most part, such rules' main purpose is to insure a financially responsible defendant so that plaintiff's loss will be compensated. They developed at a time when automobile liability insurance was not so prevalent nor so broad in coverage as it is today, and thus they are not nearly so important now as they once were. In particular, they have been rendered largely unnecessary by the advent of the so-called "omnibus clause" in most policies which makes anyone driving the auto with the insured's permission an additional insured. Nevertheless, they remain a part of the fabric of our tort law, and therefore must be noted. And in some cases they will provide an additional defendant whose own insurance policy may be "stacked" on top of the driver's policy to increase the available limits.

Joint Enterprise. As previously noted (§§ 8—10 and 8—11), partners and the principals in a joint venture are vicariously liable to third persons for each other's negligence within the scope of the business activity. The doctrine of joint enterprise is a unique creation of American courts by which, under analogous circumstances, the same principle is extended to the operation of an automobile, so that all participants are vicariously liable to third persons for the negligence of the driver.

Basically, a joint enterprise is founded upon an express or implied agreement among two or more persons to use an automobile for a common purpose, with all participants having a mutual right of direction and control over its operation. At one time, some courts held that *any* common purpose was sufficient; but today, most require some business, financial or pecuniary interest in the objective of the journey. The mutual right of control requires that all have an equal voice; thus, there will usually be no joint enterprise when an employee is riding with his employer, even though for a common business purpose. Even joint ownership or possession of the vehicle, or the sharing of the driving or expenses, are ordinarily not conclusive proof of the mutual right of control, although they may be some evidence of that right. In the final analysis, it is the express or implied understanding of the parties which is determinative, which is of course a question of fact for the jury.

Owner-Passenger. At one time, some courts held that an automobile owner who was a passenger in his own car was *vicariously* liable for the negligence of the driver on the theory that by virtue of his ownership alone he had the right to exercise control over the driving. Most courts, however, went no further than to create a rebuttable presumption that the driver is the agent of the owner-passenger. Of course, an owner-passenger who *in fact* retains the right to control the operation of the auto is *personally*—not vicariously—liable for his negligence in the exercise of that control.

Owner Not a Passenger. In the absence of a statute or the family purpose doctrine, an owner-bailor who merely permits another to use his automobile is not vicariously liable for the driver's negligence unless the driver was then his agent acting within the scope of his employment. (In most jurisdictions there is a rebuttable presumption that such an agency exists.) The single exception is Florida, which has declared an automobile to be a "dangerous instrumentality" and thus the owner is vicariously liable when it is negligently operated by another.

Family Purpose Doctrine. About half the states have accepted the "family purpose doctrine," under which the owner of an auto which he makes generally available for personal (noncommercial) use by members of his immediate household is vicariously liable for its negligent operation by such persons within the scope of the express or implied permission. In effect, the family unit is treated as a "business," and a member of that unit who uses the vehicle within the scope of that "business" subjects its owner to vicarious liability as if he were the owner's agent.

Consent Statutes. About one-fourth of the states have a form of statutory vicarious liability making the owner of an automobile vicariously liable for the negligence of anyone operating it on a public highway with the owner's consent, within the scope of the express or implied permission.

Imputed Contributory Negligence. The foregoing rules were designed for the protection of third persons injured by the driver's negligence. An interesting question often arises as to whether these various vicarious liability rules may be used in reverse, imputing the driver's negligence to the owner or other principal so as to bar his recovery under the rule of contributory negligence for harm he himself sustains as a result of the driver's negligence. As a matter of principle the answer should be no, but courts have sometimes held otherwise. See § 5—2, supra.

Guest Passengers. Guest passengers in an automobile have a status which was once thought to be analogous to that of a licensee upon real property. Based on this idea, statutes in about half the states (and judicial decisions in a few others) have limited the auto owner's or driver's duty to guest passengers.

The statutes generally restrict liability to cases where the driver's conduct was reckless ("wilful and wanton misconduct") or where the injury was caused by the driver's intoxication. Absent such a statute, some jurisdictions, by judicial decision, hold the driver liable for his negligent operation of the car and for harm caused by known defects, but not for injuries caused by defects in the vehicle of which the driver has no knowledge; the guest is said to "assume the risk" of such defects, and the owner or driver has no duty to him to inspect and discover them. Occasional cases and statutes, by analogy to the law of bailments, limited liability to the driver's "gross" negligence.

The difficult problem, of course, is to determine when the passenger is a "guest." Generally, he is not only if there is some direct or indirect pecuniary benefit to the host, as where the passenger pays for the ride or where some business interest of the host is being served by the passenger's presence (e. g. he is a prospective customer). Sharing the expenses of the trip may be sufficient, at least if agreed upon in advance (as opposed to the passenger, as a matter of courtesy, merely insisting upon paying for a tank of gasoline). Usually an owner cannot be a guest in his own car, nor can a child too young to understand his status be a guest. And a guest ceases to be such when his demand to be allowed to leave the vehicle is refused.

The guest statutes were passed largely at the urging of insurance companies who feared collusive lawsuits. Increasingly the possibility of fraud is seen as greatly outweighed by the injustice of arbitrarily denying legitimate claims, and there is a stong trend away from such statutes and similar court-made limitations on the host's duty. Some guest statutes have recently been repealed, and others, following the lead of California in Brown v. Merlo (Cal.1973) have been declared unconstitutional as arbitrary denials of the equal protection of the laws. E. g., Primes v. Tyler (Ohio 1975); Manistee Bank & Tr. Co. v. McGowan (Mich.1975); McGeehan v. Bunch (N. Mex.1975). But there are recent decisions upholding them. E.g., Sidle v. Majors (Ind.1976).

§ 8—17. Automobile Accident Compensation

Motor vehicle traffic ranks high as a major source of injuries and deaths in this country, and indeed in all prosperous countries. Until very recently, tort law, as enforced through the litigation process, has had to shoulder a large share of the responsibility for compensating traffic accident victims in order to reduce the economic disruption which these losses cause.

From the advent of the automobile, there have been those who have suggested that the costs of the inevitable traffic accidents should be shared by all those who engage in the activity. If one accepts this premise—and the number who do are steadily increasing—then it is immediately obvious that there are much better and more efficient mechanisms for accomplishing this than the traditional tort litigation process. Indeed, recalling our discussion of the functions of tort law (§ 1—2), we saw that it was never intended to compensate every injured plaintiff; for the most part, it is designed to shift the loss from a more or less innocent plaintiff to a defendant who was somehow at fault in causing plaintiff's injury. Thus, tort law requires a fairly elaborate litigation process in order to determine fault and whether plaintiff is or is not entitled to compensation—in other words, whether he *qualifies* to have the law command another to reimburse him for his losses. Today, many want to abolish fault as a necessary qualification for compensation— and thereby eliminate the need for litigation to assess fault—and simply compensate all who are injured for at least their basic economic losses and distribute these costs more or less evenly among all who own or operate motor vehicles as a part of the price of ownership or operation.

Clearly, the widespread acceptance of automobile liability insurance was an important intermediate step in the retreat from the fault ethic. Since most defendants are insured, the losses of those plaintiffs who *are* compensated are in fact already being spread among the motoring public as a group. The impact of liability on any one defendant is slight, consisting at most of a manageable increase in his insurance rates. Thus, as to each motorist, we have assessed as a cost of his driving not the full cost of his *individual* fault, but merely his proportionate share of the total fault of the *entire group* (insured motorists). Having divorced individual fault from personal liability as to *defendants,* it now seems somewhat arbitrary and unjust to require a *plaintiff* to establish an individual defendant's fault in order to qualify for a share in the common compensation fund.

Those who favor some sort of "no-fault" compensation system for traffic accident victims have supported their view in large part by leveling a number of criticisms at the existing tort-litigation system. In essence, these criticisms may be grouped as follows:

(1) *Not all traffic victims are compensated and those who are, are frequently over- or undercompensated.* This is certainly true. Of course, in some cases compensation is reduced or denied because the victim was contributorily negligent, or denied because defendant was not negligent. Those who support the fault requirement would not consider this a defect in the present system.

However, there are other reasons why some plaintiffs receive too little or too much. Some defendants are uninsured or underinsured. Insurance policy defenses occasionally permit the insurer to escape liability for plaintiff's judgment.

Some needy plaintiffs are forced to settle too cheaply. Juries, for reasons which may or may not be apparent, sometimes return excessive or inadequate verdicts. Lawyers' fees and costs reduce most awards, but benefits paid from collateral sources (e.g., health, accident and disability insurance, wage continuation plans) do not. Damages for lost income are not taxable. Large verdicts for punitive damages or noneconomic losses (e.g. pain and suffering, humiliation) may amount to a windfall. But damage awards, when finally received, are paid in a lump sum (instead of periodically as required to replace lost income or future medical expenses) which too often is quickly dissipated.

Many of these problems, and particularly those involving insurance, could be solved through modifications of the existing system. For example, about one-fourth of the states require *all* drivers to have liability insurance, and a few states have an unsatisfied judgments fund. More could. Most states have one or the other of the two types of financial responsibility laws which require either (a) one involved in an accident which injures another or (b) one who has an unsatisfied judgment against him resulting from such an accident, to furnish proof that he can satisfy claims arising from *future* accidents up to some relatively modest amount. (They are notoriously ineffective, except as an inducement to purchase minimal insurance.) Insurance against injuries caused by an uninsured motorist is generally available, but of course it pays only when it can be proved that the uninsured motorist was negligent.

Nevertheless, potential reforms of the *liability* insurance system do not meet the basic criticism that liability ought not to be required as a condition of compensation in the first place.

(2) *"Fault" is difficult and uncertain of proof, or else is easy to falsify.* To some extent this is true of every injury claim, including those not arising from a traffic accident. But certainly it is especially true of many vehicular accidents, where usually little tangible evidence of any value is available and the claim must be proved or disproved by the oral testimony of witnesses (the most important of whom are interested in the outcome) based on their memory of events which occurred during a traumatic few seconds, months or years earlier.

(3) *Litigation is too slow, cumbersome, involved, elaborate, costly, and wasteful of precious resources, especially as to relatively small claims.* The preparation and trial of a lawsuit certainly can be a time- and resource-consuming process, involving investigation, pre-trial discovery (interrogatories, depositions, etc.), preparation of exhibits and witnesses, and the trial itself, which even in the simple case requires a number of hours of the time of lawyers, a judge and other court personnel, jurors, witnesses, and various other supporting staff. Cases usually take up to

a year to prepare for trial, and delays of several years are not uncommon on metropolitan dockets; meanwhile the victims do without. And while the overwhelming majority of such cases are settled without trial, most are not settled until at least the fact-gathering process is complete, many not until suit is filed, and some not until the eve of trial is reached. Lawyers' fees and other costs are high. According to some studies, only about forty-four cents of every auto insurance premium dollar reaches the victim's pocket; the remainder pays for the cost of operating the compensation system, not counting the public funds which support the court, its personnel and facilities.

Nevertheless, it is no indictment of the litigation process merely to say that it is costly and time-consuming, and does not invariably reach the ideal result. One must ask (1) does it do substantial justice, and (2) is it worth the cost—that is, are sufficient benefits received in return or are community values sufficiently realized to justify the time, money and effort expended in the process.

So far as the automobile accident case is concerned, fairminded persons can and do differ in their answers to these questions. Most trial lawyers are of the opinion that the present negligence litigation system can be modified so that it will produce substantial justice. Reforms suggested by plaintiffs' lawyers include universal adoption of comparative negligence, compulsory auto liability insurance with realistically high mandatory limits (or no limits), compulsory "medical payments" coverage expanded to include some payment for disability, expanded court facilities, and better unsatisfied judgments funds. Lawyers who customarily represent defendants (i.e. insurers) would regulate the contingent fee, abolish the "collateral source" rule and require plaintiffs to credit their judgments with medical and disability benefits received from other sources, regulate compensation for pain and suffering, provide for arbitration of small claims, and punish fraudulent claims.

Critics of the present system charge that trial lawyers' opinions are consciously or unconsciously biased by their obvious self-interest. In their view, no amount of tinkering with the present system will remedy its inadequacies. The fault requirement will still produce erratic and inconsistent results; dishonest plaintiffs will too often prevail and honest ones suffer; costly and painful delays will still occur; and too many victims who are no less deserving of compensation than the successful plaintiffs will get nothing at all. And they believe that the litigation process is an expensive luxury which the American motorist can no longer afford, especially since it does not operate to sort out deserving and undeserving claimants.

Out of the heated debate which has raged over these issues a compromise consensus seems to be emerging. Compensate *all* victims' basic economic losses—medical and hospital expenses, and lost wages or services—and thereby eliminate the small cases where the litigation process is most inefficient; and preserve the tort claim (based on fault) for the more serious injuries, which are a small fraction of the total number of cases.

A variety of "no-fault" auto compensation plans, too numerous to catalog here, have been put forth. Most prominent among them are the Columbia (University) Plan (1932), the Saskatchewan Plan (1946), Prof. Ehrenzweig's "Full Aid" Plan (1954), Prof. Conard's "social insurance" plan (1964), and the well-known Keeton-O'Connell Plan (1965). These have spawned countless other plans, all variations on the same basic themes, some of which have reached the legislative arena. Accurate generalization is difficult, but the various plans have some common features.

(1) *No-fault compensation.* The heart of all plans is some form of compensation for personal injuries and deaths which is paid to all victims of automobile accidents, irrespective of fault. Most are funded by private first-party insurance—that is, the benefits are paid to the victim by his own insurer, as opposed to third-party or liability insurance where the victim is paid by the insurer of the person (other than himself) who was re-

sponsible for the accident. In this respect it is similar in form to other kinds of health or accident insurance, and to the optional "medical payments" coverage commonly offered with most present auto liability policies. Under a few of the plans, none of which have so far been adopted in this country (except in Puerto Rico), the government collects and administers the compensation fund. (Occasional proposals call for financing through the social security system or even general tax revenues. But unless financed by a tax on motorists, such a system is subject to the criticism that the activity [automobile traffic] does not bear the costs it generates.)

Under almost all plans, a certain basic coverage is mandatory. One cannot register or operate an automobile without it.

Benefits usually include medical, hospital and funeral expenses, lost wages, physical rehabilitation and (in the case of victims who are not wage earners) the cost of replacing his or her domestic services, all subject under most plans to maximum limits, either on each category of benefits or on total benefits. Occasionally benefits of a certain type are unlimited, as in the case of medical expenses in New Jersey and Pennsylvania.

Sometimes optional broader coverages are available, including damages for noneconomic losses (e.g. pain and suffering).

Under some plans, the benefits payable must be credited with reimbursement received from other sources, such as other medical or disability insurance, social security, workmen's compensation, etc.

(2) *Tort liability.* It is generally recognized that the cost of no-fault compensation would be prohibitive, absent an offsetting decrease in the frequency of liability claims under the tort system.   There are two schools of thought on the best method of achieving this.

(a) Most plans expressly abolish the tort cause of action, making the no-fault compensation the exclusive remedy, to the extent that the loss does not exceed a certain minimum or "threshold" level.   Under these plans, typically there is no tort remedy unless the victim's medical (or other) expenses exceed a certain dollar amount, or unless the injury sustained is one of those expressly designated as "serious," such as death, dismemberment, permanent disfigurement or impairment of some part of the body, fractures, and the like.   Under the Keeton-O'Connell Plan, tort liability is abrogated unless the compensable economic loss exceeds $10,000 or pain and suffering damages exceed $5,000 in value.

(b) Some plans contain no prohibition of tort litigation.   Their premise is that since plaintiff's insurer who has paid no-fault benefits must be reimbursed from the proceeds of any tort recovery obtained from a third party tortfeasor, those with small claims will usually be discouraged from pursuing them because they stand to gain too little. Perhaps more importantly, few lawyers would find it economically feasible to handle such claims. Proponents of this alternative believe that the savings thus achieved on liability insurance costs will more or less offset the increased cost of no-fault compensation, while preserving maximum individual freedom to resort to the tort system for those who feel strongly enough that they want to do so.

Much of the controversy between the proponents and opponents of no-fault compensation has centered around its costs. Under either of the foregoing systems, will insurance rates increase, and if so how much? Estimates vary widely. Actuarial predictions are notoriously unreliable when they depend upon predicting human behavior under new and untried circumstances. Now that a number of states have enacted no-fault legislation, accurate data should soon be available, but preliminary statistics are inconclusive.

Not counting Puerto Rico (1968), the first American state to enact a no-fault compensation plan was Massachusetts, effective January 1, 1971. Today, about half the states have such laws, although there are vast differences among them.

No-fault auto compensation legislation was first introduced in Congress in 1971. Originally conceived as a comprehensive national uniform plan, it did not pass in that form and so it evolved into the "National Standards For No-Fault Insurance

Plans Act." This bill would have permitted the various states to enact their own versions of compulsory no-fault plans, except that state laws would be required to meet or exceed the standards set forth in some detail in the federal act as to coverages, benefits, exclusions, and limitations on tort liability. In any state whose law did not meet the federal standards (or which failed to pass any law), an even stronger federal no-fault compensation act would automatically have taken effect. Opponents of the bill argued that the states were in fact passing various forms of no-fault legislation, and that they should be permitted to continue to do so; that the subject is complex with many variables, the idea is largely untried, and thus state-by-state experimentation ought to be encouraged. The opponents prevailed, and the act failed to pass in 1976. It would appear that at least for the time being, there will be no federal legislation in this area.

Some (but not all) of the arguments in favor of no-fault compensation for victims of auto accidents also apply to those injured in other ways. Thus, no-fault compensation systems have been proposed which would partly or totally replace the traditional tort remedies in areas such as products liability, medical malpractice, and premises liability, ultimately extending perhaps to all accidental injuries and deaths. See, e.g., J. O'Connell, Ending Insult to Injury: No-Fault Insurance for Products and Services (1975);

Franklin, Replacing the Negligence Lottery: Compensation and Selective Reimbursement, 53 Va.L.Rev. 774 (1967). Such proposals face even stiffer opposition than has no-fault auto insurance, and bring into sharp focus both jurisprudential and empirical questions about the functions and operation of the tort-litigation system. All that is certain is that vigorous and healthy debate will continue over these matters for some time to come.

E.   OTHER SPECIAL LIABILITY RULES

§ 8—18.   Nuisance and Environmental Law

"Nuisance" is one of those amorphous concepts in the law which cannot be concisely defined and is often misunderstood and misused. At one time or another, it has, as Prosser says, "meant all things to all men." The principal sources of confusion are (1) a tendency toward indiscriminate use of the term and (2) a failure to recognize and to focus upon the fact that it is in essence merely a form of action for particular kinds of *harm* with special rules as to when and how that harm may be redressed. It is the interest of plaintiff which has been invaded, and not the conduct of the defendant, which determines whether an action for nuisance will lie. Liability for interference with such a protected interest may be based upon defendant's intent to so interfere, negligence, strict liability for abnormally dangerous activities, or occasionally upon violation of a statute. But the character of defendant's activity or conduct is irrelevant in distinguishing nuisance from other torts; it is the nature of the harm to plaintiff to which one must look. Indeed, strictly speaking, nuisance may not be a tort at all, but merely a category of certain types of harm. Unfortunately, there are a number of cases in which the term "nuisance" is used improperly and unnecessarily, as where plaintiff is actually being (or ought to be) permitted to recover under some other tort theory.

To understand nuisance at all, it is essential to bear in mind the distinction between *public nuisance* and *private nuisance*.

Private Nuisance. Properly conceived, a private nuisance is a thing or activity which substantially and unreasonably interferes with the possessor's *use and enjoyment* of his land or an interest therein.

This interference may occur in an infinite variety of ways. For example, there may be a physical effect upon the land itself, such as by vibration, objects hurled upon it, destruction of crops, flooding, or pollution of its water or soil. Or it may consist of a disturbance of the comfort, convenience or health of the occupant, as by foul odors, smoke, dust, insects, noxious gases, excessive noise, excessive light or high temperatures, and even repeated telephone calls. Under proper circumstances it may even extend to conditions on adjoining land which impair the plaintiff's mental tranquility by the fear or offensive nature

of their mere presence, such as a house of ill re-
pute, a contagious disease hospital, stored explosives, or a vicious animal.

The important thing to remember is that the
interference must be with the *use and enjoyment*
of plaintiff's interest in *land*.   Similar interferences which affect plaintiff only personally, and
do not affect his use and enjoyment of his land,
may be some other tort but they are not a private nuisance.

It will be seen that there are situations in
which nuisance will be a concurrent remedy with
trespass to land, which, recall (§ 6—7), protects
one's right to exclusive possession against physical invasions.   An interference with that right
frequently will also be an interference with the
use and enjoyment of the land.   At one time, a
trespass had to be direct; if defendant merely set
forces in motion which eventually resulted in an
invasion of the land, the remedy (if any) was in
nuisance.   And trespass could not be maintained
for invasions of air-borne gases and particles not
visible to the naked eye.   On the other hand, nuisance, a form of the action of case, required proof
of fault and actual damages; trespass did not.   In
its modern form, trespass requires proof of fault,
but may be direct or indirect, and it has been
held that microscopic particles wafted on the
breeze may constitute a trespass.   Thus, trespass
and nuisance are now more often concurrent remedies than in earlier times.

Public Nuisance. A public nuisance is so different from a private one that it is unfortunate that the term "nuisance" is applied to both. Public and private nuisance are separate and distinct wrongs which developed independently. The area of overlap between them is not very great, and is largely accidental.

A public nuisance is an act or omission which obstructs or causes inconvenience or damage to the public in the exercise of rights common to all. It is fundamentally a catch-all collection of minor crimes, originally common law and now largely legislative in origin, to be redressed by criminal prosecution. "It includes interferences with the public health, as in the case of a hogpen, the keeping of diseased animals, or a malarial pond; with the public safety, as in the case of the storage of explosives, the shooting of fireworks in the streets, harboring a vicious dog, or the practice of medicine by one not qualified; with public morals, as in the case of houses of prostitution, illegal liquor establishments, gambling houses, indecent exhibitions, bullfights, unlicensed prize fights, or public profanity; with the public peace, as by loud and disturbing noises, or an opera performance which threatens to cause a riot; with the public comfort, as in the case of bad odors, smoke, dust and vibration; with public convenience, as by obstructing a highway or a navigable stream, or creating a condition which makes travel unsafe or highly disagreeable, or the collection of an inconvenient crowd; and in addition, such unclassified offenses as eavesdropping on a jury, or being a common scold." Prosser, § 88.

The interest or right which is interfered with must be one which is common to the *public* as a *class,* and not merely that of one person or even a group of citizens (except by statute in a few states where interference with the rights of a substantial number of persons is sufficient, even though no public right as such is involved). The pollution of a river is only a private nuisance insofar as it interferes with the rights of the riparian owners to make use of the water; but if it also kills the fish or impairs a public water supply it is to that extent a public nuisance.

In addition to broad, general criminal public nuisance statutes, all states have a number of specific provisions declaring certain things (e.g., bawdy houses, certain plants, houses where narcotics are sold, mosquito breeding grounds) to be public nuisances.

A private citizen has no civil remedy for the harm he has sustained as a result of a public nuisance if that harm is of the same kind as that suffered by the general public, even though he may have been harmed to a greater degree than others. A criminal prosecution is the exclusive remedy. But an individual who has sustained damage particular to him, different in kind from that of the public, may maintain a tort action for his damages. Thus, where dynamiting has thrown a large boulder onto a public highway, members of the public who use the highway (even those who use it much more frequently than most) have no action for the inconvenience caused by the obstruction. But a motorist who collides with the boulder has sustained damage of a kind different from that of the general public, and so may sue for his personal injuries.

Where a public nuisance interferes with plaintiff's use and enjoyment of his land, it is a private nuisance as well. And since this injury is particular to him and different in kind from that suffered by the public, he may sue for his damages under either theory. Usually it is preferable to rely on the public nuisance theory, since in such cases certain defenses (prescriptive rights, laches, statute of limitations) are not available.

Basis of Liability: Fault. Notwithstanding some early cases to the contrary, nuisance liability is not absolute. Absent a statute, defendant's interference with plaintiff's protected interest must have been intentional, reckless, negligent, or the result of an abnormally dangerous activity (see § 3—3) such that principles of strict liability will apply. The requisite intent, if that is the theory of liability, is similar to that of other intentional torts (see § 6—1), and it is sufficient if defendant created the condition or continued his conduct after he acquired knowledge of actual harm, or a substantial certainty of future harm, to plaintiff's interest.

Thus, attempts which some have undertaken to distinguish nuisance from, for example, negligence liability reflect a fundamental misconception. Nuisance is a type of harm; negligence is one basis on which liability for that harm may be imposed.

In addition, nuisance liability may be based upon violation of a statute, and in such cases (within constitutional limits) there will be no need to find fault or some other basis beyond the requirements of the statute to support nuisance liability.

Basis of Liability: Substantial Interference. Nuisance liability requires some substantial interference with the interest involved. Where the physical condition of property is affected, it is not too difficult to distinguish the substantial from the insubstantial. This is not always so, however, in cases of personal inconvenience, annoyance, or discomfort. Generally, the standard is that of the ordinary member of that community with normal sensitivity and temperament. Similarly, plaintiff cannot, by devoting his land to an unusually sensitive use, make a nuisance out of conduct on defendant's adjoining premises which would otherwise be relatively harmless. Beyond this, whether or not the harm is substantial is a question of fact.

At one time it was thought that a nuisance did not exist unless the interference was continuing or recurring; a single interference of relatively short duration was not enough. Despite the persistence of occasional pronouncements to this effect, there is no such requirement. However, it is true that certain kinds of interferences are substantial or unreasonable only because they are continuing or recurring. And where an injunction is sought, it is obviously necessary that there be a threat of future harm.

Reasonableness of Defendant's Conduct. Not only must the interference with plaintiff's interest be substantial; it must also be unreasonable to require him to bear it, or to bear it without compensation. This balancing process, weighing the respective interests of plaintiff and defendant, is of course required in any event where the basis of liability is negligence. A similar balancing process is used in determining whether an activity is "abnormally dangerous" such that strict liability is appropriate (see § 3—3). But in the case of a nuisance, it is also a prerequisite to liability for harm which is intentionally inflicted. In effect, defendant has a privilege to cause substantial harm to an interest of the plaintiff which would otherwise be protected by the law of nuisance if, on balance, his conduct is reasonable under all the circumstances.

This reasonableness test may be applied to public nuisances, unless there is a statute which establishes the standard of conduct (i.e., makes something a nuisance per se) and therefore precludes further inquiry into the reasonableness of defendant's activity. But the primary application of the requirement is in cases of private nuisance.

The rationale behind the reasonableness requirement is that in a crowded society, some accommodation to the activities of others is necessary. Some activities are socially useful (particularly those relating to industry, commerce and trade), or at least do not deserve to be prohibited or unduly burdened, and therefore will be tolerated even though they impinge to some extent on others and on the tranquility, comfort, and quiet enjoyment of their land. At the same time, some activities may fairly be required to bear the cost of the harm they cause, where that cost is reasonable under all the circumstances.

The balancing process by which reasonableness is determined is not unlike that used to determine whether conduct is negligent. Essentially, the nature and gravity of the harm is balanced against the burden of preventing it and the utility of the conduct. More specifically, among the many factors which may be relevant are: (1) the extent and duration of the interference; (2) the character of the harm; (3) the social value of plaintiff's use of his land, or other interest invaded; (4) the burden to plaintiff of preventing the harm; (5) the social value of defendant's conduct, both in general and to the particular community; (6) the motive of the defendant; (7) the burden and feasibility of defendant preventing or mitigating the harm; and (8) the nature of the locality and the suitability of the activities or uses of the land being made by defendant and plaintiff. With respect to the latter, the dominant character of a neighborhood or area may be an important factor in determining what activities are reasonable and what a nonconforming plaintiff must reasonably endure—a sort of judicial zoning.

Courts occasionally speak of an "absolute" nuisance. Frequently this means nothing more than that a public nuisance statute has established the standard of conduct and therefore the issue of reasonableness is foreclosed. But once in a while a court will attempt to establish that a particular activity, otherwise lawful, is a nuisance per se, giving rise to liability for any harm it may cause under any and all circumstances. As in the case of most other absolutes in the law, the generalization must sooner or later admit of exceptions in which case it is no longer absolute. Even where strict liability is asserted, a balancing process is required in order to determine whether the activity is so abnormally dangerous that liability may be imposed.

Remedies. The usual private remedy for nuisance is an action for damages. In cases of permanent nuisance (that is, of a type which probably will continue indefinitely), all damages must be obtained in one action. If the nuisance can be abated, plaintiff generally recovers all damages incurred up to the time of the trial. If defendant then fails to abate it (a continuing nuisance), the further invasion of his interest constitutes a new nuisance for which another action may be brought.

In cases of continuing and threatened nuisances, if plaintiff has no adequate remedy at law (which frequently is the case where real property is involved) equitable relief may be sought. When an injunction is requested, the court will undertake a further balancing process, taking into account the relative economic hardships which will result to the parties from the granting or denial of the injunction, as well as the interest of the public in the continuation of the defendant's enterprise. Thus, the court may find defendant's conduct so unreasonable that he must pay damages but not so unreasonable as to justify an injunction, compliance with which might require an unreasonably high expenditure of funds to abate or the ceasing of the activity altogether. Boomer v. Atlantic Cement Co. (N.Y.1970). Cf. Spur Industries, Inc. v. Del E. Webb Development Co. (Ariz.1972) (injunction granted but *plaintiff* must pay *defendant's* cost of abatement.)

In addition, there is a limited self-help privilege to enter upon defendant's land to abate a nuisance. Usually notice to defendant and his refusal to act is first required. Only reasonable force may be used, and plaintiff may be subject to criminal or civil liability for unreasonable or unnecessary damage, personal injuries, or a breach of the peace.

Defenses. Legislation authorizing a particular activity or use of land (e.g. zoning laws, licenses) may be used to establish that it is not a nuisance. Generally, however, the courts have tended to construe narrowly the authority given to include only reasonable conduct.

While it is no defense to an action for nuisance that others are also contributing to the harm, each defendant is ordinarily liable only for the damages which he has caused. However, it is consistently held that a defendant will be liable where his conduct along with the activities of several other persons combine to create a nuisance, even though neither defendant's activity nor that of any of the others, by itself, would have been sufficient.

Contributory negligence, assumption of risk, and the doctrine of avoidable consequences are defenses to the same extent as in other tort actions.

Defendants in nuisance cases have often alleged that plaintiff assumed the risk because he "came to the nuisance" by purchasing and moving to land next to an existing and operating source of interference. The cases generally have not supported this defense, at least where plaintiff purchased the land in good faith and not for purposes of litigation. Absent a prescriptive right, which requires actual harm to the property for a certain period of time, defendant cannot require surrounding land to endure his nuisance—at least not without compensation. A purchaser is entitled to the reasonable use and enjoyment of his property the same as anyone else. Nevertheless, "coming to the nuisance" may be one factor to be considered in determining the reasonableness of defendant's conduct or activity, and also in determining whether plaintiff has suffered damage (since the purchase price of the land may reflect the existence of the nuisance).

Environmental Law. Recent years have witnessed a dramatic awakening of interest in protection of the environment against certain abuses, principally resource depletion and pollution. Pollution frequently causes physical harm, and thus those harmed have looked to tort law—especially the law of nuisance—in their search for legal remedies to combat it.

The nuisance provisions of the new Restatement (Second) Torts have been drafted with a view toward expanding this remedy. In the area of private nuisance, the Restatement now incorporates the concept that the plaintiff may be entitled to compensation (but not to an injunction) for substantial harm intentionally caused, even though on balance the utility of defendant's conduct outweighs the harm to plaintiff, and therefore ordinarily would be considered reasonable and hence not a nuisance. In other words, even socially very useful activities should have to pay (i.e. internalize) the cost of substantial harm they cause their neighbors, and should not have a privilege or license to deposit their wastes (make noise, etc.) upon them without charge. Section 826 now provides that an intentional invasion of another's interest in the use and enjoyment of land is unreasonable if:

(a) the gravity of the harm outweighs the utility of the actor's conduct, or

(b) the harm caused by the conduct is substantial and the financial burden of compensating for this and other harms does not render infeasible the continuation of the conduct.

A new section, 829A, is added to those which spell out specific applications of the balancing test used to determine whether conduct is unreasonable, expressly providing that it is if "the harm resulting from the invasion is substantial and greater than the [plaintiff] should reasonably be required to bear without compensation."

Public nuisance, which was not dealt with in the first Restatement of Torts, has been added to the Second. A proposed definition of a public nuisance as a "criminal" interference with a public right was rejected on the ground that the requirement that the interference be a crime was unnecessary and too restrictive, since it still had to be unreasonable. And the standards for determining whether the interference is unreasonable are broadly stated as follows:

(a) whether the conduct involves a substantial interference with the public health, the public safety, the public peace, the public comfort or the public convenience, or

(b) whether the conduct is proscribed by a statute, ordinance or administrative regulation, or

(c) whether the conduct is of a continuing nature or has produced a permanent or long-lasting effect and, to the actor's knowledge, has a substantial detrimental effect upon the public right. § 821B (2).

With respect to the standing of a private citizen to sue for public nuisance, the new Restatement (Second) preserves, so far as an action for *damages* is concerned, the common law rule that he must have suffered harm of a different kind than that of the public. Any other rule could subject a defendant to an unreasonable burden of multiple suits. But it opens the door to the development of broader standing rules in suits by private citizens to *enjoin* or *abate* a public nuisance. In such cases, § 821C would require only that plaintiff (1) have a cause of action for damages, or (2) have the requisite authority as a public official or public agency, or (3) have "standing to sue as a representative of the general public, as a member of a class in a class action, or as a citizen in a citizen's action." The latter, while not itself providing any standing rules, invites the courts to fashion them as they see fit.

There are by now a large number of environmental protection statutes on the books at both the state and federal level, and many jurisdictions have an environmental protection agency. These statutes may interact with tort law in one of four principal ways:

(1) The statute may, expressly or impliedly, create a private cause of action for damages or an injunction where one would not otherwise exist.

(2) The statute may create standing for other remedies.

(3) The statute (or rules or regulations issued under it) may establish defendant's standards of conduct (e.g., permissible levels of noise or pollution) applicable in a nuisance or other tort action.

(4) The statute may preempt the field and thereby make unavailable (a) common law tort remedies, or (b) in the case of federal legislation, state statutory remedies as well. For example, this has been held to be the effect of federal automobile emission standards.

Water Rights. There are special rules applicable to the tortious interference by one with another's rights with respect to watercourses, lakes, ground and surface waters. See R. §§ 841–864.

§ 8—19. Negligent Infliction of Emotional Distress

As we have already seen (§ 6—5) the common law long refused to recognize a cause of action where the only effect of defendant's wrongful conduct was plaintiff's mental anguish, with or without some resulting physical illness. Various reasons were given—a fear of false claims, the difficulty of measuring damages, lack of precedent, a fear of the proverbial "flood of litigation," and assertions that such harm is too "remote" from the wrongful conduct and that since there can be no recovery for mere fright there can be none for its physical consequences.

The weakness of these reasons is apparent, except perhaps for the first. Spurious claims might indeed be easy to make and hard to disprove, especially where defendant never directed his conduct toward plaintiff, never made contact with him, and might not even have known of plaintiff's presence in the vicinity when he allegedly committed the act for which he is sued.

During the past half century the courts have come to realize that the risk of false claims is not a sufficient reason to deny a cause of action for legitimate ones, and so have begun to carve out exceptions to the general rule of nonliability. Note, however, that a cause of action has been given only in those cases where (1) the circumstances surrounding the actionable event create some inherent assurances of genuineness or (2) the equities favoring liability are strong, or (3) some combination of these two factors is present.

As previously noted (§ 6—5) an action for severe emotional distress was first allowed in cases where the harm was caused *intentionally* or *recklessly*. Where it can be shown that defendant intended to shock, frighten or severely upset the plaintiff (or that he knew that this was a highly probable result of his conduct) there is some objective assurance that plaintiff's injury is real, and his claim is reinforced by the social interest in deterring such conduct.

But suppose defendant is merely negligent, as where he drives his auto through a red light and narrowly misses the plaintiff. The circumstantial probability that plaintiff was in fact severely emotionally distressed by defendant's conduct is less; and in addition it can be argued that liability for the consequences of plaintiff's fright may be disproportionate to defendant's fault.

Thus, in cases of *negligent* conduct which inflicts severe emotional distress the law distinguishes three fact situations, which may be designated (1) impact, (2) zone of danger, and (3) bystander.

(1) **Impact.** Where defendant's negligence causes an impact with plaintiff's body resulting in some physical injury, plaintiff traditionally may claim damages not only for his physical injury but also for the accompanying damage to his mental equilibrium—pain, suffering, neurosis,

nervousness, humiliation, apprehension, and fright. R. § 456. Such damages are said to be "parasitic" to the damages recoverable for the physical harm. By extension of this familiar and well-accepted principle, the courts have generally permitted an action for such psychic trauma and resulting physical consequences even though the physical impact was very slight and itself caused little or no bodily harm at the point of the impact. Sufficient impact has been found in a slight blow, jolt or jar; a trifling burn or electric shock; and dust in the eye or the inhalation of smoke. The requirement has even been satisfied by an impact resulting from plaintiff's own response to the fright. Thus, the courts have gone far beyond the concept of such damages as parasitic. Rather, it appears that the true function of the impact requirement is to provide a circumstantial guarantee of the validity of plaintiff's claim.

(2) Zone of Danger. At one time, the courts denied recovery for the physical consequences of emotional distress which occurred in the absence of an impact, even though plaintiff was within the zone of danger of a risk created by defendant's negligence, and plaintiff legitimately feared injury from that risk—for example, where defendant negligently drove his car and narrowly missed striking plaintiff. But one by one the courts have abolished the impact requirement and allow such plaintiffs to recover in such cases upon satisfactory proof. The impact rule, which is now a distinctly minority view, was severely crippled when New York rejected it (Battalla v. State (N.Y.1961)), and it is doubtful that any court will ever adhere to it again when next faced with the issue.

(3) Bystander. Where plaintiff was not himself within the zone of danger, but merely witnessed a shocking event caused by defendant's conduct, most courts continue to deny recovery for plaintiff's resulting physical harm if defendant's conduct in precipitating the event was merely negligent. There is some fear of questionable claims, but perhaps more significant is the prevailing view that liability for shock to bystanders would be too great a burden when compared to the risk created by defendant's negligence.

But even here, the rule of nonliability is beginning to erode in exceptionally compelling cases. The leading decision is Dillon v. Legg (Cal.1968), where a mother was allowed to recover for the severe emotional trauma and resulting illness caused when she witnessed defendant negligently run down and kill her child, even though she was in a position of complete safety. The court found that ordinary principles of negligence law would permit recovery, since it is entirely foreseeable by one who is negligent toward a child that its mother will be in the immediate vicinity, will witness the event, and will suffer severe shock. *Dillon* has been followed in several jurisdictions in cases involving similar facts, but it has been expressly rejected in several others (e.g., Tobin v. Grossman (N.Y.1969)). So far, the cases and writers have suggested that liability in such cases be limited to situations where (1) the threatened injury is a serious one, (2) plaintiff is a member of the immediate family of the person in peril, (3) the shock results in actual physical harm to plaintiff, (4) the event is of short duration, and (5) plaintiff actually witnesses the traumatic event, or at least comes upon the scene almost immediately and witnesses its aftermath. While such limitations are somewhat arbitrary, they are seen as necessary to keep liability within reasonable bounds and to restrict it to indisputably genuine claims. E.g., compare Leong v. Takasaki (Hawaii 1974) with Kelley v. Kokua Sales & Supply, Ltd. (Hawaii 1975).

Even before *Dillon,* some cases would permit a plaintiff who was himself within the zone of danger to recover not only for the fright caused by fear for his *own* safety but also for the emotional distress caused by witnessing the peril to a close relative who was simultaneously threatened or harmed by the same negligent conduct of defendant.

See generally R. §§ 306, 436, 436A.

Interestingly (and somewhat anomalously), a number of courts which would deny liability in the *Dillon* situation will permit plaintiff to recover for the mental anguish caused by witnessing damage to or destruction of his valuable personal property caused by defendant's negligence as parasitic damages in a suit to recover for such property damage. And there is a line of cases allowing recovery for emotional distress to the next of kin caused by the negligent mishandling of a corpse. R. § 868.

Proximate Cause. In general, plaintiff may recover for emotional distress negligently inflicted only if it results in some physical illness or comparable objective bodily consequences, and then only if such consequences were reasonably foreseeable. R. §§ 436A, 313. And unless defendant had actual knowledge of some special hypersensitivity of the plaintiff, he will be liable only to the extent that plaintiff's physical response to the emotional trauma was within the normal range of ordinarily sensitive persons. These limitations, which are narrower than the usual proximate cause rules (see §§ 4—4, 6—5, supra), are in keeping with the previously-discussed policy to require objective assurance of the genuineness of claims and to prevent defendants' liability from becoming disproportionate to the risk.

§ 8—20. Prenatal Harm

Until recently, plaintiff could not recover for physical harm sustained prior to his birth. The justifications given were (1) a fetus is not a separate person, and (2) medical proof of causation would be too speculative and this would lead to false claims.

These reasons are, of course, extremely weak. It is undisputed that a fetus is capable of sustaining a permanent injury. The law has long accorded property and other rights to the unborn. And it is difficult to understand why the medical proof should be any less trustworthy here than in other kinds of cases.

Thus, this duty limitation finally succumbed to virtually unrelieved criticism. Between 1946 and 1972 the rule was totally reversed, and today a child if and when born alive may maintain an action for personal injuries suffered while in the womb as a result of defendant's wrongful conduct.

Despite some contrary dictum, it is well established that recovery may be had for injuries which occur during any stage of the pregnancy; the fetus need not have been viable or "quick" at the time. Of course, the earlier in the pregnancy the injury is thought to have occurred, the more difficult may be the proof that the injury is causally related to defendant's wrongful conduct, but this does not alter the rule.

Suppose the injuries are fatal. Where the child is born alive and subsequently dies from injuries sustained in the womb, the courts (having first allowed the action for prenatal injuries) have had little difficulty allowing the wrongful death action. But where the child is stillborn, the courts at first were hesitant to allow recovery, frequently construing the term "person" in the applicable wrongful death act to exclude the unborn. But since Verkennes v. Corniea (Minn. 1949) the trend has been to allow the action if the child was viable at the time of the injury, and this is now the majority rule. See, e.g., Mone v. Greyhound Lines, Inc. (Mass.1975).

These tort law developments present an interesting contrast to recent developments in the law concerning abortions, particularly Roe v. Wade (U.S.1973) which held that an unborn nonviable child is not a "person" within the meaning of the Fourteenth Amendment.

"Wrongful Birth." So far the courts have unanimously refused to recognize a cause of action in favor of a bastard for damages caused by having been born illegitimate, on the ground that such damages are more then offset by the benefits of having been born at all. But a number of courts have recently permitted an action in favor of the parents for negligence in performing sterilization procedures which results in the birth of a healthy child. Damages in such cases have been limited to those associated with the pregnancy and birth, and do not include the cost of the child's support. And a recent lower court opinion allows a cause of action on behalf of a deceased two-year-old child and her parents against two physicians for negligence in diagnosing and advising them which allegedly resulted in her birth with a congenital kidney disease which could not be cured and from which she died. Park v. Chessin (N.Y.Sup.1976).

§ 8—21. Dram Shop Liability

The general common law rule was that one who sold intoxicating beverages was not liable to third persons subsequently injured by the intoxicated person. The damage was considered too remote; it was the consumption and not the sale which was the immediate cause of the harm.

There were exceptions, usually cases involving sales to known habitual drunkards or to persons known to be intoxicated or nearly so, founded upon a reckless disregard of the rights of others. But the exceptions were limited, and many courts refused to allow liability even in the face of extenuating circumstances.

Largely at the behest of the temperance movement, statutes (called "dram shop acts") were enacted in many states which imposed some form of civil liability on those engaged in the business of selling such beverages in favor of third persons injured thereby. The justification was that those trafficking in demon rum ought to bear the cost of its inevitable consequential harm as a part of the cost of doing business. At one time, almost half the states had such laws; today, that number seems to be declining.

The majority of such statutes impose civil liability only where the sale was itself unlawful, such as to a minor, a person already intoxicated, or an habitual drunkard or other person whom the seller had previously been notified to deny. In some cases, actual knowledge of the illegality of the sale is required. But in some states, there is liability for even lawful sales which contribute to one's intoxication. Typically, recovery is allowed to plaintiffs injured or killed by the intoxicated person, or to members of the intoxicated person's family who incur expense or lose his support as a consequence of *his* injury or death as a result of his intoxication. Absent some knowledge requirement, liability is strict. No negligence need be shown, and contributory negligence is no defense. Of course, the intoxicated person cannot himself sue for his own injuries, nor can any person maintain an action who participated with him in the drinking (a defense called "complicity"). In some other states there is a statutory limit on the damages; and in others punitive damages are recoverable in appropriate cases.

A growing minority of states have overthrown the common law rule and have created a common law dram shop action. In most of these jurisdictions, liability is predicated on statutes which regulate the liquor business and prohibit certain sales by liquor licensees (to minors, intoxicated persons, etc.). Thus, where the sale is unlawful, it is negligence per se. And the old proximate cause limitation has been swept aside and third persons injured by the intoxicated person may sue. Here also, most (but not all) jurisdictions limit liability to those engaged in the regulated business of selling intoxicating beverages.

§ 8—22. Deprivations of Federal Constitutional Rights

A number of federal statutes have as their purpose the implementation of one or more of the rights secured to individuals by the United States Constitution, chiefly by certain amendments (I, IV, V, VI, XIV, XV).

The most important of these statutes is 42 U. S.C.A. § 1983, which implements the Fourteenth Amendment by creating a federal cause of action in tort for acts under color of state authority which deprive one of any federal constitutional or statutory right. ("State" includes political subdivisions such as cities and counties.) It provides:

> Every person, who under color of any statute, ordinance, regulation, custom, or usage, of any State or Territory, subjects, or causes to be subjected, any citizen of the United States or other person within the jurisdiction thereof the deprivation of any rights, privileges, or immunities secured by the Constitution and laws, shall be liable to the party injured in an action at law, suit in equity, or other proper proceeding for redress.

Enacted in 1871, § 1983 long lay nearly dormant, having been rather narrowly construed. But in 1961, the U.S. Supreme Court in Monroe v. Pape (Douglas, J.) breathed new life into it, holding that, contrary to popular belief, § 1983 was *not* limited to unconstitutional acts which state law purported to authorize, but rather extended to *all* deprivations of federally created rights whether lawful or unlawful under state law. "Under color of" state law thus means that the defendant, at the time he committed the act, need merely have been acting in his capacity as a state officer or employee or else have had some substantial connection with the state such that he could be said to be its instrumentality. It also ruled that the wrongful act did not have to be done with specific intent to deprive plaintiff of a federal constitutional right; § 1983 "should be read against the background of tort liability that makes a man responsible for the natural consequences of his actions."

Section 1983 is designed to prevent abuses of power by state and local officers, employees, and others acting with the authority of the state behind them. It is primarily intended to provide a remedy where state law is inadequate or, though adequate in theory, is ineffective in practice. However, it is not limited to these situations. The remedy is supplementary to remedies available under state law, and ordinarily unsuccessful resort to such remedies is not a prerequisite.

Federal jurisdiction in § 1983 cases is conferred by 28 U.S.C.A. § 1343, irrespective of diversity of citizenship or the amount in controversy. Trial by jury is available. States courts have concurrent jurisdiction of § 1983 claims.

The most significant feature of § 1983 is its enormous breadth. *All* constitutional rights guaranteed by the Fourteenth Amendment and all rights created by federal statutes are within its scope. Included are (1) First Amendment rights—freedom of speech, religion, the press, assembly, and association; (2) illegal arrest, and the use of unnecessary force during an arrest; (3) unlawful searches and seizures; (4) assault, bodily injury, and wrongful death (e.g. police brutality); (5) the right to consult an attorney; (6) reasonable access to the courts; (7) coerced confessions and other denials of the right against self-incrimination; (8) bail; (9) malicious prosecution; (10) false imprisonment; (11) the right to a fair trial (e.g., knowing use of perjured testimony, right to an impartial and unbiased tribunal); (12) various prisoners' rights (e.g., right to medical care, First Amendment rights, and protection against cruel and unusual punishment, or summary punishment), including rights of juveniles and those committed to institutions for the mentally ill; (13) invasion of privacy (e.g., police harrassment, the privacy of one's body); and (14) other due process and equal protection rights, whether personal or property (Lynch v. Household Finance Corp., U.S.1972), such as freedom from discrimination based on race or sex; rights to due process in public and other employment, public housing, license issuance and revocation, grant or denial of other valuable privileges (e.g., bar admission), pension rights, social security benefits, rights to public utilities, students' rights; protection against summary garnishment, seizure or destruction of property; and voting rights—to list only some.

Since *Monroe,* there has been a dramatic increase in the number of § 1983 cases in the federal courts, to the point that they are now a significant fraction of the docket. With the broadening of the areas in which state and local government touch the lives of all persons, it is safe to predict a continuing increase in the volume of such cases.

Plaintiffs may include anyone whose rights have been violated, white, black, or otherwise, and even aliens and corporations where appropriate.

Ordinarily, the defendant will be a state or local officer or employee, since liability exists only for rights denied by state action. *Monroe* held that, at least as to actions for damages, municipalities are not "persons" and are *not* proper defendants; the same is probably true of the states. (In addition, the eleventh amendment is a bar to suits against the states in federal courts.) Except for these entities, however, the coverage of the act has been increasingly liberalized. Many state agencies have been held proper defendants. And even private persons may be held to have acted "under color of" state law where (1) they act in concert with state officers or employees, or (2) they purport to act pursuant to state law, or (3) they act under the authority of some state which purports to give them the power to so act, such as a state statute authorizing summary garnishment, or (4) there is a substantial state nexus with defendant's activities, as where defendant is subject to extensive state regulation (e.g., an insurance company or public utility) or receives significant state aid, either directly as in the case of grants or tax exemptions (i.e. private universities) or indirectly as where defendant is permitted to use public property or facilities (e.g. a Y. M.C.A. regularly allowed to do so). There is a large and growing body of law as to what is state action; the courts will now look to all state involvement, support, encouragement, sanction, aid, and regulation, and the test is whether the totality of these factors is sufficiently substantial to give a "color" of state law to defendant's activities.

The nature, extent and interaction of (1) the fault required to support liability, (2) defenses, and (3) immunities in § 1983 cases are in the process of development and are not yet fully worked out. The corresponding rules of analagous torts will certainly play an important part in this process, as Justice Douglas suggested in *Monroe,* but cannot be controlling since there may be overriding policies applicable to § 1983 which are absent in the usual tort case.

As to fault, it is at least clear that no specific intent to violate another's rights is required. Here, tort law may be of its greatest value. The emerging rule seems to be that if there is an analogous common law tort, the fault required in a

§ 1983 action will ordinarily be the same. Thus, while there is authority to the contrary, there are cases in which there may be liability for a negligent interference with a protected right.

Defenses and immunities are a different matter. It is apparent that if all of the common law immunities of government and governmental employees (see Chapter 11) were available in § 1983 cases, the act would be emasculated. It is also noteworthy that the statute itself makes no reference to any immunities, and some have argued persuasively that it was intended that there be none. Nevertheless, at least in actions for *damages,* the courts have given absolute or qualified immunities to certain defendants as a matter of policy, apparently on the theory that such immunities are necessarily implicit. Thus, judges (Pierson v. Ray, U.S.1967), legislators (Tenney v. Brandhove, U.S.1951), public prosecutors (Imbler v. Pachtman, U.S.1976), and public or court-appointed criminal defense counsel (Minns v. Paul, 4th Cir. 1976) are *absolutely* immune from damages suits under § 1983 for acts within the scope of their duties (an area yet to be delineated). Others have a qualified immunity, which is to say immunity for acts committed (1) in good faith, (2) with probable cause, or (3) in the exercise of their discretion, or some combination of these three. Examples include the state governor (Schever v. Rhodes, U.S.1974) and probably other high executive officials, and school officials exercising disciplinary authority (Wood v. Strickland, U.S.1975). In certain cases, the courts speak of a "qualified immunity," but what they really mean is that defendant's good faith or probable cause negates the existence of the intent required for liability.

The full effect of 42 U.S.C.A. § 1988 on § 1983 actions is yet to be determined. Section 1988 provides, in effect, that in suits under § 1983 (and certain other civil rights statutes) if issues arise as to which there is no applicable rule of federal law, or there are gaps or deficiencies in the federal law, then the law of the state in which the federal court is located may be applied. Under this provision, state law has been used to determine survival of the action, the statute of limitations, and the nature and extent of the remedy for wrongful death. On the other hand, federal common law is generally held to determine the measure of damages in the interest of uniformity, and thus for example punitive damages may be awarded even though the law of the state in which the federal court is sitting does not allow them. Some have argued, with some force, that the federal courts should fill gaps by fashioning federal common law consistent with the purpose of § 1983, rather than to borrow under § 1988 the various state laws which may themselves be inadequate or inconsistent. How far this will be done remains to be seen. Perhaps decisions such as Moragne v. States Marine Lines, Inc. (U.S.1970) will be an impetus in that direction. But it is at least clear that state law rules which are barriers to liability (such as very short special statutes of limitations applicable to suits against state employees and common law tort immunities) will not be applied if they significantly impair the § 1983 remedy.

There are other federal statutes upon which an action for damages for discrimination may be based. These remedies are broader than § 1983; no state action is required. These include § 1981 (personal rights), § 1982 (property rights), §§ 1985 and 1986 (conspiracies), § 2000a (public accommodations), § 2000d (federally funded programs), § 2000e (employment discrimination) and §§ 3601–3631 (housing discrimination). A remedy for age discrimination is provided in 29 U.S.C.A. §§ 621–634.

Since § 1983 is limited to acts under color of state law, it does not reach deprivations of constitutional rights by *federal* officials and employees. However, it is now recognized that interference with any federal constitutional right, at least by federal personnel, gives rise to a cause of action under the Constitution itself without the necessity of implementing legislation. Therefore, a person whose constitutional rights have been violated by a federal officer or employee may sue him in federal court under the provisions of 28 U.S.C. A. § 1331 (which gives jurisdiction to the federal courts of civil actions arising under federal law) if the amount in controversy exceeds the required

$10,000. Bivens v. Six Unknown Named Agents of Federal Bureau of Narcotics (U.S.1971). In response to this case, Congress removed exclusions for certain intentional torts by investigative and law enforcement personnel from the Federal Tort Claims Act. This principle provides a remedy for violations of constitutional rights by officers and employees of the District of Columbia, who are beyond the reach of § 1983. District of Columbia v. Carter (U.S.1973). And it has even been suggested that *Bivens* might be the basis for a direct action against a municipality which cannot be sued under § 1983. The full scope of *Bivens* is yet to be determined, but it seems clear that it is not limited to fourth amendment violations. See, e.g., United States ex rel. Moore v. Koelzer (3d Cir. 1972) (fifth amendment); Paton v. La Prade (3d Cir. 1975) (first amendment); Butler v. United States (D. Hawaii 1973) (same); Wounded Knee Legal Defense/Offense Comm. v. Federal Bureau of Inv. (8th Cir. 1974) (sixth amendment). See R. § 874A.

Finally, it should be noted that racial discrimination by private citizens has been held actionable under the common law tort of infliction of emotional distress. See § 6—5, supra. Cf. R. § 866.

CHAPTER 9

DAMAGES FOR PHYSICAL HARM

§ 9—1. Compensatory Damages

When defendant's tort injures plaintiff's person or property, his basic remedy is compensatory money damages. In almost all cases, this will also be his only remedy.

The common law rules of damages for physical harm reflect three fundamental ideas:

(1) Justice requires that plaintiff be restored to his pre-injury condition, so far as it is possible to do so with money. Thus, he should be reimbursed not only for his economic ("out-of-pocket") losses, but also for his noneconomic damage (loss of physical and mental well-being).

(2) Most noneconomic losses are capable of being translated into dollars.

(3) When plaintiff sues in tort for an injury which he has sustained, he must recover all of his damages arising from that injury, past and future, in a lump sum and in a single lawsuit. R. § 910.

General vs. Special Damages. For purposes of pleading and proof, there is a distinction between general damages and special damages. *General* damages are those awarded for harms and losses which are a natural and usual consequence of the tort and injury asserted. These harms and losses may be proved even though plaintiff did not specifically allege them in his complaint. For example, a battery which causes bodily harm normally results in physical pain, and so "pain and suffering" may be proved under a complaint for a battery which alleges only that plaintiff suffered "great bodily harm" or "a broken leg." *Special* damages are those awarded for all other compensable harms and losses. Such harms or losses must be specifically pleaded so that defendant will be on notice that damages for them will be claimed. Medical expenses, lost wages, and damages for any unusual effects of the injury (e.g. traumatic neurosis) are illustrations of special damages in a personal injury case. R. § 904.

Which items of damages are general and which are special depends, of course, on (1) the tort and (2) the general or specific injuries alleged. No hard and fast rules can be laid down, nor are they necessary for our purposes. Note, however, that in personal injury cases it has become common usage to refer to all plaintiff's economic or out-of-pocket losses as "special damages" or simply "specials," and to his noneconomic losses (such as pain and suffering) as his "general damages," irrespective of the allegations in the pleadings. Although technically inaccurate, this usage sometimes appears in judicial decisions and other legal writing.

Nominal Damages. If plaintiff establishes defendant's liability for some tort but is unable to prove any actual damages, nominal damages may be awarded. R. § 907. As the name implies, they are damages in name only, usually one cent or six cents or one dollar. Such awards are largely confined to the intentional torts (e.g. trespass to land) where actual damages need not be alleged or proved. Occasionally they may be given in other cases where plaintiff proves that he sustained some actual damage but is unable to establish the amount.

Damages for Personal Injury. Where plaintiff proves a compensable injury to his person, he may in general recover for all adverse physical and mental consequences of that injury. R. § 924. While the specific elements of damage for which recovery may be had vary somewhat among the torts, and will differ a little from one jurisdiction to the next even for a particular tort, the following types of harms are commonly compensable.

(1) *Economic Loss.* Past and future pecuniary losses and out-of-pocket expenses proximately caused by the injury are recoverable, including (a) reasonable medical expenses (doctor, hospital, nursing, tests, medicines, devices, physical therapy, and travel to obtain these services); (b) lost wages, earnings or profits; (c) the cost of substitute labor hired to do work which plaintiff can not perform because of his injury; and (d) the cost of custodial care, if any, required because the injury has left plaintiff more or less incapable of caring for himself.

Future losses and expenses need not be established to a certainty, either as to their incidence or amount. The jury need only find it more probable than not that they will be incurred and have some reasonable basis beyond sheer speculation for their computation. Thus, where the injury impairs plaintiff's earning capacity, he may recover for future lost earnings even though not employed at the time of his injury if the jury can find that more probably than not he would be employed in the future and can determine the probable type of employment and rate of earnings. It may take into account probable future wage increases. In the case of a child, it may even find that he probably would have gone to college and obtained skilled employment, if such a finding is supported by some evidence.

Impaired earning capacity is frequently a subject of expert testimony by an economist or actuary.

(2) *Physical Pain.* Past and future physical pain—commonly referred to as "pain and suffering"—is compensable. Within broad limits, its valuation is left largely to the jury's discretion.

An oft-debated question is whether plaintiff should be permitted to use the so-called "per diem" argument to the jury in which he suggests that his past and future pain be valued in units of time (e.g., $20 per day, $2 per hour) or whether he should be limited to suggesting a lump sum for such damages. The authorities are split, with a substantial minority refusing to allow the "per diem" argument on the ground that it enhances the effects of sympathy and lends a spurious sense of accuracy to what is fundamentally sheer speculation.

(3) *Mental Distress.*   In addition to physical pain, most courts will permit plaintiff to claim damages for some or all of the following mental harms: (a) fright and shock; (b) anxiety about the future, both physical (e.g. premature death, physical disability, illness, the effect on plaintiff's unborn child) and economic (whether for himself or others), unless plaintiff's fears are clearly unfounded and unreasonable; (c) loss of peace of mind, happiness, or mental health, ranging from depression through neuroses and psychoses; (d) humiliation, loss of dignity, or embarrassment caused by the physical injury, disability or disfigurement; (e) mental distress resulting from loss of the ability to enjoy a normal life; (f) inconvenience caused by the injury.

(4) *Physical Impairment.*   In lieu of compensation for the mental distress caused by a physical impairment of plaintiff's body, some jurisdictions purport to base compensation on the physical impairment itself.   In other words, where the injury impairs (temporarily or permanently, partially or totally) his eyesight, hearing, use of an extremity, consciousness, ability to conceive or bear children, or any other bodily function, or where plaintiff is disfigured, the jury is told to

value and compensate that loss as such and not
merely its mental consequences. (Such compensation is, of course, in addition to that awarded
for any economic loss and pain resulting from
that injury.) Of course, as a practical matter it
probably makes little difference whether the jury
is instructed to base compensation on the physical impairment or its mental effects, since in either case it is in reality the latter which is being
valued.

Pre-Existing Conditions. As previously discussed (§ 4—4), defendant's liability for damages
is not mitigated by the fact that some pre-existing physical infirmity of the plaintiff was responsible for all or part of the consequences of plaintiff's injury by defendant. If plaintiff is especially predisposed or vulnerable to some illness or injury, defendant whose tort precipitates it is liable
for the harm it causes even though under the
same circumstances a normal person would not
have suffered that illness or injury. The same is
true where the injury re-activates a previous condition which had been brought under control, or
aggravates an existing condition.

A corollary rule is that defendant is liable for
the aggravation during treatment of plaintiff's injuries, even where such aggravation is due to the
negligence of another, so long as plaintiff exercised reasonable care in selecting those in whose
care he placed himself.

Present Value. If plaintiff is awarded damages for losses which he will incur in the future, he will be over-compensated unless these damages are figured at their present value, due to the fact that (1) they are received by him in a lump sum at the conclusion of the trial, and (2) money will earn interest. R. § 913A. For example, assume that plaintiff is awarded $1,000 to compensate him for lost income which, but for his injury, he would have earned ten years in the future. Presumably he can now take that $1,000 and invest it at, say, six per cent interest. Thus, ten years hence he will have not $1,000 but $1,791. Therefore, in order to provide him with $1,000 ten years from today, that $1,000 must be discounted to its present value—a sum which, together with the interest (compounded) which it will earn, will equal $1,000 in ten years. At a discount rate of six per cent, this would be about $558.

Typically, the jury is told to discount its award for future economic loss to present value, but is not told how to do so or what rate to use. Frequently this is a subject of expert testimony by a statistician, economist or actuary.

In most jurisdictions, damages for future *non-economic* harm (pain and suffering, mental distress, disability, disfigurement) are *not* reduced to present value.

Inflation. In calculating damages for future economic losses, may the jury take into account the probable continuing decline of the purchasing power of the dollar due to inflation? May plaintiff introduce expert testimony of the probability of such continued inflation? At one time the general rule was that the court would not sanction the jury's consideration of inflation on the ground that its future effects were too speculative. But now that inflation is generally regarded as inevitable, the majority of jurisdictions will allow it to be the subject of evidence and argument. See, e.g., Feldman v. Allegheny Airlines, Inc. (2d Cir. 1975); Seaboard Coastline R.R. v. Garrison (Fla.App.1976). In some states inflation is held to offset the discount rate and they cancel each other out, so that in these jurisdictions plaintiff's future economic loss is simply not reduced to its present value.

Taxation. The Internal Revenue Code exempts compensatory damages for personal injuries from income taxation, even though they may include damages for past and future lost earnings. 26 U. S.C.A. § 104. The general rule is that the nontaxability of such damages may not be the subject of evidence, argument or instructions to the jury on the grounds that (1) plaintiff would thereby be deprived of the tax benefit given him by Congress, and (2) the future effects of taxation cannot be calculated to an acceptable degree of certainty. R. § 914A. However, a few courts recognize an exception in cases where plaintiff's income loss is very high and thus the windfall would be unacceptably large if the tax benefit is

ignored.   See Felder v. United States (9th Cir.
1976).

Collateral Source Rule.   As a general rule,
plaintiff may recover the reasonable value of the
expenses, services and lost time from work attributable to his injury (e.g. doctors' fees, hospital
and other medical expenses, his wages while absent from his employment), even though he did
not in fact pay for them (as where they were furnished as a gift or as a matter of professional
courtesy) or he was reimbursed for such expenses from a collateral source (that is, a source other than defendant or which defendant did not
fund).   R. § 920A.   Examples of these collateral
sources include private health and accident insurance, workmen's compensation, social security,
disability insurance, wage continuation plans, sick
leave, veterans' benefits, and public aid.   (Distinguish payments received from or on behalf of a
joint tortfeasor in settlement of his potential tort
liability to plaintiff for the same injury; defendant *is* credited with these payments.   See § 9—4,
infra.)   The justification for the rule is that it
would be more unjust to give defendant the benefit of these payments than to permit an innocent
plaintiff to recover them twice, especially since in
most cases plaintiff himself arranged for the collateral benefits and paid for them.   (There is, of
course, no double recovery where plaintiff must
repay the collateral source out of the judgment
he obtains from defendant, as in the case of bene-

fits received from workmen's compensation, public aid, and the military services.)

In some (but not all) jurisdictions, plaintiff (or the person furnishing them) may even recover the value of nursing services gratuitously furnished plaintiff by friends and relatives, on the ground that defendant is not entitled to the benefit of these services.

The collateral source rule is not without its critics, and courts occasionally allow exceptions to it, but in general it appears too well established and accepted to be changed except by statute. Some automobile accident compensation acts (§ 8—17) modify or abolish it, but otherwise there is as yet no discernible movement to do so by statutes of general application.

Mitigation. Under the doctrine of avoidable consequences, plaintiff is required to make reasonable efforts to mitigate the consequences of his injury and to take steps to prevent further harm, and defendant is not liable to the extent that he fails to do so. For example, absent some legitimate reason for not doing so, plaintiff is required to make a reasonable effort to seek medical treatment for his injuries.

In some jurisdictions, this is extended to include safety precautions required or available *prior* to the injury, such as the wearing of seat belts or safety helmets, and defendant is not liable for those damages attributable to plaintiff's failure to make use of them. However, the majority rule is to the contrary.

Mere negligence in failing to mitigate damages is no defense to an intentional or reckless tort.

Of course, plaintiff may recover as an item of damages any expenses reasonably incurred in attempting to mitigate his harm, whether or not his efforts were successful, and also damages for further harm sustained as a result of reasonable efforts to mitigate his harm.

Conversely, where defendant's tort caused harm but also conferred some benefit on plaintiff, that benefit may be considered in mitigation of plaintiff's damages if it is equitable to do so.

Attorneys' Fees and Litigation Costs. The universal American rule (with exceptions not pertinent here) is that the prevailing party in litigation may not recover as damages his attorneys' fees or other litigation costs in the absence of a statute expressly authorizing them. Statutes typically provide for the recovery of minor litigation expenses, such as filing and service fees, but little else.

This fact is often used to bolster arguments in favor of certain damages rules, such as the collateral source rule, the rule against a deduction for tax benefits, and damages for pain and suffering. It is said that any windfall which plaintiff receives as a result of these rules is more than offset by the fact that plaintiff must pay his own attorneys' fees and most other expenses of litigation out of the award he receives.

Harm to Personal Property. For harm to personal property which does *not* amount to a conversion, plaintiff at his election may recover either:

(1) The difference between the value of the property before the tort and its value afterwards; or

(2) The reasonable costs of repair and restoration to use of the chattel, or attempts to do so, plus any diminution in its value remaining thereafter.

Ordinarily, plaintiff may recover the reasonable costs of repairs or restoration even though they exceed the value of the chattel before the harm, unless a reasonable person under the circumstances then known to him would simply have junked it and obtained a replacement.

In addition, if recovery is based on the cost of repair, he may recover any costs or damages reasonably incurred during the time he was deprived of its use (such as the cost of renting a substitute) proximately resulting from the loss of use.

The measure of damages for the conversion of personal property is its value at the time and place of conversion, plus interest from that time. Plaintiff may also recover any damages proximately resulting from loss of its use, including (in lieu of interest during that time) the cost of renting a substitute, until such time as a replacement was or could have been obtained.

Some courts will permit plaintiff to recover damages for the mental distress proximately caused by the trespass or conversion.

Damages for conversion of a chattel are mitigated if plaintiff accepts a tender of its return, or in certain cases by the tender alone.   R. § 922.

Harm to Real Property. Damages for past invasions of land include (1) the difference in the value of the thing damaged (or if it cannot be separately valued, the value of plaintiff's interest in the land) before and after the invasion, or, at plaintiff's election, the reasonable costs of restoration, (2) compensation for loss of use, and (3) damages for (a) bodily harm, (b) harm to chattels, and (c) mental distress (such as discomfort, inconvenience and annoyance) resulting from the invasion.

In certain cases, plaintiff may be required, or may elect, to recover for future invasions in the same lawsuit. The measure of damages for future harm is either the permanent decrease in the value of the land or the cost of preventing future harm.

§ 9—2. Consequential Damages

Where defendant causes injury to the person of *A,* that injury will often cause damage to *B.* Such indirect or consequential damage to third persons will sometimes give rise to a separate cause of action. Such actions have generally been limited to spouses, parents, and the employer of the injured person, absent an intent to cause an injury to the third person.

Spouse. At common law, a husband was entitled to the domestic services of his wife, and to the earnings from her employment outside the home. Accordingly, when defendant's tort physically injured or incapacitated the wife so that she was unable (temporarily or permanently) to perform them, the husband was given a cause of action for loss of her services. In time the measure of damages was broadened to include his loss of "consortium," which consists of her society, companionship, affection and sexual relations.

The wife, however, had no corresponding right to the services of her husband. She was entitled only to his support, and only he could recover for an injury which impaired his earnings or earning capacity. Hence, she had no action for loss of his services or by extension his consortium.

Beginning in 1844, Married Women's Acts or Emancipation Acts were passed in all American jurisdictions giving married women a legal identity separate from their husbands. For a long time this had little effect on either the husband's action or the denial of the wife's action, except that (1) the wife alone could now recover for her lost earnings and (2) a few courts abolished the husband's action, interpreting the act to mean that the husband was no longer entitled to an action for loss of his wife's services and throwing out with it his action for loss of consortium.

Most courts, however, continued to allow the husband's action for loss of consortium and also for loss of domestic services actually performed. As the recognition of equal rights for women increased, so did criticism of the denial of a similar cause of action for the wife. A few courts yielded in the case of certain intentional torts. Finally, Hitaffer v. Argonne Co. (D.C.Cir. 1950) overthrew the ban and recognized the wife's action for harm to the marital relation caused by a negligent injury to her husband, and a number of jurisdictions have since followed suit. This trend undoubtedly will continue, especially with the aid of recent interpretations of the various constitutional provisions on equal protection. Certainly the old distinction cannot survive the adoption of equal rights provisions which are now a part of some state constitutions and may soon be an amendment to the federal constitution.

Ordinarily either spouse may recover medical expenses which he paid or incurred as a result of a tortious injury to the other, to the extent that the injured spouse does not recover them in his own action.

Parents. At common law (and yet today, believe it or not) a father is legally entitled to the services and earnings of his unemancipated minor child. Thus, he (or the child's mother, if she has sole custody) may recover for loss of those services against one who negligently injures the child. A few courts permit, in addition, the award of damages for loss of the child's society, companionship and affection, but at present the majority of jurisdictions do not.

In addition, the parent may recover medical and other expenses which he paid or incurred as a result of the child's injury, and future expenses which will be incurred during the child's minority.

Children. Despite some sentiment in support of it, the courts so far have denied a cause of action to a child for loss of his parent's care, support, training, guidance, companionship, love and affection resulting from a negligent injury to the parent.

Nursing Services. The authorities are divided as to whether a member of the injured person's family may recover the value of nursing services gratuitously furnished to him.

Nature of Action. The action of a spouse or parent for consequential damages is separate and distinct from that of the injured spouse or child, and in most jurisdictions either action may be brought independently of the other. As a practical matter, all such claims are usually brought in the same lawsuit, and a few courts, fearing double recovery and the burden of multiple suits, require it.

Most courts regard the action for consequential damages as derivative, and therefore defendant usually may invoke any defense (e.g. contributory negligence) which would have been available in a suit brought by the injured person. Thus, one suing for consequential damages must first prove that the injured person could have succeeded in a lawsuit of his own, and must then establish *his* right to recover and negate any defenses asserted against him.

Whether the actions are brought separately or together, there does exist a danger of double recovery for the same elements of damage. Contrary to the views of some courts, this is not a sufficient reason to deny the action for consequential damages altogether, but care must be taken to see that the damages recovered by persons other than the one injured do not duplicate those awarded to the injured person, and vice versa.

Employers. At common law, a master had a property interest in the services of his servant sufficient to support a cause of action against one whose tort deprived him of those services. But times have changed, and with them the nature of the employer-employee relationship. While there is still authority (some of it relatively recent) supporting the existence of the cause of action, most current decisions have refused to recognize it, in cases where the injury to the servant was negligently inflicted. Steele v. J & S Metals, Inc.

(Conn.Super.1974); Phoenix Prof. Hockey Club, Inc. v. Hirmer (Ariz.1972). The action is preserved by statute in one or two states.

§ 9—3. Punitive Damages

If defendant's wrongful conduct is sufficiently serious, tort law permits the trier of fact to impose a civil fine to punish him and to deter him and others from similar conduct in the future. R. § 908. Punitive damages—also called exemplary or vindictive damages or "smart money"— are not really damages at all (even though they are paid to plaintiff) since presumably plaintiff has been made whole by the compensatory damages awarded in the same action. They are justified as: (1) an incentive or reward for bringing defendant to justice, especially where plaintiff's actual damages are so small that suit would otherwise be prohibitively expensive; (2) punishment for criminal or quasi-criminal offenses which often escape or are beyond the reach of the criminal law; (3) compensation for damages not normally compensable, such as wounded feelings and attorneys' fees and other expenses of litigation; and (4) the only effective means to force conscienceless defendants to cease practices known to be dangerous or tortious and which they would otherwise continue because it is more profitable to pay (or insure) compensatory damages for the harm they cause and continue them.

Punitive damages are of common law origin, but may be expressly allowed, prohibited, or reg-

ulated by statute. Generally they are not recoverable as a matter of right, but only in the
discretion of the jury when justice and the public
good will be served.

The common law of four states (Louisiana,
Massachusetts, Nebraska and Washington) does
not permit them. They may be recovered, however, even in those states if allowed by statute
(e.g. under the Massachusetts wrongful death
act). A few states permit them primarily on the
theory that they serve compensatory functions;
in Connecticut they are limited to the expenses of
litigation. They may *not* be awarded in F.E.L.A.
and Jones Act cases, nor sometimes in certain
types of cases in particular jurisdictions (e.g. survival or wrongful death actions in some states).

To justify an award of punitive damages, defendant must have acted from a wrongful motive,
or at least with gross or knowing indifference to
the rights or safety of another. His conduct
must have an element of outrage, similar to that
which is a crime. An intentional tort usually will
suffice. Most jurisdictions also allow them in
cases of reckless or "wilful and wanton" misconduct. Of these, some courts permit them whenever such conduct is found; others require, in addition, a finding of a kind of "malice," which in
this case means a conscious and deliberate disregard of a high probability of harm. Negligence,
even gross negligence, is not enough, although
some courts have defined the latter as synony-

mous with wilful and wanton misconduct and as so defined sufficient to support punitive damages. A fortiori, strict liability in any form will not do.

In most states, the fact that defendant's conduct also happens to be a crime does not prevent the assessment of punitive damages in a civil tort action. The double jeopardy argument has totally failed, and so has the contention that such damages amount to criminal punishment without the accompanying safeguards and standards of proof required by criminal law and procedure. But courts will occasionally look to the criminal fines for similar misconduct as guidelines when reviewing the excessiveness of punitive damages.

Most jurisdictions require that plaintiff prove some actual damages as a prerequisite to an award of punitive damages. But proof is usually all that is required, and a verdict for compensatory damages is not an absolute necessity. An award of nominal damages will often support a verdict for substantial punitive damages, as where the tort is particularly offensive or outrageous but no substantial damage resulted from it. On the other hand, the courts will often (especially in personal injury or property damage cases) use the amount of the compensatory damages as a guideline in judging the excessiveness of the punitive damages, and sometimes require that there be a reasonable relation between their amounts, or at least between the character of the harm and the amount of the punitive damages.

Since the function of punitive damages is ordinarily punishment and deterrence, evidence of defendant's financial circumstances is usually admissible as bearing on the amount of such damages which will be necessary to accomplish this purpose.

The whole concept of punitive damages has always had its critics, and courts frequently state that such damages are not a favorite of the law and will be scrutinized with care. Until recently, however, such awards were relatively rare and were ordinarily affirmed. But lately plaintiffs have been seeking such damages, and juries have been awarding them, with increasing frequency and sometimes in very large amounts. Thus, there is some indication that the courts are becoming increasingly watchful and may begin to place new limits on them.

One lively controversy concerns vicarious liability situations. A majority of jurisdictions have held that punitive damages may be assessed against an employer for any tort committed by his employee (within the course of the employment) for which punitive damages against the employee would be justified. But a substantial minority, supported by the Restatements of Torts (§ 909) and Agency (§ 217C) do not allow punitive damages to be awarded against an employer based upon the acts of his employee, except where (1) the employer authorized the doing and the manner of the act, or (2) the employee was unfit and the employer was reckless in employing him, or (3) the employee was working in a "managerial capacity," or (4) the employer or one of his managerial agents ratified or approved the act. These rules have particular significance in the case of corporations, which act exclusively through agents and employees.

Another problem arises where tortious conduct gives rise to multiple claims, as where many items of the same product sold to the public have the same defect which causes injury to a number of persons. If there is no class action and all the claims are brought separately, it may be appropriate to limit or deny punitive damages in each case (and especially the later ones) in order to prevent astronomical liability. See Roginsky v. Richardson-Merrell, Inc. (2d Cir. 1967).

Another question of lively current interest is whether punitive damages are insurable. Assuming that the language of defendant's liability insurance policy may fairly be read to cover them, is such coverage contrary to public policy and therefore void? On the one hand, it would be easy enough for the insurer to expressly exclude them, and his failure to do so may well have misled the insured. On the other hand, punitive damages are to punish and deter, and that purpose is substantially impaired (if not defeated) by permitting the wrongdoer to shift his punishment to his insurance company. There seems to be general agreement that where the liability for punitive damages is vicarious, as in the case of a corporate defendant, punitive damages are a business risk which may be insured, at least where the tort is not that of management and where the conduct was merely reckless and not an intentional wrong. There is a split of authority as to whether one may insure his own personal liability for punitive damages. The majority view seems to be that he may not, but a substantial minority of courts hold that he can if the tort was not wilful.

§ 9—4. Allocation Among Tortfeasors

Joint Tortfeasors. It is not uncommon for a plaintiff who has suffered physical harm to claim against two or more tortfeasors, usually simultaneously. This was not always so. Recall that earlier rules of tort law were oriented toward placing responsibility on a single wrongdoer. And under older rules of procedure, joinder of more than one defendant in a single tort action was possible only where all such defendants acted in concert in committing the tort, either directly (where each did a tortious act pursuant to a common plan) or where one was vicariously responsible for the tortious act of another under principles of conspiracy or joint enterprise such that a mutual agency existed.

Tort law now recognizes that the negligence (or other wrongful conduct) of more than one person, each acting independently and without a common design, may be concurrent causes of plaintiff's injury for which all may be subject to liability. For example, a passenger in an automobile may be injured by the combined negligence of its driver and the driver of another vehicle. There may be a violation of a common duty; the manufacturer, wholesaler and retailer of a defective product may all be liable to a user injured by it. Or one person may be directly liable and another vicariously liable for the same act, as in the case of a tort committed by an employee in the course of his employment.

Modern rules of civil procedure generally permit joinder in a single action of all defendants whose liability to plaintiff arises out of a single event or transaction, or even out of closely related events. But irrespective of whether such persons are sued separately or together, or are not even sued at all, multiple tort liability creates issues as to how the plaintiff's damages are to be allocated among the different persons liable for them.

Divisible Damages. It sometimes happens that different persons may be liable for separate, identifiable parts of plaintiff's harm. For example, two hunters in separate hunting parties each negligently fire at the same time; one wounds plaintiff in the arm, the other in the leg. Absent concert of action, each is liable only for the harm traceable to him. This is essentially a problem of proof of causation, previously discussed. See § 2—1, supra.

Indivisible Harm. Where two or more persons are responsible for the same harm, all whose tortious conduct is found to be a proximate cause of that harm are jointly and severally liable for all of the plaintiff's damages, along with anyone who is vicariously liable for that conduct. Each is liable for the entire harm, and plaintiff ordinarily may sue any one of them, or some or all, jointly or separately, obtain judgments for the full amount of his damages against as many as he can, and then collect his judgment from one or any combination of them, as he chooses. R. § 882. Of course, he is entitled to only one *satisfaction* for his damages, but an unsatisfied judgment against one does not bar a subsequent action against another.

All persons who are jointly and severally liable to one plaintiff for the same harm are customarily referred to as joint tortfeasors, even where each acted independently and there was no joint enterprise or concert of action involved, and irrespective of whether they are sued in the same action (or indeed at all). In such cases "concurrent tortfeasors" might be a more accurate term, since only their liability is potentially joint.

Release and Covenant Not to Sue. Plaintiff may, of course, enter into an agreement with a tortfeasor by which he promises to relinquish his claim against him in exchange for a consideration. This transaction is called a settlement. By far the greater number of all tort claims are settled without trial.

One form of instrument by which this may be accomplished is a release, in which plaintiff completely surrenders his claim. His cause of action against the released tortfeasor is extinguished. What of his claims against other potential defendants for the same harm? While plaintiff may have rights against several persons arising out of a single injury he has but one cause of action, and thus the traditional common law rule was that a release of one released that cause of action and therefore released all others potentially liable for the same harm.

This led to the development of a device known as a covenant not to sue, under which plaintiff (usually by express language in the instrument) does *not* release his claim against that person, nor his cause of action, but instead merely agrees to forego any further attempts to enforce his claim against that alleged tortfeasor, by suit or otherwise. (A slight variation is a "covenant not to enforce" in which plaintiff promises not to try to collect any judgment he may obtain, or has obtained, from that particular tortfeasor.) Usually such covenants expressly reserve plaintiff's rights against other tortfeasors. But even in the absence of such a reservation, a covenant not to sue or not to execute is held not to release or extinguish plaintiff's claims against others who may also be liable for the same harm. The consideration received in exchange for such a covenant is always less than the full amount of the damages which plaintiff claims; otherwise his cause of action is fully satisfied and the instrument is in reality a release, and will be so construed. The amount received under such a covenant is credited against any judgment plaintiff subsequently obtains against other tortfeasors, but of course has no effect on later settlements with others.

Whether a particular instrument is a release or a covenant is a question of construction not always free from doubt. It is the parties' intent as derived from the substance of the document which controls, and not the document's form or designation. Having rejected the tyranny of labels, the courts are increasingly realizing that there is no logical reason why an instrument which is in form a release of one tortfeasor should ipso facto discharge others if the parties expressly agreed that it shall *not* do so and if it is *not* intended as a full satisfaction. Accordingly, a substantial number of courts now hold that under these conditions a release of one tortfeasor does not release others liable for the same harm, and statutes in nearly half the states are to the same effect, together totalling perhaps three-fourths of the American jurisdictions.

The Restatement goes one step further, holding that a release does not discharge others liable for the same harm unless the agreement expressly so provides. It characterizes the requirement that there be an express reservation of rights in the instrument as a "booby-trap for the unwary." R. § 885.

Loan Receipt Agreement. Another settlement device which has the sanction of at least some courts is the so-called "loan receipt" agreement, whereby one tortfeasor "loans" the plaintiff a sum of money, without interest, to be repaid *only* if and to the extent that plaintiff is successful in his claims against other joint tortfeasors, and *only* from the proceeds of any amount which plaintiff eventually obtains from the others. Plaintiff ordinarily promises to use his best efforts to pursue such other claims as he may have. Such an agreement is advantageous to the first tortfeasor to settle, since it gives him the prospect that the entire loss will be shifted to others, and this in turn may tend to induce settlements by other tortfeasors who might otherwise have to bear the full amount of the damages if the case goes to judgment. (These effects may be altered by the rules of contribution and indemnity, to be discussed.) A few jurisdictions (e.g. Florida) have indicated that they will give effect to the terms of virtually any form of settlement agreement which the ingenuity of counsel can devise.

Contribution. If plaintiff obtains a judgment against two or more joint tortfeasors, he may collect that judgment from any one or less than all in any disproportion he pleases. At this point plaintiff's convenience and assurance of satisfaction are the main considerations; he is allowed to get his money the best way he can. If, as a result, one such defendant does in fact pay less than his proportionate share of the judgment, it might seem logical and fair that he should reimburse the other defendant(s) who, due to the luck of the collection process, paid more. The English and early American common law so held, except in cases of intentional torts or acts in concert where the wrongdoer's equities were too weak to justify the court's aid. But during the past century, the majority of U.S. jurisdictions overextended this exception and denied all common law contribution among joint tortfeasors irrespective of the basis of liability, including cases of negligence and strict liability.

The common law is superseded by statutes in over half the states which provide for contribution in some form. (Some are patterned after the Uniform Contribution Among Tortfeasors Act, a desirable model.) Several jurisdictions continue to allow contribution by judicial decision, never having followed the majority rule disallowing it. Perhaps a dozen states still generally deny contribution. As comparative negligence becomes the universal rule, so too will contribution among joint tortfeasors. Similar rationale supports both principles. See R. § 886A.

Of those states allowing contribution, a majority allocate the damages among the defendants in proportion to their relative fault, much as in the case of the allocation between plaintiff and defendant under the pure form of comparative negligence. In the remainder (which includes almost all those without a statute) the damages are divided equally. Certain defendants (e.g. employer and employee) are grouped together and charged a single share.

Contribution is still generally (but not universally) denied to wilful tortfeasors.

Suppose plaintiff has sued and obtained a judgment against fewer than all joint tortfeasors. Should contribution be allowed against one against whom there is no judgment? Some of the statutes say no, but the better rule allows it (subject, of course, to satisfactory proof of liability).

It is generally held (in the absence of a statute requiring otherwise) that a tortfeasor who settles prior to trial, and therefore against whom there is no judgment, may nevertheless obtain contribution from other joint tortfeasors. He must, of course, prove the others' liability to the plaintiff, the amount of the damages, and the reasonableness of his settlement.

In an action for contribution, the party seeking it must ordinarily establish that the tortfeasor from whom contribution is sought was subject to liability to the injured plaintiff, if no judgment has been obtained determining that liability. Thus, it is usually held that even defenses which only the contribution defendant could have asserted against the injured person, such as intrafamily or governmental immunity, privilege, an auto guest statute, or the immunity provided an employer under the workmen's compensation act, will bar contribution. There is, however, some authority to the contrary. Of course, the fact that the statute of limitations has run on the injured person's claim against the contribution defendant is no defense in the action for contribution.

Indemnity. Contribution must be distinguished from indemnity, with which it is often confused. Rights to both coexist in most jurisdictions, and indemnity is available even in those which do not allow contribution.

Contribution is an equitable sharing of the loss; indemnification is a shifting of the entire loss from one tortfeasor to another, by operation of either (1) a prior agreement of the parties or (2) law, based on equitable considerations. While in theory the main justification for denying contribution—that the courts will not assist a wrongdoer—is equally applicable to an action for indemnity, the fact is that every jurisdiction permits indemnity at least to some extent.

Subject to restrictions imposed by statute and occasionally by public policy, parties entering into a relationship or engaging in an activity may contract in advance that one will indemnify the other for any tort liability (short of intentional wrongdoing) arising therefrom. Such agreements are relatively common, for example, in the construction industry among owners and contractors and subcontractors.

Indemnity by operation of law is based upon the concept of unjust enrichment. R. § 886B. It is allowed in a variety of situations for which no concise tests or standards can be articulated. Generally speaking, it lies when there is a significant or qualitative difference between the blameworthiness of two defendants, both of whom are nevertheless legally liable to the plaintiff for his injury, such that the primary responsibility for the harm rests upon the defendant against whom indemnity is sought. It is frequently said that where the misconduct of the indemnitee (the one seeking indemnity) was merely "passive," or his fault only "secondary," indemnity will be granted against one (the indemnitor) whose wrongful conduct can be described as "active" or a "primary" cause. Such formulations are useful in some situations, but by no means do they encompass all, and they are not sufficiently precise to use in deciding cases.

Indemnity is always allowed in favor of one (such as an employer, partner, or automobile owner) whose sole basis of liability is vicarious responsibility for the tort of another. The same is true where the indemnitee acted pursuant to directions received from the indemnitor which he reasonably believed to be lawful; or where he was induced to act by a misrepresentation of the indemnitor upon which he reasonably relied. Indemnity is allowed where the indemnitor is responsible for a defective or dangerous condition which caused injury to the plaintiff, and which the indemnitee innocently or negligently failed to discover (e.g. the wholesaler or retailer of a defective product).

Thus, while there is no rule that a negligent defendant cannot have indemnity, neither is there a general principle that one who was merely negligent may always obtain indemnity from one whose conduct was intentionally wrongful or reckless. The indemnitee's fault usually may consist, at most, of a sort of benign neglect, such as the failure to discover and eliminate a danger.

An interesting recent New York case, Dole v. Dow Chemical Co. (N.Y.1972), overturned the "all-or-nothing" indemnity rule in that state. Rejecting the use of "active-passive" and "primary-secondary" concepts, the court ruled that henceforth the damages in an indemnity action would be apportioned according to the respective faults of the parties—a comparative negligence rule applied to defendants, very similar to some types of contribution. It thereby sidestepped the New York contribution statute, which required an equal division of the damages and which could only be invoked between parties to a joint judgment. Shortly thereafter, the New York legislature adopted comparative negligence and also broadened its contribution statute.

Note that the *Dole* rule does not apply in cases of indemnity based upon vicarious liability. Rogers v. Dorchester Assocs. (N.Y.1973).

Indemnity is sometimes allowed in favor of one who is held liable for additional harm caused plaintiff by the subsequent negligence of another. For example, the original tortfeasor who is held liable for all of plaintiff's damages, including those attributable to the aggravation of his injuries by the negligence of the treating physician, may be allowed indemnity from the physician for that portion of the damages for which the physician was responsible. Other courts have reached the same result under a theory of subrogation.

PART III

TORT AND CONTRACT

CHAPTER 10

TORT AND CONTRACT

§ 10—1. Parties to the Contract

As we have seen, the duty upon the breach of which a tort action may be founded can arise from either of two sources: (1) a general obligation which each of us has to carry on our activities with proper regard for the interests of others; and (2) specific obligations which arise out of some relationship between two or more persons. One such relationship is a contract, which creates by agreement of the parties certain enforceable obligations which the law in most cases would not otherwise impose.

When one party to a contract fails to render the agreed performance, the other party may not only lose the benefit of his bargain, but may also suffer other kinds of injury, including physical and pecuniary harm, as a direct result. Assuming the breach to have been intentional, reckless or negligent, may the party wronged elect to sue in tort, or is he confined to his action for breach of contract? For a variety of reasons, plaintiff will usually prefer to sue in tort if he can. For example, typically the tort measure of damages will be more favorable to him.

General Rule: Misfeasance vs. Nonfeasance. For reasons mainly historical, but also because of a fear of unwarranted extensions of liability, the general rule is that where defendant's duty arises because of a contractual relationship between the parties, he is not liable in tort for harm caused by his breach of that contract where the breach consists of his failure to commence performance at all. But once having begun to perform, he will generally be liable in tort for his intentional, reckless, or negligent misperformance, whether consisting of acts or omissions to act. For example, one who contracts with plaintiff to cut down a tree on his property will not be liable *in tort* if he simply never arrives on the premises and the tree falls on plaintiff's house before another contractor can be engaged. But once he appears and starts to cut down the tree, he will be liable if he does so negligently, or if he negligently abandons the work halfway through, with the same result. His liability is the same as that of one who gratuitously undertakes to perform some task and does so negligently. Both are liable where their misperformance creates a foreseeable, unreasonable risk of harm to the recognized interests of the plaintiff.

The difficulty lies in determining exactly where nonfeasance ends and misfeasance begins. Many forms of conduct can logically be characterized as either. Omissions to act during the course of an ongoing activity are readily seen as misfeasance. But, perhaps for unspoken policy reasons, firing an employee and expelling a theatre patron have been held to be nonfeasance. In general, however, the question is whether defendant's performance (as distinct from his promise or his preparation) has gone so far that it has begun to affect the interests of the plaintiff beyond the expected benefits of the contract itself and may be regarded as a positive act assuming the obligation beyond the mere promise to perform.

Exceptions; Liability for Nonfeasance. When the common law first began to allow an action for breach of an undertaking, it was against those engaged in the common or public callings —common carriers, innkeepers, public warehousemen, and other public servants and utilities. It was a form of tort liability, and it was soon extended to nonperformance and even to defendant's refusal to enter into a contract at all. Gradually this evolved into the action of assumpsit, a contract action in its later stages, which became the principal remedy for breach of any contract. But the original principle has been carried forward in tort law, and such defendants remain liable in tort for nonperformance.

In addition, there are certain other relations (which may or may not be based on a contract) in which the law imposes a duty of affirmative care and for the failure of which there may be tort liability. For example, a bailee must act affirmatively to care for the goods; an employer must take steps to provide a safe place for his employee to work; a possessor of land must make the premises reasonably safe for invitees.

Such duties arise independently of the terms of the contract, and thus the tort action is limited to that which the law requires. If the contract provides for a different or greater duty, then to that extent its nonperformance must be enforced in a contract action. For example, when defendant agrees to board plaintiff's pet dog, the law will impose a duty to feed it independent of the contract, and for the failure to do so there may be a tort action; but for the failure to perform a promise to give it a rabies shot, the sole remedy is in contract.

Another exception to the general rule is that a promise made without any intent to perform it may be fraud for which a tort action in deceit will lie.

Election: Tort or Contract Action. Where the facts permit, it would seem logical to allow plaintiff to elect to bring his action in either tort or contract as he sees fit. In general, the courts have so held, at least where the issue is one of procedure (jurisdiction, venue, joinder of parties, etc.) or where plaintiff is claiming only pecuniary loss or property damage. But where the action is one for personal injury, many courts have ignored the pleadings and characterized the suit as one in tort for purposes such as determining whether the action survives or which statute of limitations is applicable.

Unjust Enrichment: Restitution. Where defendant's tort results in the unjust enrichment of defendant at plaintiff's expense, the law generally allows plaintiff to "waive" his ordinary tort remedy and sue instead for restitution of the benefit, under a completely theoretical and fictitious "contract" by which defendant impliedly promises to repay his wrongful gain to plaintiff who lost or was deprived of it. Originally a common law tort action, a form of assumpsit, it is now called "quasi-contract" and has some of the advantages of a contract action. It derives from equity and is subject to equitable principles and limitations.

§ 10—2. Liability to Third Persons Not Parties to the Contract

The duties arising under a contract between *A* and *B* will sometimes affect the interests of *C*, a nonparty, such that *A*'s or *B*'s nonperformance or misperformance of the contract may cause harm to *C*. For example, an auto mechanic's negligence in repairing an automobile causes it to crash and injure *C*, a passenger in another vehicle. May *C* sue the mechanic in tort?

Under the common law as it existed in this country until well into the twentieth century, the general rule was that as to duties created by con-

tract, one who was not a party to the contract
had no cause of action in tort for harm he suffered as a result of the parties' misperformance
or nonperformance. In effect, as a nonparty he
had no standing to complain of the breach, even
in a tort action; he was not in "privity of contract" with the defendant.

This rule is another of those duty limitations
which served to keep tort liability within manageable bounds until the maturation of our econo-
my and the development of the institution of liability insurance. It appears to have originated,
or at least to have had its first clear statement,
in the notorious 1842 English case, Winterbottom
v. Wright. The Court of Exchequer there held
that the breach of a contract to keep a mailcoach
in repair after it was sold gave no cause of action
to a passenger in the coach who was injured
when it collapsed. The holding was that there
could be no action on the contract itself, but certain dicta, particularly that of Lord Abinger who
foresaw "the most absurd and outrageous consequences, to which I can see no limit" "[u]nless
we confine the operation of such contracts as this
to the parties who entered into them," were tak-
en to mean that there could be no action even in
tort. This principle was generally followed and
extended to the misperformance of any contract.

As in the case of most duty limitations, the
courts soon found themselves busily engaged in
creating exceptions to it. The exceptions prolif-

erated, and today the privity barrier is largely down and relatively few vestiges of the *Winterbottom* rule survive. Ordinary principles of negligence and proximate cause for the most part now delineate the liability of a contracting party to one with whom he is not in privity.

The classic example of the erosion of the privity rule is the history of the law of products liability, discussed elsewhere.

Nonfeasance. Just as there is no tort liability between the parties for harm caused by the nonperformance of a contract, absent some recognized exception, so there is generally no tort liability to a nonparty injured thereby. Thus, one who is hired to repair an auto but never even begins performance is not liable to a third person injured by the defect.

But here also there are exceptions, and liability to third persons for failure to commence performance may be imposed in situations where the courts have determined that a contract between *A* and *B* creates a sufficient duty toward *C* to justify it. Illustrations of such situations include: (1) the failure of a telegraph company to transmit a telegram; (2) the nonperformance by an agent of his contractual duty (a) to supervise property or persons over which he has been given control (e.g., a herd of cattle) or (b) to take certain precautions for the safety of third persons (e.g., a railroad crossing guard); (3) nonperformance of a contract to maintain, inspect or re-

pair an instrumentality which foreseeably creates
a substantial risk of harm to third persons (e.g.,
an elevator, a boiler, scaffolding); and (4) in
some jurisdictions, nonperformance by a landlord
of his contract to repair the premises. In a number of these cases, defendant's conduct might just
as easily have been classified as misfeasance,
bearing futher witness to the illusory nature of
the distinction.

One oft-cited example of nonliability in tort for
nonperformance of a contract is found in cases
exonerating water companies from liability for
fire damage caused by their failure to perform
their contractual duty to maintain adequate water pressure in their lines—e.g., H. R. Moch Co.
v. Rensselaer Water Co. (N.Y.1928) (Cardozo,
J.). A similar result is usually reached in cases of
failure to furnish other utilities and municipal
services. Again, such cases could just as readily
be deemed misfeasance, and the real reasons for
these holdings are based upon fears of unduly
burdensome liability.

Misfeasance. Once defendant has commenced
performance of his contract, the general rule today is that he will be liable to nonparties for his
tortious misperformance, subject of course to the
usual rules of proximate cause and any other applicable limitations. The privity rule is now virtually dead in cases involving the sale of goods,
and nearly so in cases involving the performance
of services. Thus, our auto mechanic who negli-

gently performs repairs on an automobile will be liable to third persons injured as a result, when and to the extent that their injuries are a foreseeable result of his negligence. An attorney who negligently drafts or directs the execution of a will may be held liable to disappointed intended beneficiaries.

It must be emphasized, however obvious it may seem, that even though privity is no longer necessary, liability to third persons does not automatically follow from the misperformance of a contract. For the most part, privity was an arbitrary duty limitation which could not be justified in terms of the underlying principles from which liability or nonliability ought to flow. But in certain cases, the privity limitation rather inartfully expressed a valid concern that liability not be so disproportionately burdensome that otherwise desirable activities be made prohibitively risky or expensive. Removal of that limitation merely laid bare the underlying dilemma and forced the courts to deal with that directly. For example, when privity of contract was required, that in itself would prevent an accountant who negligently prepared a financial statement from being liable to third persons who sustained pecuniary loss in reliance upon it. Now that privity is no longer necessary, the courts have had to face the real problem, which is the risk of very large potential liability to an indeterminate class of persons who may reasonably rely on the statement. The solution has been to limit liability for pecuniary loss

for a negligent misrepresentation to those persons
for whose benefit and guidance the accountant
(or other actor) knows the information to be intended. This is, in effect, a special proximate
cause rule. In the area of products liability, an
analogous problem is the scope of the manufacturer's liability to "bystanders" (i.e., persons other than the user or consumer injured by the product), and the solution has been either to deny liability to bystanders or to limit liability to those
bystanders whose exposure to the product the
manufacturer can reasonably anticipate.

PART IV

IMMUNITIES

CHAPTER 11

IMMUNITIES

§ 11—1. Government and Its Employees

An *immunity* is a defense to tort liability which is conferred upon an entire group or class of persons or entities under circumstances where considerations of public policy are thought to require special protection for the person, activity or entity in question at the expense of those injured by its tortious act. Historically, tort litigation against units of government, public officers, and charities, and between spouses, parents and children, has been limited or prohibited on this basis.

It is frequently said that immunities differ from privileges (see § 7—1) in that the latter are narrower in scope and operate when the presence of certain facts make defendant's conduct nontortious. Thus, a privilege negates the existence of the tort, whereas an immunity recognizes that a tort has been committed but provides a defense to liability because of defendant's favored status. While perhaps technically accurate, this distinction is largely semantic and is frequently not observed, and courts and writers sometimes use the two terms interchangeably. Moreover, in recent

years there has been a strong trend to abolish or
limit immunities, and to the extent that they remain in force at all, often it is not because of defendant's favored status but because the utility of
the particular conduct in question is such that
the burden of liability would be disproportionate
to the risk created. Hence, what is left of the
traditional immunities tends to resemble duty
limitations or privileges.

Governmental or Sovereign Immunity. The
most important tort immunity is that of units of
government, which is frequently referred to as
sovereign immunity.

The sovereign immunity concept has dual aspects, and this duality has caused controversy and
confusion. One aspect is procedural, the other
substantive. In its original form, under English
common law, the rule was fundamentally procedural. A lawsuit could not be brought against
the Crown (the sovereign) in the Crown's own
courts without its consent. (This disability
would, of course, apply not merely to tort actions
but to all others as well.) But the doctrine eventually came to be regarded as also embodying a
rule of *substantive* immunity from *tort* liability,
as reflected in the oft-quoted phrase "the King
can do no wrong," which was usually interpreted
as meaning that the sovereign was incapable of
committing a tort.

One might have expected that the United
States, founded as it was upon a premise of the

supremacy of the people over those who govern them and a rejection of the notion of the divine right of kings, would also have rejected the notion of sovereign immunity. But the opposite is true; the doctrine was unquestioningly accepted into the fabric of the American common law. Ironically, in England the Crown had long provided other means of redress for injuries caused by royal and governmental agents.

In this country, there are three distinct levels of government—federal, state and local. Initially, each of these was uniformly held to be entirely immune from tort liability. That immunity has by now been largely eliminated at all levels, but each has had a different history and there are important differences among them with respect to the nature and scope of their liability.

United States. From the beginning, it was taken for granted that the United States could not be sued without its consent, Cohens v. Virginia (U.S. 1821), and this is still the rule. R. § 895A. Congress in 1855 created the Court of Claims to adjudicate contract claims, and the Tucker Act of 1887 gave jurisdiction to the Court of Claims and the federal courts of certain non-tort claims, including those arising under the fifth amendment (prohibiting the taking of private property without compensation). But, with minor exceptions, there was no remedy against the United States for torts committed by the government against its citizens (except by private bill in Congress) until Congress adopted the Federal Tort Claims

Act in 1946. 28 U.S.C.A. §§ 1346, 1402, 1504, 2110, 2401, 2402, 2411, 2412, 2671–2680.

Under this statute, the federal district courts have (exclusive) jurisdiction over suits against the United States "for money damages . . . for injury or loss of property, or personal injury or death caused by the negligent or wrongful act or omission of any employee of the Government while acting within the scope of his office or employment, under circumstances where the United States, if a private person, would be liable to the claimant in accordance with the law of the place where the act or omission occurred." 28 U.S.C. A. § 1346 (b). Trial is without a jury.

The Act contains a number of exceptions, mostly preserving immunity for specific governmental activities (e.g., tax assessment and collection, failure to deliver mail, military combat in time of war, actions arising in foreign countries). In addition, there are two important general exceptions. First, the United States is not liable for "any claim arising out of assault, battery, false imprisonment, false arrest, malicious prosecution, abuse of process, libel, slander, misrepresentation, deceit, or interference with contract rights"; except that the Act *does* apply to "acts or omissions of investigative or law enforcement officers of the United States Government" with respect to claims "arising, on or after the enactment of this proviso, out of assault, battery, false imprisonment, false arrest, abuse of process, or malicious prosecution." 28 U.S.C.A. § 2680(h). (The proviso was added by amendment in 1974 to assure the availability of adequate remedies for abuses of power by federal law enforcement personnel. See § 8—22, supra; Boger, Gitenstein & Verkuill, The Federal Tort Claims Act Intentional Torts Amendment: An Interpretive Analysis, 54 N.C.L. Rev. 497 (1976).) While it is sometimes said that (except for the proviso) the Act is limited to negligent acts or omissions, there are intentional torts which are not excluded and for which actions may be brought, such as trespass and invasion of privacy.

Second, the federal government is not liable for acts done with due care in the execution of a statute or regulation, even though it is invalid, or for "an act or omission . . . based upon the exercise or performance or the failure to exercise or perform a *discretionary* function or duty on the part of a federal agency or an employee of the Government, whether or not the discretion involved be abused." 28 U.S.C.A. § 2680 (a) (emphasis added). Much litigation has centered on whether the act in question involved the exercise of discretion or was merely ministerial, because almost any act by any governmental employee is arguably the product of the decision of some one who had the power to decide to act or not. The concept refers to decisions made at the planning or policy level, and for the most part does not include conduct at the lower or "operational" levels of government even though the exercise of some judgment may be involved.

In addition, the United States is not subject to strict tort liability, since the Act waives its immunity only for a "negligent or wrongful act or omission." Laird v. Nelms (U.S.1972).

Agencies of the federal government share its immunity. Sometimes a statute will expressly or impliedly authorize suits against a particular agency; but if the claim is cognizable under the Federal Tort Claims Act, that is the exclusive remedy.

States. The doctrine of sovereign immunity has been uniformly held applicable to the state level of government. R. § 895B. (An early decision that this did not apply to suits against the states in federal court, Chisholm v. Georgia (U.S. 1793), was nullified by the eleventh amendment.) Most states adopted the common law rule of sovereign immunity in both its substantive and procedural aspects. Some state constitutions codify the procedural aspect of the doctrine, but expressly or impliedly allow waiver; a few expressly prohibit the giving of consent to suit.

Various justifications, all of them rather weak, have been advanced for adhering to the doctrine: there should be no liability for negligence in the performance of a duty imposed by law; a tort cannot be committed by an entire people; whatever the state does must ipso facto be lawful; a government employee who commits a tort must thereby be acting outside the scope of his authority and employment; tort compensation is not a proper use of public funds; tort liability would cause inconvenience and embarrassment to the government; and, occasionally, just "public policy." The most likely reason for its persistence is a fear that governmental tort liability would precipitate a large scale milking of the public treasury and fiscally disastrous consequences—a fear which is increasingly seen as unwarranted and outweighed by the injustice of immunity. Thus, all states have now consented (usually by statute or constitutional provision) to allow tort claims in some form and to a greater or lesser extent. Some are limited to particular types of claims (e.g. motor vehicle accidents); in many states there is a special court, agency or procedure for claims against the state. Some merely authorize the purchase of liability insurance and permit claims to the extent of the insurance.

One could assume that a constitutional or statutory provision authorizing the state to be sued would be construed to waive the state's *substantive* tort immunity as well; but there are decisions holding that it does not, in the absence of an express and specific provision to that effect. However, the more recent decisions are usually willing to imply the waiver in such cases.

Given the general trend toward abolition of special liability limitations, the vigorous criticism to which the doctrine has been subjected, and the weakness of its rationale, one might expect to find the courts abrogating sovereign immunity in those states where it is no more than a common law rule. But until recently, no court had done so. Besides the usual judicial reluctance to overturn long-standing rules of nonliability was the fact that in most jurisdictions the state had made *some* provision, however minimal, for allowing tort claims, thereby (arguably) making the subject one of legislative concern. But finally, in Muskopf v. Corning Hosp. Dist. (Cal.1961), the state's tort immunity was judicially abolished. Approximately a dozen states have since followed suit, but several jurisdictions have continued to refuse to do so (e.g., Hannigan v. New Gamma-Delta Chapter of Kappa Sigma Fraternity, Inc. (Mass.1975)) (at least until legislature has had a reasonable time to act). At least one court abolished the state's substantive tort immunity, leaving it to the legislature to implement a constitutional provision authorizing it to consent to suit. Holytz v. City of Milwaukee (Wis.1962).

Even where the state's sovereign immunity is discarded, of necessity certain special common law defenses unique to governmental activities remain. For example, a state is not liable in tort for the actions or inaction of its courts or legislature, nor ordinarily for the judicial or legislative acts of state administrative officers and agencies. Nor is it liable in tort for the basic planning and policy decisions of state officials involving the exercise of official discretion. See R. § 895B (3) (b) and Comment *d*.

Local Governments. Units of local government below the level of the state are in a separate category. The distinction between state and local governments derives from the fact that municipalities are regarded as having a dual character. In one sense, they are a branch of government, deriving their governmental powers from their parent state. But in another sense, they are corporate entities, much like private corporations, organized to provide various services to the residents of their areas, such as water, electricity, waste disposal, and sometimes hospitals, schools, libraries, transportation, and others. For this reason, units of local government are often referred to as municipal corporations.

The first local governmental entities were cities, towns and villages. Today, we have these and many more—counties, townships, special purpose districts of various kinds, and other separate governmental entities such as transit and utility companies. In some jurisdictions certain of these are state agencies, and thus are governed by the state immunity rules. If not, they are regarded as local governmental entities and the rules governing municipalities apply.

Russell v. Men of Devon (K.B.1788) is usually cited as the first articulation of local governmental immunity. At that time, the idea of a local governmental *entity* had not yet developed and the action was, in effect, against the entire population of the county. Thus, one basis for denying liability was the fact that there were no corporate funds out of which to pay a judgment.

Nevertheless, the *Russell* case was followed in this country, and local governmental immunity was at one time the universally accepted rule in the United States. It was rationalized on grounds similar to those previously noted which were offered in support of state immunity. But it was subject to the same criticisms; predictably, exceptions to it soon developed. The most important of these was based on the "governmental-proprietary" distinction arising from the dual character of municipal corporations. When the entity was acting in its governmental, political, or public capacity, it was immune. But when acting in its corporate, private, or proprietary capacity, it was subject to tort liability to much the same extent as any private corporation.

As might be expected, the courts have had considerable difficulty distinguishing between governmental and proprietary functions, and there is substantial disagreement and inconsistency among the cases on this issue. Moreover, as sentiment favoring liability has increased, a trend is discernible to find acts to be "proprietary" whenever possible. The result is hopeless confusion.

Other exceptions developed. Local governments are always liable in nuisance. An important intermediate step on the road to abrogation was taken in many jurisdictions which held that where the local government had purchased liability insurance (as most had, since they were liable for some activities), immunity was thereby waived to the extent of the insurance coverage. In addition, local governments were sometimes held liable for particular activities, such as the maintenance of public ways, or for activities voluntarily undertaken, or for misfeasance. In addition, statutes began to impose liability for certain activities, such as operating motor vehicles.

Finally, beginning with Hargrove v. Town of Cocoa Beach (Fla.1957), the courts began to overthrow local governmental immunity entirely. Largely unrestricted by constitutional or statutory provisions, local governmental immunity until recently has remained much more a common law doctrine than state immunity, and thus the courts are freer to abolish it. Accordingly, *Hargrove* has attracted a large following—so far, at least twenty states. But a few states have declined the invitation.

As in the case of the state's immunity, the abolition of the immunity of local governments has been held not to affect certain pre-existing defenses peculiar to the activities of government. There is no tort liability for judicial and legislative functions, nor for the exercise of an administrative function involving the making of a basic policy decision. R. § 895C(2) and Comment *g*.

Comprehensive Statutes. A number of state legislatures have now enacted comprehensive statutes governing the tort liability of state and local governmental units and their employees. At first these statutes were passed in response to decisions abolishing immunity, and many of the acts are patterned after legislation enacted in California in 1963; some follow the Federal Tort Claims Act. Several states have since obviated the need for judicial abrogation by similar legislation. The statutes typically recognize general governmental liability, but reinstate limited immunities or defenses for particular kinds of activities.

Governmental Officers and Employees. The personal tort liability of governmental officers and employees for their job-related conduct is *not* identical to that of their governmental employer. As a general rule, in the absence of a statute, their common law liability is somewhat broader. But they are also the beneficiaries of certain special immunities.

As a general proposition, a governmental officer or employee is personally liable for his torts. R. § 895D. However, when exercising a judicial or legislative function, he shares the traditional immunity of his employer.

The highest executive officers of the federal and state governments are also absolutely immune from tort liability, except perhaps when they have so far exceeded the scope of their official discretion as to be acting clearly beyond the bounds of their authority, as when acting purely out of personal spite or malice.

Lower level executive and administrative employees possess a qualified immunity. When performing a discretionary function, they are immune from liability so long as they act honestly and in good faith. But with respect to ministerial acts, they are subject to the ordinary rules of tort liability. As to the distinction between discretionary and ministerial acts, see R. § 895D, Comments *f* and *h*.

The scope of the common law tort liability of public officers and employees is, of course, subject to statutory modification, and there are many such statutes. State governmental tort immunity acts usually apply to government employees, often making their liability coextensive with that of the government. Federal and state employees are generally liable for constitutional violations (see § 8—22, supra), but even here some (but not all) of the traditional immunities have been judicially preserved. And occasionally a statute will immunize the employee even though the government is liable for his act (e.g., negligence in the operation of a motor vehicle by a federal employee, 28 U.S.C.A. § 2679(b)).

Statutes frequently alter the usual rule that an employer may obtain indemnity from an employee for whose tort he is held liable, either by prohibiting indemnity, or, occasionally, by reversing it and requiring the government to indemnify the employee.

Public employees ordinarily may be held personally liable for punitive damages, but such damages usually may not be assessed against a governmental entity in the absence of statutory authorization.

§ 11—2. Charities

At one time, all but one or two American jurisdictions held that charitable, educational, religious, or benevolent organizations and enterprises were immune from tort liability.

The rule was derived from an 1846 English case, which justified it on the ground that the funds of the charity should not be diverted from the donor's intended charitable purpose to so remote a use as the payment of tort claims. The parent case was overruled in England in 1866, a fact which seems to have gone unnoticed here. Moreover, that justification runs counter to well-established principles of trust law; trust assets may generally be used to satisfy tort liabilities incurred in administering the trust.

Another supposed justification is that the principle of respondeat superior does not apply to charities because they derive no profit from the employee's service. The defect in this argument is that the principal justifications for respondeat superior (see § 8—10, supra) have nothing to do with whether the employer profits from his employee's work.

With respect to the beneficiaries of the charity's services some courts have held that they, in effect, impliedly assume the risk of the charity's negligence by accepting its benevolence. Clearly, this is quite unrealistic. One should be able to expect even a charitable enterprise to conduct itself with reasonable care, and we have seen that principles of tort law require one who undertakes to act, even gratuitously, to exercise ordinary care.

Some have suggested that charities in rendering a public service should be treated the same as a governmental unit. Aside from the fact that the justifications for governmental immunity have been discredited and the immunity itself largely abrogated (§ 11—1), the functions of charities and government qua government are seldom similar and therefore the analogy is false.

The most likely reason for the immunity is that it is thought to further a public policy which strongly favors and supports charitable enterprises, whose beneficent work might be hampered if their assets must be used to pay tort claims. But first legal writers and then the courts accepted the now-prevailing view that tort liability is a legitimate expense of any enterprise, however benevolent and worthy, and the public policy favoring charity is outweighed by the injustice of tort immunity, especially now that liability insurance has reduced the burden to manageable levels.

President and Directors of Georgetown College
v. Hughes (D.C.1942) (Rutledge, J.) effectively
demolished the underpinnings of charitable immunity, and started an avalanche of decisions
overthrowing it. At least two-thirds of the states
now reject it entirely, and this is the Restatement
position (R. § 895E). The rest have all abolished
it in part. A few have abrogated the immunity
of charitable hospitals but retained it as to religious institutions and other charities. Some limit the immunity to recipients of the benefits of
the charity. Some have abolished it to the extent
that defendant is covered by liability insurance or
to the extent that the judgment can be satisfied
out of nontrust assets. And almost all will impose liability in certain situations, as when the
tort is that of a managing agent, or when committed during fund-raising activities, when not
directly connected with the charity itself, or when
it is a nuisance. Some jurisdictions have statutes
which purport to impose a partial immunity, either generally or as to certain charities, but there
would appear to be some question as to the constitutionality of at least some of these.

§ 11—3. Spouses, Parents and Children

In many jurisdictions, if the person injured and
the tortfeasor are (or were) either (1) husband
and wife or (2) parent and child, the tortfeasor
may have immunity from suit or liability.

Husband and Wife. At common law, neither spouse could sue the other during the marriage, but only because it was procedurally impossible. A woman lost most of her separate legal identity during marriage. Her husband acquired many of her rights, and became liable for her torts. She could not sue or be sued without joinder of him as plaintiff or defendant. Thus, there could be no tort litigation inter se because the husband would have had to be on both sides of the same lawsuit.

In the United States, beginning about 1844 statutes (called Married Women's Acts or Emancipation Acts) were passed in every jurisdiction which gave a married woman a separate legal identity and separate ownership of her own property. These statutes were construed (where possible) to permit the wife to maintain an action against her husband for torts against her property interests and for torts involving only pecuniary loss (e.g., deceit). By necessary implication, the husband was given the same rights against his wife. But most jurisdictions refused to go further, and held that such legislation did not remove the bar to actions between spouses for personal torts not involving property. A few of these acts expressly prohibit interspousal litigation.

Preservation of the common law interspousal tort immunity after the passage of the Married Women's Acts required the courts to find new justifications for it, such as: (1) preservation of the peace and harmony of the home; (2) prevention of a flood of spurious litigation; (3) the availability of other remedies to the injured spouse, such as divorce or criminal prosecution; (4) protection of liability insurers from collusive suits; (5) avoidance of the danger that the tortfeasor spouse would share the benefit of the proceeds of the claim obtained from the insurer; and (6) legislative preemption (the statutes themselves being held to make the matter one of legislative concern). The immunity was thus transformed from a procedural to a substantive one.

All of these justifications have been refuted to the satisfaction of most legal writers and many courts. Domestic disharmony is perhaps a *cause* of litigation, but rarely an effect; either there is no tranquility left to preserve by the time the litigation stage is reached, or else the real object of the suit is liability insurance. In the latter case, there is no reason to suppose that the trier of fact is any less able to detect spurious or collusive claims here than elsewhere. Remedies under the divorce or criminal laws are manifestly inadequate, and do not compensate for the injury. The possibility of a benefit to the wrongdoing spouse does not justify denying the injured spouse a remedy, especially since the latter is presumably capable of protecting his or her rights in the compensation fund. And, absent a controlling statute, the immunity remains of common law origin and subject to judicial control.

Thus, the trend has been to abolish this immunity; so far, about half the states have done away with it entirely. The Restatement (Second) rejects it (§ 895F). And many of the remaining states (a few of which have statutes expressly preserving it) recognize exceptions, as where the marriage has been terminated (by death or divorce) or where the tort occurred prior to the marriage. Some jurisdictions allow actions for intentional torts. And almost all courts now hold that plaintiff may sue one who is vicariously liable for his spouse's tort, even though his spouse is personally immune.

Parent and Child. The common law recognized no such legal unity of a parent and his child. Property and contract actions between them have always been permitted, and so have actions for torts involving property interests or pecuniary loss. And while authority is scant, there is no reason to think that the same would not have been true in other common law countries as to personal torts. But in the United States, the first reported decision on this issue was Hewlett v. George (Miss.1891), which held (citing no authority) that a minor child could not sue her parent for false imprisonment. Following this case, it soon became the general rule that a parent and his unemancipated minor child were each immune from suit by the other for a personal tort, whether intentional or negligent in character.

Justifications were given for this immunity analogous to those offered in support of interspousal tort immunity. It was said that to allow parent-child tort actions would : (1) undermine parental discipline; (2) permit collusive lawsuits; (3) upset the even allocation of family resources; (4) foster useless litigation, since the parent or child might eventually inherit the recovery from the other's estate; and (5) violate a general social policy that the parent is the head of the household and as such should have an immunity like that of a sovereign.

These justifications, like those for the husband-wife immunity, have now been largely discredited on similar grounds. The principal difference in the rationale of the parent-child immunity relates to the possible effect of parental liability upon the parent's authority to discipline the child, and this authority would seem to be adequately protected by the privilege to discipline, previously discussed (§ 7—7). Whatever merit remains in the bases of this immunity is now generally regarded as outweighed by the injustice of denying compensation to one who has been tortiously injured, especially when one or more of the foregoing justifications are absent.

Thus, about one-third of the states have now abolished this immunity generally; this is the Restatement position (R. § 895G). Note, however, that this does not mean that the liability of a parent will be the same as if the plaintiff was a

stranger. Aside from the privilege of discipline,
it is sometimes said that there is no liability
where the alleged negligent act involves an exercise of parental discretion in the provision of
food, clothing, housing, and other necessities and
care, or that a parent is not liable for the ordinary risks inherent in intrafamily activities and
relations. In some cases the courts may simply
be saying that defendant's conduct was not negligent under the circumstances, one of which was
the family relation; but other courts may be preserving a portion of the former immunity. Future cases will have to develop the scope of this
new liability.

Among the remaining states, a number of exceptions to the immunity have evolved. Most
now hold that there is no immunity for bodily
harm intentionally or recklessly inflicted. In
some jurisdictions there is no immunity where
the risk is unrelated to the status of the parties
as parent and child, as in the case of harm inflicted in the course of a business activity of the defendant. Some will allow an action where the
parent-child relation has been terminated by the
death of either party, or for the wrongful death
of the other parent. And it is generally agreed
that the immunity of the parent or child is a personal one which does not protect a third party
who is vicariously liable for the tort of either,
such as his employer.

It is uniformly held that the immunity extends only to unemancipated minor children, and that it does not apply to persons who only stand in loco parentis.

Siblings and Other Kin. Brothers, sisters, and other kin are not, by reason of their relationship, immune from tort liability to one another. R. § 895H.

*

INDEX

References are to Pages

INDEX

INDEX

References are to Pages

[*426*]

[427]

INDEX
References are to Pages

[432]

INDEX